P9-DEI-818

NOW YOU KNOW

KITTY DUKAKIS

with JANE SCOVELL

SIMON AND SCHUSTER
New York   London   Toronto   Sydney
Tokyo   Singapore

Simon and Schuster
Simon & Schuster Building
Rockefeller Center
1230 Avenue of the Americas
New York, New York 10020

Copyright © 1990 by Katharine D. Dukakis

All rights reserved
including the right of reproduction
in whole or in part in any form.

SIMON AND SCHUSTER and colophon are registered trademarks
of Simon & Schuster Inc.

Designed by Carla Weise/Levavi & Levavi
Manufactured in the United States of America

1 3 5 7 9 10 8 6 4 2

Library of Congress Cataloging in Publication Data
Dukakis, Kitty.
Now you know/Kitty Dukakis with Jane Scovell.
p. cm.
ISBN 0-671-68458-2: $19.95
1. Dukakis, Kitty. 2. Dukakis, Michael S. (Michael Stanley),—1933–
3. Governors—Massachusetts—Wives—
Biography. 4. Massachusetts—Biography.
I. Scovell, Jane, 1934– . II. Title.
F71.22.D84A3 1990
794.4'04'092—dc20
[B]   90-39952
CIP

TO THOSE I LOVE—
ESPECIALLY MICHAEL

NOW
YOU
KNOW

I'm Kitty Dukakis and I'm a drug addict and an alcoholic. I am also the wife of the governor of Massachusetts, and, not so long ago, came perilously close to becoming the first lady of the United States of America. I say "perilously" only for myself, not the country. I believed then, I believe now, Michael Dukakis would have been a great president. However, had my husband been elected to the highest office in the land in 1988, it could have been very dangerous for me. At the time of the presidential campaign, I was addicted to alcohol. Had the vote gone differently, had Michael and I moved into 1600 Pennsylvania Avenue, I am certain the first crisis would have sent me out of control. I am equally certain, thrust into the smothering, protective confines of the White House, I would not have been able to seek proper help. There is ample evidence to support my feeling. The White House has sheltered a number of persons with addictive disorders, and you don't have to go far back into the history books to find them. After her husband left office, Betty Ford, the wife of our thirty-eighth president, revealed her dependency, and, thus far, no political personality has proved as influential and helpful as she. Other White House occupants have suffered in silence and never openly disclosed their pain and shame. So what? Whispers, backstairs gossip, and media allusions did it for them. Rumor is often more harmful than fact. We hear the innuendoes, the suggestions, the snide stories. Unsubstantiated, they are circulated and generally accepted as truth. My heart aches for those poor souls trapped into a life of quiet desperation while living on White House display. The White House. For a while, after the defeat, I thought a lot about it. I would love to have lived there. Realistically, I wasn't ready for it. I was an alcoholic trying to stay in control. Sometimes I succeeded; other times, I did not. I did manage to refrain from drinking in situations that might have given me away; consequently, few people saw me drink, especially during the campaign. The truth is, I didn't drink that much. In public, I had one cocktail, sometimes two, at the end of the day. Now and then, I would overindulge at home. It may not seem like the portrait of an alcoholic, but I assure you, it is. I learned the hard way: I was a substance abuser.

During the presidential campaign, whenever possible I flew on a small aircraft rather than Michael's huge plane. The big transport could hold over a hundred people and was always jammed with staff and reporters. We called it the Sky Pig because it was so awful. It shook when it took off, it shook when it was in the air, and it shook when it landed. I was shaken up all over the United States. I much preferred my sturdy, steady, little plane, which we affectionately dubbed Sky Heaven.

Sky Heaven held twelve people including the crew. (Though having my own plane may sound extravagant, I assure you, we did not willy-nilly incorporate another aircraft into the campaign. We did extensive research and discovered it was cost-efficient for me to have my own wings. I'm pleased to say, Sky Heaven did save us money.) After an exhausting day's work, my road staff and I would board the plane. Marlene Dunneman, the flight attendant, would have drinks ready. For most of us, vodka was the beverage of choice and our airborne happy hour commenced when we flew off to the next stop. As I said before, I always had one drink.

One drink.

Oh, but I thought about that one drink constantly. One drink, and I spent hours picturing it being poured. I could feel the glass in my hand, imagine the cool liquid sliding down my throat. When happy hour (God, what a misnomer that is!) actually arrived, I would sit, strapped into my seat with the vodka on the tray beside me. I never attacked my cocktail in wild-eyed, *Lost Weekend*–like frenzy. No, I was far too controlled for such behavior. Outwardly, I seemed calm. Inside, I was seething. My whole being was concentrated on that glass. After a jam-packed schedule of meetings, rallies, breakfasts, luncheons and the like, after making speeches and addressing issues, this moment became the focal point of my day. And while I didn't actually stiff-arm my drink, I would drain the contents far more quickly than anyone else. I'd finish and then look around at the others who were still sipping. I felt guilty, so awfully guilty, and ashamed. I wanted another, yet, I knew I shouldn't ask for more. I could not afford to; I had work to do and an image to maintain. Moreover, I didn't want my staff to know *how much* I needed that pick-me-up. I didn't even want to know myself. And so, I would stop at one, or, once in a great while, two. Some, those who remember how arduously and enthusiastically I campaigned and how little I seemed to require alcohol, may find my confession hard to accept. Others—alcoholics like myself —will understand.

One of the attendant myths about alcoholism suggests that alcoholics cannot function properly. It's not true. There are many successful, very successful, people in this world who are alcoholics. They can be steps away from losing control, yet their precarious positions remain undetected. They hold important jobs in industry and in the professions; they are not stumblebums. Neither was I. After all, it *was* just one or two drinks. However, I was not totally unaware of what was happening. Buried way back in my brain was a warning I had received at the Hazelden Clinic back in 1982.

I had gone to Hazelden because of my addiction to drugs. I had been taking diet pills for twenty-six years. I began because, though I only weighed a bit more than I do now, I wanted to be "thin," and I wanted to lose weight quickly and painlessly. My doctor prescribed alphamethylphenethylamine, or, amphetamines. No big deal, my own mother took diet pills and so did most of her friends. It seemed everyone was taking them. We now know amphetamines have another name: speed. It's mind-boggling to think that doctors—good doctors— were blithely prescribing amphetamines. So many of us were on speed during the late fifties and sixties, it almost constituted the norm. When the American Medical Association presented findings in the late 1960s showing that continued use of diet pills was a form of substance abuse, most people stopped using them. Not I. I couldn't give them up. I was dependent upon those pills. I was addicted to them. For twenty-six years I had taken them and everything I accomplished during that quarter of a century plus I attributed to the chemicals ruling my body. I actually felt that without them, none of these achievements would have been possible.

As a result, I had led what was in effect a double life. On the one side, I began college, married, had a son, divorced, went back to school, received my bachelor's degree, married again, had two daughters, taught modern dance, and, as the wife of the governor, became involved in all sorts of social programs. And you know what? I took no real pride in my achievements because, on the other side, I remained convinced that everything I attained derived from the pills.

Why didn't anyone realize I was a drug dependent? Why? Simple. I always was viewed as high-strung, hyperactive, a "ball of fire," a "bundle of energy." Okay for strangers not to realize what was happening, but how come my husband didn't catch on? I was on amphetamines when Michael Dukakis met me; he never knew me any other way. Further, I left no clues. I was an expert, a commando at sneaking those pills. I hid them. My husband never saw a telltale bottle or prescription. When at last he found a cache of amphetamines, he immediately confronted me. I pretended it was a one-shot deal and convincingly pooh-poohed the whole thing. I promised Michael I wouldn't take them again. I broke my promise. Addicts tend to break promises.

The insidious diet pills held sway until the summer of 1982. I could no longer live with myself. I had become a short-tempered, unhappy woman. I knew it was the amphetamines. I wanted out. I turned for help to Dr. Al Peters, my sister Jinny's husband. (Al has permitted me to reveal that he is a recovering alcoholic and actively involved in helping others.) I asked Al whether there was a program for people who took drugs. He put me in touch with a physician who recommended Hazelden in Center City, Minnesota. I entered Hazelden on July 14, 1982. While in treatment there, I considered myself addicted only to specific drugs, the diet kind. My counselor believed differently and cautioned me about turning my addiction onto other tracks, like drinking. I thought she was way off base. Drinking had never been a problem for me. I was a nice Jewish girl from a good family and everyone knows nice Jewish girls don't drink. I left Hazelden convinced I had conquered my habit, my only habit.

Back in the outside world, I went along with my counselor's admonition about alcohol and attended support group meetings. It was a halfhearted effort; I simply couldn't identify. If I had gone the distance and really committed myself to a structured program, things might have turned out differently.

For about eight months, I did not indulge. No one questioned my total abstinence because I had a built-in excuse. To cover up my Hazelden stay, everyone was told I had hepatitis. When I returned, I couldn't drink—for "health" reasons. Then, one evening, at a small dinner party, my host poured wine into my glass. I remember thinking, "It's no big deal. It's just a glass of wine." I felt like having it and I did. I had maybe two glasses of wine. I drank slowly, as though they were merely pleasant accompaniments to the meal, just like the advertisements tell us. They weren't. No matter how casually I tried to treat it, I was pulling the trigger.

Soon, I returned to a sporadic pattern of drinking—one or two vodkas before dinner and perhaps a glass or two of wine with my meal. I really didn't give it a thought; I firmly believed, right up until the run for the presidency, that I had my dependency under control. During the campaign, whatever excess drinking I did was done in private. In the waning days of the race, a bottle of Stolichnaya began to appear in the hotel suites I occupied; not *my* room, but the quarters in which my executive assistant was housed. There was a connecting door and it wasn't locked; I passed through that door many times.

At ceremonies and in public I continued to restrain myself. Ask the crew of Sky Heaven, ask my staff, ask my family. No one saw me drinking. No wonder people had trouble accepting my declaration of dependency. Even those closest to me expressed doubts when I entered Edgehill Newport, a drug and alcohol rehabilitation center in Rhode Island, two months after the election. Upon hearing the news, violinist-conductor Alexander Schneider reassured his friend and colleague, my father, Harry Ellis Dickson, "Don't worry, Harry, Kitty's not an alcoholic." Smart as he is, Sasha Schneider, an original member of the Budapest String Quartet and one of the most extraordinary men I've ever known, could not see straight when it came to my problem. I fooled a lot of savvy people. "You're not an alcoholic, Kitty, you're a bit hysterical, that's all," an old friend advised. I guess my friend figured it was better to be deemed hysterical than alcoholic. Thank God I did not listen to the opinions of others. If I had yielded to their views of my condition, I might still be denying. Alcoholism is a disease, and one does not choose to be diseased. Still, for an awfully long time, those words, "You're not an alcoholic," rang in my ears and enabled me to ignore my own symptoms.

"You're not an alcoholic, Kitty."

Right! I was not an alcoholic.

Tell me, though, what *would* you call someone who, after the presidential defeat, woke up in the morning, waited until her husband left for work, canceled all her appointments, and began to drink anything she could get her hands on, starting at 9:00 A.M.?

What would you call someone who at first tried to mask her multiple trips to the liquor closet and then defiantly screamed at her own son to mind his own goddamn business when he questioned what his mother was doing?

What would you call someone who raided her own liquor cabinet, drank, alone, in her kitchen, then staggered up the stairs of her house and reeled into her bedroom? What would you call someone who drew the curtains to block out the sun, stumbled over to her bed, and lay there until she fell into a stupor? What would you call someone who did this day after day after day.

And what would you call someone who, one terrible afternoon, lay in her own vomit on that bed until her husband, summoned by the frightened son, rushed home to rouse his wife and lovingly, tenderly, removed the filthy clothing, washed the vomitus from her body, and cleaned up the mess?

What would *you* call that someone? You would call her Kitty Dukakis and you would call her an alcoholic. That's what I told you up front.

Up front. That's also what I am. The cat has never gotten this Kitty's tongue. I'm blunt and I say what I mean. For years, my outspokenness got me into more *public* trouble than taking pills or drinking did. I'm impatient. Whenever I'm after something, I think of the old song, "Oh, I want what I want when I want it!" I cannot tolerate ineptitude or, worse, indifference. I have always been a social activist and am proud of it. I care about people, all people.

Do you want to know one of the things that, personally, hurt me most during the presidential campaign? It was an article in the *Baltimore Sun* that appeared after I visited a shelter for the homeless. According to this scathing piece, I danced into the shelter like some modern Lady Bountiful to have my picture taken and exploit the downtrodden. While I never responded to the *Sun*'s slur, it truly upset me. My husband has often remarked that I'll slough off a ton of positive material and zero in on one negative comment. He's right. It's not that I can't take criticism; everyone in public life has to accept the slings and arrows, they come with the territory. However, I do react to malicious attacks that, indirectly, can hurt innocent people.

Had the *Sun* reporter done her homework, she would have discovered that the plight of the homeless was not a new initiative for me. I did not go waltzing into a shelter for the first time during my husband's campaign, a fact the paper should have researched and respected. I became involved in 1983, when the cause of the homeless emerged as a national issue. I was cochair of a commission on the homeless that moved thousands of people from shelters, hotels, and motels into permanent housing, while raising $1.3 million for the fund for the homeless. It is just one of the activities with which I have been vigorously involved. I have been active with the United States Holocaust Memorial Council for ten years. I began the Harvard Public Space Partnerships Program at the Kennedy School of Government. In 1974, inspired by Lady Bird Johnson's efforts, I initiated the Open Space Beautification Program in Massachusetts. I organized a task force on Cambodian children and went on fact-finding tours of refugee camps in Thailand in 1981 and 1985. I serve on the board of trustees of the Refugee Policy Group and on the board of directors of Refugees

International. I have seen firsthand the devastating effects of indifference at home, and of war overseas. I am proud of what I have been able to do for the less fortunate but no less deserving. Don't pin medals on me, don't pat my back, but don't stab me in the back, either.

As part of my recovery, I've been taught to let resentments go and not harbor grudges (they often provide an impetus to drink). I'm working on it. I built up a lot of resentment about that *Baltimore Sun* article, and now, I've "given it away." That's a phrase I learned at Edgehill Newport. I've learned many adages over the past year or so, and they make good sense. One of the most helpful is "A day at a time."

One day, about two weeks before the presidential election, Bob Barnett, a Washington lawyer and literary agent, contacted my press secretary, Paul Costello. At the time, the polls showed Michael didn't have a chance; defeat was certain. Still, I would not give up and went through all the campaign activities with forced fervor. I had to stuff all my feelings and it was very wearing. That's just before I began binge-drinking in the privacy of my home. Bob Barnett knew nothing about my problem; no one did. He was impressed by my public persona. Paul and I met with him and Bob told us he thought my story would make an interesting and provocative book. Further, he was convinced I'd do well on the lecture circuit. Paul agreed; in fact, he told Bob he had been thinking along the same lines and wanted me to do a journal of the campaign. Despite their assurance, my first reaction was "Who, me?" Although the saga of seeking the presidency contained all the necessary ingredients for an exciting narrative, I could not imagine my personal participation being important enough to warrant a book. As for public speaking, who would want to hear me! I was skeptical. The campaign, yes; Kitty Dukakis, no. Neither Bob nor Paul would accept my demurs, and finally they got me to agree. At the end of our meeting, I told Bob Barnett to go ahead and set up meetings with publishing houses.

The election took place on November 8, 1988. To say the rug was pulled out from under me when Michael was defeated would be far too feeble a description; the *world* was pulled out from under me, a world of constant activity, motion, energy—everything I thrive on. I felt as though I had been squashed in a giant compactor; all the breath went out of me. Michael was hurting too; I knew it, everyone knew it. Now is not the time to go into a lengthy discussion about my husband, but I will say, up front, I honor and cherish him even more today. We have a special relationship that the media recognized as unique and is still trying to fathom.

I suppose the most widely publicized story—*positive* story, that is—about Michael and me concerned the 1988 St. Patrick's Day parade in Chicago. We were marching in frigid weather and I was freezing. I asked Michael to put the back of my collar up to block the wind. Michael leaned over and—as he fixed my coat—whispered in my ear. "Tonight if I'm asleep, wake me up. Don't let a moment go by." I cut in fast, "Your microphone's on!" My dear husband had forgotten he was wired; his personal message had been broadcast. Michael smiled. He wasn't embarrassed. We're comfortable with each other. We love each other and we don't care who knows it. (After the election, we received a charming gift. Someone sent a cross-stitch pillow cover embroidered with the legend, "Wake me up, don't let a moment go by.")

From the very beginning of our relationship, Michael has enriched and enhanced my life. His mother, Euterpe, once was asked what I brought to her son. "Happiness," she quickly answered. I treasure that response and have tried to live up to it. Alas, after the election, I could not bring anything to Michael—I was too crushed. In different ways, we both were licking our wounds. Two mornings after the election, he was working in his office at the State House while I was drinking in our bedroom on Perry Street.

Lots of people tried to reach me, but most were unsuccessful—the phone was usually unplugged. I didn't want to talk to *anybody*, not my husband, not my children, not my sister, not even my father. Why didn't my family see what was happening? The question keeps coming up. How could my husband live in the same house with me, sleep in the same bed with me, and not know what I was doing? Again, alcoholics will understand. When it comes to covering our tracks, we're consummate artists. At first, it was easy to fool Michael; all I had to do was go through the formal motions of normalcy when he was home in the morning and at night. While he was away, I entered my netherworld of alcohol. Eventually, I became totally immersed and too far gone to deceive anybody. That's precisely when Michael called for help.

During the last weeks of 1988, Bob Barnett had gone about the business of getting appointments with publishing firms. Then, he had to get hold of me. I had pretty much confined myself to my bedroom. Bob is persistent. He kept calling until he finally got through, on one of the rare occasions when the phone was connected. Brushing aside my mush-mouthed responses, he eagerly outlined the schedule. He had no idea he was talking to a woman on the brink of collapse. I forced myself to pay attention. I desperately needed something to do and viewed work-

ing on a book as a possible salvation, anything to bring
me out of the doldrums. Bob's enthusiasm was catching.
I agreed to fly down to New York and meet with publishers. For the next few weeks, during my sessions
with editors, I hardly drank. Sure, I hit the bottle when
I was safe at home, but never when I was negotiating. I
think I had one vodka when we met with the last pub-
lisher. Once again, my selective sobriety gave me a false
sense of security. I could still control my drinking, or so
I deluded myself.

Looking back, I don't know how I got through those
sessions. I sat in the executive offices of the most pres-
tigious publishing houses in America and talked with
some of the most brilliant editors in the business about
a book based on my life. My life? My life was worthless.
I could not imagine anyone wanting to publish, let alone
read, a book about Kitty Dukakis. Who the hell was I?
A woman who had stopped taking pills and now was
drinking. Thank heaven, my agent did most of the talking; he had a far higher estimation of my worth than I.
To be honest, some of the publishers felt the same way
I did; they weren't interested in me. (Some had been
burned following the 1984 presidential election when
they paid large advances for books about that campaign
that bombed.) Ironically, I agreed with their opinions
more than with those who thought I was worthy. Talk
about the emperor's new clothes! I felt like a fraud, a
sham. I had been exposed to public scrutiny and unrelenting questioning from the press and had come
through with flying colors, yet I truly believed that had
been a fluke. I just knew that any minute I would be
revealed. What a tremendous strain! The pressures of
the campaign had barely subsided and I was in another
hot pot, only this time, I was alone. What could I possi-

bly have to say! I'm talking self-worth and self-esteem, and I had remarkably little. Like all of us, my feelings about myself come directly out of my childhood, and, a long time ago, I was judged and found wanting by one of the most important people in my life, my mother, Jane Goldberg Dickson.

"You're just pretty," Mother told me when I was a little girl. "You have the looks, but your sister has the personality." What a thing to say to a child! I have a son and two daughters of my own; I cannot imagine making such a stunning statement to any of them. My mother not only laid this on *me*, she repeated it to my younger sister. Jinny was understandably wounded at being dubbed less attractive, and I was furious at being classified as merely "pretty." How I envied Jinny for having "personality," and how little I thought of myself for having nothing except what I had been given at birth! My lovely, lively sister and I laugh about Mother's judgment now, but, when we were children, her assessment of our respective virtues was devastating to our egos. It's a miracle we didn't kill each other. Like all siblings, we tried. Jinny and I fought like mini-Amazons.

My dad tells the story of one occasion when he was conducting a concert to which he planned to take us. A local acting company was presenting Shakespeare's *Midsummer Night's Dream* and Dad's orchestra was going to perform Mendelssohn's Overture and Incidental Music. Dressed and ready to go, Jinny and I naturally began to squabble. Dad was busy with last-minute preparations. Annoyed by our shrieks and shouts, he called out for us to pipe down and stop fighting. Jinny and I were around seven and eight years old at the time; we needed referees, not reprimands, and continued to battle.

Dad struck his head in the door and said, "If you two don't stop, I'm not going to take you!" We'd heard that one before, too. The second the door closed, Jinny and I were at it again.

"That does it!" cried our father. He turned on his heels and left the house without us. We could not believe it. He had never carried through on any of his threats before.

The funny thing is, my dad has never forgiven himself for leaving us at home. To this day he talks about that event as though it were the worst crime committed against his progeny. It's even funnier because neither Jinny nor I was that upset then, and certainly not now. Left in the lurch, we continued fighting and our rounds carried us through the afternoon. At the end of the day, my father returned and sheepishly handed us two pail-and-shovel sets. He felt so guilty, he bought presents. I can't speak for Jinny, I know only that I much preferred having the pail and shovel to having to sit through a concert.

This episode is illustrative of my dad. He was, and is, so outgoing, so warm, and so giving, he naturally makes everyone around him feel good, even when he's punishing them.

My mother was a different story. She was the most private person I have ever known. Beautiful, restrained, refined, reserved—these are the words to describe my mother. So much of what I felt about myself came from her. She died in 1977 and, for seven years after her death, I never bought a dress without assuring myself she would have approved. Dad's volubility and Mother's restraint were the two poles. Since Mother was around the greater part of the time, I was raised under her watchful, critical eye.

I was eighteen years old and a counselor at camp when Billie Isber, a cousin on my mother's side, came to visit her daughter Carolyn. I had a long conversation with Billie, mostly about my mother. I was concerned because she was going through the change of life and reacting rather negatively. While we were talking, Billie inadvertently revealed a secret my mother had kept hidden from almost everyone, including her two daughters. My mother was an adopted child, and the couple my sister and I knew as grandfather and grandmother were really adoptive grandparents. When my cousin mentioned this, I was thunderstruck. I don't think anyone could hear such a tale and not be profoundly affected. Poor Billie was aghast; she assumed I knew. I was a wreck. When camp was over a few days later, I packed up my bags, piled them in a friend's car, and drove home.

My dad was away at Pierre Monteux's conducting school and Mother was alone. I went into the house and found her dusting the furniture, a cigarette dangling from her lips.

I made her put away the dustcloth and sit down. I told her what Billie had said. "Why did you keep this from me? Why didn't you let me know?" I pleaded passionately. I guess I wanted Mother to say it wasn't true, or, short of that, to give me some reason why I hadn't been told, something to hang on to.

Mother looked at me and replied, flatly, "Well, now you know."

She got up and started dusting again. As far as she was concerned, that was the end of the matter. As far as I was concerned, there had been an enormous breach of trust.

That traumatic moment haunted me for years. Indeed, until I began this book, I never knew the full story.

While searching for my "roots," Mother's true origins were revealed. The basic fact is, my restrained, reserved, and proper mother was an illegitimate child.

A scant year after my mother admitted she was adopted, I started using amphetamines. Does it have any bearing? I don't know. I only know, when I recognized my addiction and ceased taking diet pills in 1982, it was merely a step toward recovery and not a triumphant victory. I did not fully comprehend that I could not use drugs or drink in any form without risking a relapse. I did not know it was only a question of time.

I signed a book contract with Simon and Schuster in January 1989, returned to Perry Street in Brookline, and systematically began to destroy myself. Okay, I was going to write a book about my life, especially the campaign experiences. I had a million stories in my head: Could I get them out? Worse, what if I told them and they were deemed ordinary and inadequate? I was terrified. I went for the oblivion provided by alcohol. I left the campaign trail, picked up the booze trail, and reached rock bottom. Then, through a series of discoveries and disclosures, I managed to pull myself together enough to acknowledge my intense need for help. I entered Edgehill Newport. I have to say it took more courage for me to declare my alcohol dependency to the world than anything I had ever done. It was humiliating. The woman who had gone around the country lecturing on drug dependency, and how she had kicked the habit, now stood before the world confessing she was addicted to alcohol. Frankly, I believed my confession would end my love affair with the public; I thought I'd be censured and dubbed a phony. Who would care about such a fraud? Who would read a book by an avowed dissembler? I didn't care. I only cared about getting sober. And, beyond that, getting back to my loved ones. When I left Edgehill Newport, I was on the way to sobriety. My family and friends were wonderfully supportive. And I was deeply moved by the public's response. My life did not begin and end with the 1988 presidential campaign; it appears I really have a story to tell.

August 1989

February 1990

Six months ago, when the preceding preface was written, I truly believed I knew where I had been and where I was going. I was five months sober, and, to all intents and purposes, drug-free. I had started my lecture tours and my speeches had been well received. Following months of intense dialogue, the manuscript for my book had been completed and submitted, and, with minor revisions requested, a spring publication date was scheduled. True, Michael was having problems in the state, and though I was concerned for him, everything seemed to be falling into place for me. I had returned to my family, and, paradoxical as it may sound, was looking forward to the future a day at a time. Convinced I had roused my demons and routed them, I was eager to get on with my life.

In rereading the original preface, I am struck by both

my utter confidence and what proved to be my relative ignorance. I tried to be up front. I thought I was on top of everything. I knew I had a dependency problem that encompassed alcohol as well as drugs, and my guard was up. You'll notice when I said I was drug-free, I added "to all intents and purposes." The whole truth is, when I left Edgehill Newport, I was taking Prozac, an anti-depressant.

I have suffered from severe depression for the past eight years. Though no one has been able to tell me what actually causes my depressions, it is significant that these moods began after I left Hazelden—after I stopped taking amphetamines.

I had mixed feelings about taking the Prozac, but my doctors convinced me medication was necessary until my body adjusted. By the end of May, I was feeling so good, I asked the psychiatrist to take me off medication. He agreed, and gradually I stopped. Mid-September, I started feeling a little down, the faint beginnings, I feared, of those fall depressions. I told Michael and, to-gether, we consulted with the therapist. I did not want to return to the medicine and instead went ahead with an Outward Bound experience that had been arranged months before. In that program, I could test myself without being threatened. Outward Bound proved an invigorating and gratifying challenge. For a time, I felt fine—but only for a time. I could not gather sufficient residual strength to provide the support I needed.

In October, I went on a whirlwind speaking tour; ten engagements in less than four weeks. The old pattern of leaping from excitement to excitement, event to event was set in motion. When the run was over, I felt empty. I had no other lectures until February. I returned home at the beginning of November, settled in, and slowly, surely, began to withdraw. My resources had dried up. Nothing mattered. Nothing loomed on the near horizon of activity. There was little to do at home and I could not bear going to the State House. Politically, financially, and emotionally, Beacon Hill was a disaster area as Michael valiantly battled to revamp the Massachusetts economy. Beset with his own problems, my husband still tried to help me. He begged me to tell him what was troubling me. I would not—I could not—answer. I was unable to reach out to him or anyone else. My lethargy escalated. I could not face working on book revisions and refused to meet with my collaborator. I canceled appointments with my therapist. I was going to fewer meetings. And, one Monday evening in November, because I desperately needed something to make me feel better and because there was no liquor in the house, I drank rubbing alcohol.

I need to say right here, I did not want to kill myself. I have never wanted to kill myself. I am not suicidal. I only wanted to "get away" for a while. It was a slip, but it wasn't the last one. It's like Al Jolson used to say, "You ain't heard nothin' yet!" Within the next six weeks, on two other occasions, I again attempted to "get away," once with pills and then with a mixture of liquids I blush to name. I never took enough stuff to kill myself, just enough to escape, to block things out. Each episode took place at my home and neither was reported or recorded by the media. In December 1989, with strictest secrecy and under an assumed name, I entered a psychiatric hospital in New York State.

Because I am a public person, there is a certain amount of interest in what happens to me. I would like to put that attention to positive use. In the process of trying to bring my life into balance, I've uncovered aspects of my existence to which I hope others can relate and from which I hope they can learn. I know there are many, many people out there who could benefit from hearing about my experiences. I'm fortunate. I'm getting help; most others who are suffering are *not*, and their lives are filled with unrelieved misery. It makes whatever reticence I might have had about revealing myself inconsequential. Knowledge and understanding can help erase the stigma attached to mental illness. I know, firsthand, there is hope. I'm beginning to feel good about myself. I certainly feel good about this book. I'm eager to share my story.

I

EARLY
STAGES

Mon. Feb. 20, 1989

Dear Kit,

It was good to see you on Saturday, your old, smiling, healthy, beautiful self. Your references to Mother and her preoccupation with perfection for you and for Jinny and for me rather surprised me. Perhaps it is a fault within me that I didn't realize its importance and the effect it had on you. You know Mother never even complimented me on anything I did. I didn't seem to mind it, because I knew she loved me and I also knew she was proud of me. As she was of you. Mother never seemed to be overly impressed by any of our attempts or accomplishments. I must confess my own shortcomings in expressing my feelings, and it is only lately that I am able to say to you that I love you. I had always felt that feelings were understood and did not need verbalizing. And I was wrong, and I'm much more comfortable now saying what I feel. I have been almost afraid to acknowledge your qualities, your talents, your varied and wonderful abilities, although I burst with pride and thankfulness when others do.

Dear Kitty, the world from now on is your oyster, and I know you will make the most of it.

I LOVE YOU,
DAD

ONE

I was raised in privileged circumstances. I don't mean we were fabulously wealthy and dwelt in a big mansion with servants. Far from it. At the time of my birth, my parents lived in unpretentious quarters on Lothian Road in Brighton, Massachusetts. The privileges I'm speaking of came from ambience, not affluence. My dad was a working musician, a violinist and conductor who played with popular bands as well as serious concert orchestras. In the vaudeville act called "Grace Hushen and Her Melody Boys," my dad, dressed in flowing white shirt and pants and wearing a red sash, was one of the boys. In more formal garb, he played with WPA bands like the State Symphony Orchestra and the Commonwealth Symphony.

Like most women of her time and of her social standing, my mother was a housewife. Unlike many of them, she could have worked; she'd been trained as a nurse and had a degree in social work. Mother chose to stay at home because my father's salary, though not magnificent, was enough to live on, and, at the time, I'm sure both my parents adhered to the archaic principle, "A woman's place is in the home." There was not a lot of extra cash around and they had to watch expenses, but compared to most families struggling in the wake of the Depression, they were doing okay.

I was born in Cambridge, Massachusetts, on the day after Christmas, December 26, 1936. My father, Harry Ellis Dickson, had also been born in Cambridge, to Ethel and Ellis Dickson. Dad was a first-generation American. The Dicksons came from a shtetl outside of Kiev, Russia. According to family lore, on the boat carrying them to America, my great-grandfather had a falling out with his brother and swore never to speak to him again. Great-grandfather was so enraged he dropped his surname, Duchin, and changed it to Dickson. The Duchins were a musical family; Dad's cousin Eddie became a popular pianist and band leader in New York. His son, Peter, has carried on the tradition. Though I've seen Peter many times, I don't think my dad has ever met him. The Duchin name continues on; my father is the last Dickson.

When Dad was around eight years old, his parents moved to Somerville, a blue-collar suburb of Boston adjacent to Cambridge. My grandfather was a tailor; he was also left-handed, which must have made it awkward for him to ply his trade. Nowadays, you can get special equipment from scissors to sewing machines; it was different then. Being left-handed put you in league with the devil. When I was young, if a child showed left-handed tendencies, he was pushed into using the right hand. Presumably it would make it easier for him, since most people were right-handed. Fortunately, we don't think that way anymore. A lot of kids who would have been traumatized have been allowed to do what came naturally, like my son, John. He's a lefty. His father's family was 100 percent right-handed, so I figured it came from my side. Funny how traits, all kinds of them, can skip a generation or two, and then surface. Along with the occasional tendency to the left hand, I've also discovered a couple of alcoholics and drug dependents among my straitlaced forebears.

My Dickson grandparents were traditional, simple people. Though my grandmother was known as "Bubbe," for some reason we called my grandfather "Papa" rather than "Zaideh," the Yiddish term. Family was the most important thing in my grandparents' lives. I loved them dearly though I was a little frightened of Papa; he was gruff. Looking back, I guess he had a right to be. I don't imagine life could have been so easy for a left-handed, Jewish tailor. Despite the hardships, Dad always spoke positively of his childhood. He was in the middle, a boy sandwiched between two girls, Ruth and Lily. Jewish homes stressed education in the arts as well as the sciences, and Dad began studying the violin as a child. He was precocious in many ways and was graduated with honors from Somerville High School at fifteen. By then, music ruled his life, and instead of going to Harvard, he went to the New England Conservatory of Music. If you ask my dad what he would have done differently, he'll say, "I wish I had become a surgeon." I think he's just giving lip service to an antique ideal. The scalpel cuts out what is wrong, but music cuts to the heart of what matters. I cannot imagine my father being anything other than a music maker.

As children, Jinny and I adored hearing the tales of

my father's youth. They made fabulous bedtime stories. My father is one of the greatest storytellers imaginable, and not just for children. He really has the gift of gab and always has been in demand as a speaker. For years, his pre-concert lectures delighted Boston Symphony audiences. He's also written books on his musical experiences.

At bedtime, though, Jinny and I were interested in hearing and rehearing the tales of his childhood rather than anecdotes about the Boston Symphony Orchestra and its illustrious conductor, my dad's "boss," Serge Koussevitsky. One of our favorite accounts concerned the Somerville High School Snake Dance. To celebrate graduation, the students formed a line and did serpentine twists and turns through the city streets. Dad, the youngest and smallest guy in the class, had to lead the column. His parents, like so many immigrants, were wary of these weird American games and customs. Don't forget, their past was studded with memories of anti-Semitism and unprovoked attacks on Jews. I'm sure they thought their boy would be subjected to catastrophe by being exposed at the front of this wacky snake business. They couldn't stop him; he had to participate in the school activity, so they resorted to other means. At the appointed time, Dad took his place and began the long, devious march through Somerville. Lo and behold, every time he turned a corner, there would be his Uncle Barney standing on the sidelines. "I thought I was going crazy," said my father, "everywhere I went, I saw my uncle." Though Jinny and I knew the story and the punchline by heart, we'd look at Daddy expectantly, waiting for him to deliver the denouement, which he always did with a flourish. The explanation for Barney's ubiquitous presence? At his sister Ethel's request, her bachelor brother spent the entire afternoon running ahead of the line to make sure his nephew was safe. I'm sure Uncle Barney was far more exhausted by the snake dance than any of the actual participants.

After four years at the New England Conservatory, Dad crossed the Atlantic to attend, on scholarship, the Hochschule für Musik in Berlin. As Dad recalls, "At that time, there was little choice, musicians *had* to go to Europe to study." He arrived in Germany in 1931. Though the National Socialist party was on the rise, Dad's German pals and fellow students thought it was a joke and viewed Adolf Hitler as a ranting clown rather than a threat. Two years later, when Dad left Germany, all those laughing friends had become Nazis. In a bizarre moment in his life, my father actually sat in the second row at Adolf Hitler's inaugural.

Although they were both Americans, my parents met in Germany, through one of those coincidences that could drive a professional matchmaker crazy. Dr. Shubow, Dad's dentist, had a sister, Rochelle. She was, according to my father, a very ambitious pianist and had gone to study with Artur Schnabel in Berlin. On the voyage over, Rochelle met a vivacious, energetic woman from New York, Mabel Goldberg. The two women spent quite a bit of time together strolling on the deck and eating in the dining room. Mabel was on her way to Germany's capital city to visit her daughter Jane. After they arrived in Berlin, Mabel introduced her daughter to Rochelle. A few weeks later, Dad wrote to Rochelle Shubow and advised her of his imminent appearance in Deutschland. Many students were living overseas, and Rochelle decided it would be fun to give a party for American friends. On Dad's second night in Berlin, he went to the gathering. Among the guests was Jane Goldberg. She was working with disturbed children in a special section at Spandau, the prison that achieved notoriety after the Second World War as the residence of Nazi war criminals. Many of us remember the enigma of Spandau. Outmoded, rundown, a financial drain, it was maintained by the West German government until only one criminal, Rudolf Hess, remained. The huge fortress was kept going just to accommodate a single prisoner. I can recall seeing grainy newspaper pictures of the solitary old man walking in the prison yard. I did not feel sorry for him. It's hard to sympathize with murderers no matter what their age. After Rudolf Hess's death in 1987, Spandau closed. In the 1930s, though, it was thriving, and one section had been set aside for the care and treatment of disturbed children. This was my mother's specialty, and she was working with those troubled youths when she met Dad.

At Rochelle Shubow's party, Dad and Mother hit it off. Afterwards, they started seeing each other. He liked her, and, at the same time, felt sorry for her. "She was strong in her own way," he told me, "but there was something waiflike and vulnerable about her." Though he was attracted to her, my father was nervous about dating this beautiful young woman; indeed, he was a little jittery about dating at all. His teachers in America had cautioned him to stay away from the ladies and to stick to his studies.

"They didn't mean I shouldn't see women, they just meant I shouldn't get serious because it would interfere with my music," he explained. "All those admonitions from my professors were ringing in my ears. As a result, I was scared stiff of your mother. Even though we began to see each other on a regular basis, I tried to be a little indifferent. I remember Mabel invited me to join them for Christmas in Switzerland; I refused. I think I assumed a detached pose to protect myself. After all, I was not supposed to get serious." The irony is, despite his teachers' counsel, my father married the very first woman he met in Berlin.

My mother was nineteen when she and my father were introduced. She had been in Europe for close to a decade. First, she had been placed with a family in the middle of France. Then, at the age of fourteen, she was taken from the Midi and placed in a progressive school in Switzerland. Later, she received degrees in nursing and social work. Ostensibly, my mother became a juvenile expatriate because her mother believed children, not just musicians, should have a European education. Mother was trilingual—she spoke English, French, and German. Because she was in Europe for so long, my father claims, when he met her English was her worst language. Later, she spoke it perfectly, though a bit more formally than her peers and without any regional accent. One of the rumors circulated during the presidential campaign had to do with my mother's birthplace. It was said she was born in Europe, as though there were something wrong with that. In fact, both my parents were born in America. My husband's parents were born in Greece. He was born here, and thus, according to the Constitution of the United States, was eligible to run for the presidency.

When my father came to visit me at Edgehill Newport, I wanted to talk to him about Mother, particularly my resentments toward her. The staff psychiatrist questioned me about my parents' relationship and asked what I knew about their courtship. I had to admit I knew almost nothing. I asked Dad to fill me in. Realizing I needed to hear the truth and not bedtime stories, he opened up to me for the first time. I was surprised to learn that Jane Goldberg had set her cap for him; it was hard to believe my reserved mother would "chase" after anyone. I guess she knew a good thing when she saw it and her feelings overcame her natural shyness.

When Dad told her he would be leaving Germany for America, she arranged to return too. As it turned out, she left before him, and before Hitler's ascent as well. She and my father corresponded off and on. Dad returned to America and the letter writing continued, only now the postmarks read Boston and New Rochelle, New York. My parents might have remained pen pals had not my father been asked to give a concert with an orchestra in New Rochelle. Immediately, he wrote his friend Jane and informed her he was coming to town. Mabel Goldberg told her daughter to invite the young man to stay overnight. Dad accepted the invitation and spent the evening with Mother and the ubiquitous Mabel. He claims that, when he returned home, he realized he had to marry Jane. According to him, his own mother reacted most unusually to his romance.

"You would think," says he, "a Jewish mother would be on the lookout as far as her only son was concerned and not want him to get married. But, when I came back from Europe, she took one look at the way I was moping around and said, 'You're unhappy without this woman, I think you should marry her.' My God, she hadn't even met Jane and she was urging me to the altar! This was not a classic Jewish mother reaction."

And so they were married on October 13, 1935, and were together until her death forty-two years later.

My father joined the Boston Symphony Orchestra in 1938, and retired in 1987. During those years, he was a first chair in the violin section of the BSO and associate conductor of the Boston Pops. Dad has told some of his story in his own book, *Gentlemen, More Dolce, Please!*, a lively look at the life of a symphony player. It's delightful and I laugh out loud when I read it. I find in writing my own book that discussing my father is not so difficult; I've always been close to him. As a young girl I worried I'd never find a man like him to marry. No question, I *am* a daddy's girl. We are akin in many, many ways. Though I did not inherit his musical gifts, I'm sure my interest and involvement with dance was a direct outgrowth of his influence. I think like my dad. We're both very ambitious; we want to show people we can do something and we do it. Still, we don't believe in ourselves. When asked about me, Dad has allowed that I can *appear* vain and egotistical, yet I'm actually the opposite. He's right—I haven't such a high opinion of myself. He claims to have an even lower opinion of *him*self! It surprises people to hear that my charming, erudite father is plagued with self-doubt. He agonizes over his public appearances; in fact, he says he's more scared before concerts now than ever before! You would never believe it if you saw him in front of a crowd. He's so relaxed and informative; he seems born to the podium.

My dad is over eighty and one of the most remarkable octogenarians you can imagine. He's physically and mentally fit and retains his delicious sense of fun. Author, wit, musician, lecturer, and you know what his comment is? "In the back of my mind, all my life, I've always felt I got away with things." When my father makes remarks like that, it knocks me out—I guess because I've often felt the same way myself. Our similarities are obvious and maybe that's why I can talk about him candidly, without fear of upsetting him and/or me.

. . .

My mother is a different story. I'm not only wary of discussing her, I'm terrified of betraying her. We had problems. There was often friction. Among other points of contention, I always felt she favored my sister, who was born fifteen months after me. I was right, and in order to make up for Mother's partiality, Dad favored me, but not at Jinny's expense. When he'd introduce us, he'd say, "These are my two daughters; one is much better than the other." He left it to us and to others to figure out which one. It was only a joke, and we loved it. Dad's inherent warmth put us at ease. Mother was cut from a different cloth, a harder, more abrasive fabric. Black was black, white was white. No grays. Mother's reasons for treating me the way she did were typical of Mother's thinking processes. From the beginning she felt I was equipped by nature to take care of myself. Jinny needed assistance. Once, Jinny overheard Mother talking on the phone about her daughters. Jinny listened as Mother told her friend that I was a beautiful baby. When my little sister was born, however, she resembled, in Mother's words, "a red weasel." "I couldn't look at her," was Mother's comment. I guess because she "couldn't look at her," Mother proceeded to try to boost the "red weasel" while tearing me down. No question, Jinny was much closer to her. According to Dad, Jinny wasn't the renegade I was. She was into mischief, more a scamp than a rebel. I fought my mother's directives even as I had to obey them. My conflicts with her were a reflection of her constant bickering with her own mother.

Wait.

Before I get into an innate maelstrom, it's probably an appropriate moment to look directly into Mother's unconventional background. The more I delve into her past, the better I am able to understand my own.

My mother was the illegitimate child of Margaret Buxbaum. The Buxbaum family, Hungarian Jews, lived on the second floor of an apartment house at 535 East Eighty-first Street in New York City. Margaret was the oldest of nine children. Her best friend, Kitty Byrne, lived on the third floor in the same building. Margaret and Kitty's brother were attracted to each other and began dating on the sly (because he was a Catholic and Margaret was a Jew, they could not be seen together in public). In the early 1900s, the old religious and familial sanctions against interfaith alliances were in full force.

When Margaret's parents found out about the clandestine meetings, they were aghast. It was unthinkable for their child to be consorting with a gentile, and they forbade her to see him again. It's not on record how the Byrnes felt; I'm sure they were equally upset. I don't know what pressures were brought to bear on the young man. All I know is, he and Margaret *were* separated. Not totally; she was pregnant. Sadly, her lover, my grandfather, dropped out of the picture.

In 1990, people live together openly and have children without marrying, but for most of this century, and certainly at the time of my mother's birth, illegitimacy meant shame for the woman and disgrace for the family. Dad told me that, when he first heard the story from my mother, he got the impression Margaret had been married and then deserted by her husband. Later, Dad was informed Margaret wouldn't marry because her family opposed the union. The true story was blurred by generations of protective inventions; eventually, the distortions superceded the facts. My mother felt the circumstances of her birth were nobody's business and remained closed on the subject, even with my father. When I began searching out my roots, I learned some of the story from the youngest Buxbaum child, Birdie, who was about four, little more than a baby herself, when Margaret Buxbaum got pregnant.

We believe Margaret gave my mother up for adoption right away, but did so with a proviso: She had to go and live with the adoptive family as a nanny. Through Rabbi Stephen Wise, the Buxbaums located a couple who wanted to adopt. Mabel and Henry Goldberg were wealthy and educated; they had formidable pedigrees and their families had been in America for generations. Henry was a tall, distinguished-looking man, originally a Kentuckian. Mabel was born a Weil. The Weils, an old German-Jewish family, were affluent merchants, and so were their kin, the Stroocks. There were Dreyfusses in there, too. All in all, my adoptive antecedents were impressive. I don't want to get into the social hierarchy of Jews, although I will say German Jews have always been considered (or do they consider themselves?) to be far removed from their Eastern European kin. Putting it another way, under ordinary circumstances, the German Weils would not be likely to have the Hungarian Buxbaums, and definitely not the Russian Dicksons, to tea. The Goldbergs were not upset about my mother's bloodline; she was a beautiful baby. They adopted her and gave her their name. Later, they would adopt another child, a little boy they called Paul. And, even later, toward the end of the 1920s, they would get a divorce.

True to her expressed desire, Margaret Buxbaum moved in with the Goldbergs and acted as her own daughter's nursemaid. During her stay, she never revealed her identity to the little girl. Margaret served in the household for three years, then left to marry a nice

Jewish man. She had three children by him, all, unbe-
knownst to them, half-siblings of my mother. The oldest
daughter was named Mabel in honor of Margaret's former employer.

Margaret must have been a buffer between Mabel and
Jane, two strong-willed females. My mother was around
nine when she found out she was an adopted child. During one of their frequent battles, frustrated and furious
at my mother's behavior, Mabel shrieked the truth.
What exactly did she say? I don't know. From then on,
mother knew Margaret Buxbaum was her birth mother.
Mother never revealed to me how she felt at that moment. I don't know if she ever told anyone her true
feelings, or if she was even capable of expressing them.
Her guiding principles were: Never show people what
you are actually feeling; don't reveal yourself to others.

She tried to superimpose her defenses on me. I've had
to work hard to break them down. I know my mother
was proud of me; she would talk glowingly about me and
defend me, but *always* to others. She never praised or
complimented me directly. If I complained she'd say,
"You've been given all the gifts, you don't need my compliments. You get them from everybody else." Then,
when I received attention from others, Mother would
counter with, "People say nice things but praise from
outsiders doesn't count. Strangers aren't going to be
there for you when you really need them. Your own flesh
and blood is always there." She made similar statements
to my father. "I'm not related to you by blood but I'm
related to my children," she'd tell him. Daddy would
answer back, "So am I." Obviously, Mother's outlook
arose from her conflicted feelings about her adoption.
Her attitude toward blood ties was intensified because
she was given away.

She never publicly recognized her true mother even when her identity was revealed. She never knew her real father. Mother went through a lot of rage and a lot of pain. Unfortunately, she took some of it out on me. There had to be some jealousy on her part.

Dad used to say, "Try to be kind. Think of the sort of background your mother came from and try to understand." I heard him say this so often it became a litany, yet it didn't make any sense to me. I didn't know about my mother's background until I was eighteen and I didn't put the entire puzzle together till I was fifty-two! The truth is, Mother had difficulty with relationships; she couldn't even sustain the one she shared with her birth mother. Over the years, she became somewhat estranged from her, and, eventually, Margaret was acknowledged as nanny, period.

When Jinny and I were little, Margaret came on several occasions to take care of us, and many, many times we were sent to stay at her apartment at 1515 Selwyn Avenue in the Bronx. Can you imagine this charade going on for so long? We were her grandchildren and she couldn't acknowledge us. We called her Aunt Margaret and she was loving, sweet and dear, and full of hugs and kisses. Her easygoing personality was the antithesis of Grammy Mabel.

One time, when we were seven and eight years old, Jinny and I were having lunch with Margaret. Margaret sneezed and her false teeth flew across the room. At the sight of the flying choppers, my mouth fell open and so did Jinny's. We didn't know what to do. Margaret laughed and retrieved and reinstalled her plate. Had the same incident occurred with Grammy Mabel, she would have given us a lecture on improperly installed prostheses. Mabel kept a stiff upper lip. Not Margaret.

I positively adored staying at Aunt Margaret's and much preferred going there than to Grammy Mabel's in New Rochelle. Sometimes, when Jinny and I were sent away for a week, one of us stayed with Margaret and the other with Grammy. I was happiest in the Bronx. The family was warm and affectionate and made me feel at home.

The kitchen was the focal point of the apartment. Margaret was a fabulous cook and made delectable Hungarian food. Thanks to her, I was introduced to all manner of culinary wonders. Food featured heavily in Aunt Margaret's life, and it showed—she was quite overweight. Her husband, Uncle Sam, on the other hand, was a skinny, skinny man. They were an incongruous pair. We called them Mutt and Jeff.

Margaret's father, Henry Buxbaum, lived with her, and I met him too. We called him Pop and he lived to be ninety-four. Pop was blind. He'd call me over to his side and when I stood next to him, would reach out and touch my face. Drawing his hand over my features, he'd say, "You're beautiful." Birdie told me he did the same thing with her daughter. The difference was, he could acknowledge Birdie's child as kin. He could not admit I was his great-granddaughter. How sad.

After the Second World War, Margaret's middle child, Bob, attended Boston University and lived with us for a while. One night, my mother went out for a walk with Bob and told him he was her half-brother. He began to cry and then said, "You mean Jinny and Kitty are my nieces?" That was the most important thing to him. Mother told him not to say anything to his mother. Sure.

He returned home and, of course, talked to his mother. Margaret was furious and called my mother, crying, "You are never to say anything about this matter again." You see, her husband, Sam, never knew the story, nor had she told her daughters. But now Bob was in on the secret.

When Mother died, Dad called Bob in California and suggested he tell his sisters, Mabel and Barbara, the truth—Jane Dickson was their half-sister. At first, Bob resisted. With Mother dead, what would the revelation accomplish? In the end, he yielded and the sisters were told. The younger one, Barbara, attended my mother's funeral.

I had learned of Margaret's blood ties to mother and me when I was eighteen, but Mother had forbidden me and Jinny to do anything about it. Margaret seemed to feel the same way. Our relationship continued as always. Margaret saw my son, John, her great-grandson, on two occasions. The last meeting occurred when I was living in Cambridge, and one of Margaret's nephews was graduating from Harvard. She came up for the ceremony and dropped by my place for a visit. John was two and a half. Margaret played with him for a while, hugged and kissed him, but never stepped over the self-imposed boundary to acknowledge her real identity. She died not long after.

My mother did not refer to their true alliance again. It was as though it never happened. I saw my mother cry on only two occasions: once, when she was dying, and earlier, when I was sixteen and we received word that her adoptive mother, Mabel, had died in California. Mother began to weep and continued for quite a while. I know she felt strongly about her birth mother, too, yet I do not recall her shedding any tears at the news of Margaret's death.

. . .

While the alleged reason for mother's early exile to Europe was education, I believe she was sent for purposes other than merely receiving a proper schooling. Henry and Mabel Goldberg were not getting along. Their marriage was awash and they probably wanted to clear the deck. They were moneyed and could afford to ship their children off to the best schools.

The separation from her family must have added to Mother's feelings of alienation and isolation. First, the stigma of her birth, and then, at ten years of age, banishment from home. Poor Mother. No wonder she was so awfully contained.

Birdie told me that Grammy called her when plans were afoot to send my mother to Europe. Mabel drove her old Ford motorcar over to the Buxbaums' and made an in-person proposal to Birdie. "I want to send you to Europe to be a companion to Jane," she told the astonished teenager. Though Birdie did not know it, she was mother's half-aunt. Birdie thanked Mabel for the opportunity, but declined. She didn't want to be a companion; she wanted to live her own life. Later, when Birdie realized what she'd turned down, she was sorry she had not accepted the offer. The ties between the Buxbaum and Goldberg families were quite strong. Birdie named her first daughter Jane, after my mother.

While mother was overseas, her parents divorced and went their separate ways. My grandmother, Mabel Weil Goldberg, took on her mother's maiden name, Williams, so my Grandmother Goldberg became Grandmother Williams. And what a character she was!

I talked to my dad about her and he spoke of her with utmost respect and utmost incredulity: "Mabel was a kooky lady. Brilliant, but definitely kooky. She did everything full speed; she had no neutral. At the age of fifty-five, she went back to Columbia and received a Ph.D. in social work. I don't think she did much with it, but, by George, she got it! She was domineering and took charge of everything. She came from wealth, but, in New Rochelle, she was a supporter of leftist causes. She was an inveterate reader, and an inveterate smoker. She was also quite generous, and so impulsive. Impulsive, strange, and wonderful! 'Course I got along better with her than your mother did. They fought all the time."

Dad's right, Grammy *was* extraordinary. Young girls, however, don't necessarily want a phenomenon for a grandmother. It's not so comforting. I much preferred Aunt Margaret's easygoing manner to Grammy's intellectualism. You had to be on your toes with Mabel, she was into everything. She fancied herself a kind of lay doctor and dispensed advice along with medication. When Jinny or I visited her, inevitably we'd find ourselves in the examining rooms of doctors and dentists. Grammy concentrated on orthodontia for Jinny and orthopedics for me. I did have a problem with my feet. When I started dancing at the age of ten, it became apparent I could not do classical ballet. I have double bones—more accurately, ganglia—in my ankles, a condition that made it impossible for me to do a fifth position. I switched to modern dance, where my inability to achieve the ultimate stance didn't matter. I didn't care; I wasn't thinking in terms of a career or anything like that; I just liked to dance.

Grammy's "takeover" personality attracted a lot of people. Hortense Carlisle, Kitty Carlisle Hart's mother and an awesome lady in her own right, was a close friend. Kitty Carlisle was an actress, and, for a while, so was her namesake. I performed for nearly five years with the Tributary Theatre, a children's acting group. By the way, I was called Kitty both for Ms. Carlisle and my aunt Kate, who died young just before I was born. My birth announcement read Katharine Dickson, and in parentheses, Kitty. Katharine is spelled with a second "a," like Katharine Hepburn. Sometimes, Michael calls me Katharine, my dad often will call me Kit, but to most everyone else I'm "Kitty."

After her divorce, Grammy Mabel Williams never remarried. Neither did her ex-husband, my grandfather, Henry Goldberg. He was with the Columbia Grammar School in New York City for years. Also for years, he maintained a relationship with Florence Leonard, the head of the Florence Leonard School for Girls, which was part of the Columbia Grammar School. My grandfather was divorced, Florence Leonard had never married, and yet they never legally wed. They were together for nearly thirty years without, as they used to say, benefit of clergy. I always thought of them as a couple. Florence was like a third grandmother. I'll never forget the time Henry and Florence came up for my eighth-grade graduation from the Runkle School. They stayed at a small hotel on the corner of St. Paul and Beacon streets in Brookline. When I went up to their suite, my grandfather made sure to show me he and Florence stayed in separate bedrooms. I laugh so hard when I think about it now! My grandfather's unsanctified alliance, along with the original divorce from Mabel, added an exotic touch to my background. I knew maybe two Jewish kids whose parents were divorced; in those days, it simply didn't happen. Well, I had divorced *grandparents*; my grandmother was off-the-wall, and my grandfather was living in sin. And I didn't even know the whole story!

TWO

Despite the turbulence of my mother's background, our own family life was, in many ways, quite ordinary. After I was born, Mother and Dad moved into a two-family house at 34 Beaconsfield Road in Brookline. Fifteen years later, we transferred our headquarters to Amory Street near the Brookline-Boston line. Later, when Jinny and I had left home, Dad and Mother moved to a small house in South Brookline. I've lived in other areas of the United States —Texas and California—but basically I've spent the majority of my life as a resident of Brookline, Massachusetts.

Last year I was questioned about my oh, so solid roots, and asked if I had any desire to live anywhere else in the world. I said "no," adding quickly, ". . . except, maybe, Washington." I'm very happy to be where I am. I love this town. I grew up here, went to school here, and so did my husband. Brookline is an extraordinary community with a long history. It always has been known as an elite suburb, both in terms of its affluent citizens and its institutions. Originally, the population was divided into a prosperous, Protestant Yankee upper class and an Irish Catholic blue-collar stratum. The minority upper class controlled the development of the town and it prospered. Repeated attempts to annex Brookline back into Boston were successfully defeated and its independence preserved. At the last census, Brookline's population was 55,062 (a figure that did not include my granddaughter, Alexandra Jane Dukakis, born February 1, 1989).

Brookline has everything, including a glorious landscape of more than fourteen thousand trees of infinite variety. I grew up conscious of beautiful surroundings and it made a lasting impression on me, instilling in me a belief that everyone has a right to live amidst the splendors of nature. My mother was an avid and accomplished horticulturist. She had a real green thumb and a deep appreciation for every form of vegetation. I believe she was happiest at work in her garden. I inherited some of mother's love of flora, and, if not her intensity of interest, at least a general appreciation.

Each year, the town of Brookline publishes a street list of persons twenty years and over. The street number is followed by the resident's name, age, occupation, nationality, and previous residence. When my parents moved to Brookline they were duly inscribed at #34 Beaconsfield Road. In looking through the Brookline street lists for the ensuing years, I noticed that, while my father was registered consistently as Harry E. Dickson, occupation, musician, my mother was listed variously as Jane

C. Dickson, Jane K. Dickson, and—at last and correctly —as Jane G. Dickson. Her occupation went from the catchall "housewife" to the slightly more elevated phrase, "at home." This listing is indicative of the times. Women and their occupations were not as important as men and theirs. The males were the heads of the households; the women were either brushed off as housewives or as being "at home." If you think my statement has a slightly feminist ring, you're right. I am a feminist. Furthermore, the seeds of my feminism were not sown in the sixties with the birth of *Ms.* magazine or the polemics of Gloria Steinem, Betty Friedan, Germaine Greer, and others. When I think about it, I'm pretty certain I know exactly when I started to have feminist leanings— it was while we lived on Beaconsfield Road.

We were not a pious family. My mother had been brought up without any Jewish education and, though my dad had come from a religious background, he followed Mother's lead. We didn't even belong to a synagogue, except for one year when my sister nagged my father to join. All her friends were going to temple and she wanted to be part of the procedures. We joined but weren't members for long. Among other things, Daddy went crazy because the cantor sang off key.

Our heritage remained a part of our lives only because of my grandparents, Bubbe and Papa Dickson. They had moved to Roxbury, and almost every Friday night we went to their house, where we were served the traditional Sabbath dinner. I loved those Friday evening gatherings; I wasn't as enchanted, however, with the subsequent Saturday morning rituals. On Sabbath mornings, I sometimes went with my grandmother to an old shul in Roxbury, then a Jewish stronghold. Like all females, we were forced to sit upstairs in the "ladies' balcony." Orthodox synagogues separated men from women; they still do. During the services the low, keening voices of the men below filled the little synagogue. They obviously had a right to stand there and to pray there, for, as they recited and thanked God every morning, they were born men not women.

Meanwhile, upstairs in the stifling confines of the balcony, the distaff members of the congregation, including my grandmother and me, sat bunched together, looking down on those chosen men dressed in their fancy shawls and special hats—another part of the ritual not shared by the women. It didn't seem to bother Bubbe—she accepted most things and was not, by nature, rebellious. I, however, hated sitting in the shul's gallery. It made me furious to be packed off upstairs while my boy cousins, Bill and Ronnie Skloff, stood among the elite down below. My feelings were not only hurt, they were activated. Who wanted to be stuck up in a lousy balcony while all the action was going on downstairs? Not I!

I remember, too, being the subject of discussion among the mezzanine denizens. The ladies looked me over and mumbled, under their breath, "shiksa." I was about four and a half when I heard that term for the first time: It is Yiddish and means a non-Jewish girl. At the very word, my grandmother would turn excitedly and shush her friends. She'd purse her lips, look over to the side, and pretend to spit, saying something that sounded like *"p-tui, p-tui!"* I learned, later, she was spitting to ward off the "keenahori," the evil eye. "It's not true!" my grandmother cried vehemently. "She's not a shiksa. She's Jewish on both sides!" My grandmother never knew my mother was only half-Jewish and that my sister and I had gentile blood. I think it would have killed her. What killed me was having to sit up in the balcony like a second-class citizen simply because I wasn't born a man. *P-tui! P-tui!*

While my family lived modestly, either in a two-family house or, later, in an apartment, most of my friends lived in big fancy houses at fancy addresses on the best streets in Fischer Hill and Chestnut Hill, exclusive sections of Brookline. A few Brookline areas were more than exclusive—they were restricted. I didn't pal around with those kids, anyway, since most of them went to private schools. My friends were my classmates at the Runkle School and later Brookline High. Though I loved my girlfriends dearly, I noticed their home lives were different from mine. The deviations were obvious. They had maids and house servants, and some of their parents didn't sleep in the same bedroom. Several of my friends had fathers who owned shoe factories in Maine, fathers who would be gone all week and come home on the weekends. Looking back, I'm sure some of those men had two families, one down east and one in Brookline.

My house was different, primarily because my dad was a musician and worked at night, which meant that he was around a good deal during the day. Most fathers, of course, cleared out in the morning and didn't return till dinner time. And while my father was home, he wasn't totally available, since he practiced the violin a lot and we were not supposed to interrupt him. I can't describe how unusual it was to grow up with your father "working" in the house.

Not that Dad confined himself to the inside, and not that his activities constituted "work" as most think of it. Thanks to Dad, there was something wonderfully exhilarating about the goings-on at Beaconsfield Road and

Amory Street. Lots of times, I'd come home and find my father and some of his colleagues playing string quartets in our living room. Yes, with him around, the ambience of our house was decidedly different.

Mother's presence was steady, a slow burning flame rather than the sparks my father set off. She ran a tight ship, demonstrated in part by her obsession with cleaning. She devised methods for scouring hard to reach places like the interstices of tile in the bathroom, and would get down on her hands and knees with a toothbrush to attack the grit. (I had to clean the bathroom every Saturday morning before I went to the movies, and it remains the one housekeeping chore, besides making my bed, that I can do blindfolded. If the truth be known, despite my mastery of hospital corners, Michael makes the bed more often than I.) Mother kept our house pristine and guarded the premises like some hygienic Cerberus. We always had to take our shoes off when we came in the house lest we track mud over her floors. She really went into high gear during spring cleaning; everything came out of every closet, every drawer, and every cupboard in every room. She ruled over her domestic kingdom with a bottle of Lysol in one hand and a scrubbing brush in the other.

I had problems with Mother—big ones. Even so, she, Dad, Jinny, and I formed an exceptionally close family unit, close and volatile. As kids, Jinny and I fought constantly. We were so different, and those differences created havoc, especially in our teens. We were fourteen and fifteen when mother asked us to share a bedroom so Dad could have a private study. We agreed and moved in together. You couldn't have found two more unsuited roommates in all the world. It was hell for two years, for both of us. *She was neat, I was messy.* Jinny drew a string across the room to separate our sides. When people came in, she'd quickly tell them which was her dominion. *She was frugal. I was extravagant.* She babysat and kept all her money. I never had money because I spent whatever I got. (I dearly love them both, but I still say, if my sister and Michael Dukakis were married, they'd have the first nickel they ever made. They really would.) *I was quick. Jinny was deliberate.* We'd go to the corner and buy ice-cream cones, and I'd finish mine in three minutes. She'd still have hers, and I would wheedle her into sharing it with me. *Jinny was dispassionate. I was emotional.* I could not bear injustice, or what I considered to be unfair treatment. One winter evening, Dad came into my bedroom for his nightly visit. I told him about a previous event at summer camp that had disturbed me; I think a counselor had picked on one of my bunkmates. Anyhow, I choked up as I related the story. Jinny screamed out from across the hall, "Daddy, why is Kitty crying now? It happened last summer!"

I could go on and on about the differences between my sister and me. Despite them, we have much in common. Growing older has drawn us even closer. Jinny's a much less public person than I. She's very content with the simple things in life, and I'm not. That's part of the disease of alcoholism. Jinny's been teaching kindergarten for over twenty years. She's a fabulous teacher and loves what she's doing. I couldn't do the same thing for that many years if my life depended on it. It can't have been easy for Jinny being my little sister. Then again, Mother was in her corner and bolstered her up between rounds. I was envious of their relationship, but I had Daddy, and that made things easier to bear.

In my family, whatever our feelings toward each other, we did have feelings, and we expressed them.

When I went to play at my friends' homes, I was struck by the coldness between family members, particularly parents and children. I began to think there was very little love in those houses. The parents, while very much involved with their kids on the one hand, seemed distanced by an impersonal quality that had to do, I'm sure, with the first generation–second generation, Jewish-American syndrome. The parents had made it financially, yet many of them didn't know how to wear their riches gracefully. They showed off.

If I found their behavior annoying, how hard it must have been for my mother! She came from old, albeit adoptive wealth, and her family had been in America for generations. She was well educated, truly cultured, and she lived in a modest, little two-family house while her husband struggled to make a decent living. Sure, whenever things got really tight, Grammy Mabel would step in, but handouts are hard to take, especially for someone as proud as my mother. She grew more and more resentful as the years went on, particularly toward my dad's family. It got to the point where she didn't want to see Bubbe and Papa, and yet we spent almost every Friday night there. I think she reacted so bitterly because my dad had roots, and she didn't. She came from such a dysfunctional family. She was like a Henry James heroine plodding through the world of Shalom Aleichem —a character in search of a suitable setting.

She was also a bit of a snob. Mother looked down her nose at materialistic people and there were plenty of them in Brookline. Up-and-coming families poured into our town from less affluent suburbs. In an effort to better themselves, many spent money like crazy. Some of them were the parents of my school chums. If she found their values wanting, she'd say they were "Coolidge

Cornernish." Since Coolidge Corner was a predominantly Jewish area, Mother's remark could be interpreted as anti-Semitic, but I don't think so. I heard her speak out against prejudice too many times for me to believe she would stoop to it herself. Further, if anyone ever made anti-Semitic remarks, she would go nuts. As I've said, we weren't religious Jews, we didn't go to temple except for those early excursions with my grandparents. But since I grew up in a totally Jewish neighborhood, I didn't think about whether or not the people I liked were one religion or another. I had both Jewish and Christian friends; the majority were Jewish simply because most people in my geographic area were Jewish.

I remember my first brush with anti-Semitism. When I was in the eighth grade, a bunch of us would stop at the Beaconsfield Garage for Cokes on the way home from school. There was a soda machine inside the garage and we'd help ourselves. One afternoon, I was getting a drink from the machine and, as I started off toward my friends, a young mechanic pulled me aside. I'd seen him many times and wasn't particularly frightened. He held my arm, looked down at me, and said, "Why are you with those kikes all the time?"

Though I'd never heard the word before, I knew, instinctively, what it meant. "I'm Jewish, too," I said to the mechanic.

"You are not!" he answered vehemently.

"Yes, I am!" I replied just as strongly.

"What's your last name?" he asked.

"Dickson."

"You're not Jewish," he repeated and walked off.

I began to cry and went home. I told Mother, and, as I remember, she just sloughed it off. She'd been through the same experience many times; people did not take her for Jewish and said things. Well, now it had happened to me, and I didn't like it. I found it painful then, and I still do. To protect myself from that time forward, when meeting new people, I would almost immediately identify myself as a Jew. Michael used to tease me by saying, "How many minutes is it going to take before Kitty lets everybody know she's Jewish?"

In a way, my affirmation was a safety measure; I didn't want to hear any anti-Semitic cracks. Declaring myself was defending myself, or so I thought. In general, I was ethnically proud as a kid. Periodically I was embarrassed by the materialism, the Coolidge Corner stuff. Now, I think I'm more patient and tolerant. There are all kinds of people in the world.

I looked up the word "perfection" in the dictionary, and among the synonyms are flawlessness, superiority, excellence, precision, and purity. What a terrifying lineup —and those are all the qualities my mother expected of me. She exercised such rigid standards on herself, and, consciously or unconsciously, applied them to me. Notice, I say "me," not "us." Jinny remained exempt from a lot of Mother's perfectionist zeal, outside the circle of criticism. But, while Jinny was not chastised excessively, like the other members of the family, she was never showered with praise, either. Showered? We didn't even experience a mild drizzle. Mother didn't have time for praise.

The truth is my dad didn't bestow compliments readily, either. He expected and accepted the best. Recently, he has confessed he's sorry he wasn't more lavish in praise; he just wasn't brought up to flatter. Despite his reticence to verbalize compliments, I always felt my dad's love and understanding. I didn't with my mother.

Mother was too single-minded. For her, there was always *one* way to do things or one person to see. There was *one* gastroenterologist, *one* obstetrician-gynecologist, *one* ophthalmologist, *one* dentist. There was *one* store to buy children's clothes in, and there was *one* way to be properly dressed. Mother never went into Boston without wearing her white gloves, in an age that had long ago eschewed such niceties. It didn't matter. She had been taught a lady always wore her gloves, and my mother was a lady.

Her old-fashioned formality was a minor blessing and a major curse. It was nice to have a mother who looked exactly right and comported herself like a duchess, but it was awful to live up to the exacting standards she set. I couldn't do it. I was a shy, quiet child. Jinny was rambunctious and allowed to go her way. Mother wanted me to buckle under, and for a while I did. Sometimes my decorum paid off. I got to do things while Jinny was left out. I was about six years old when Mother informed me I was going to meet Dad's boss, Serge Koussevitsky. The prospect terrified me. I was in awe of Koussevitsky the way most children of the thirties and forties were in awe of Franklin Delano Roosevelt. Koussevitsky was a conductor of the old school. A tyrant on the podium, Koussevitsky looked upon the Boston Symphony as his children, and he was absorbed in his orchestra members' activities on and off the stage. He was the "little father" and knew what was best for them. He thought he was benevolent; the players had another name for it.

Koussevitsky loomed over our lives. In a funny way, he *was* part of the family. Every day, Dad came home with a Koussevitsky story; before Jinny and I ever knew what an ulcer was, we knew Koussie, as Dad called him, had given one to our father. There were so many afflicted players in the Boston Symphony, the orchestra members formed an "ulcer club." Nonetheless, Koussevitsky believed the Boston Symphony Orchestra was one big happy family, and in many ways he was right. Except for my father's family, all of our social life centered around the symphony players. They were my extended family; many were close friends of my parents. Mother's four or five intimates were symphony wives like herself. They met periodically for lunch and went shopping together. They couldn't do anything on a regular basis, however, because of their husbands' erratic schedules. Since there were no rules and regulations governing the members of the orchestra, they were at the mercy of the conductor.

Helen Krips, the wife of the assistant concertmaster, sister of Mike Wallace, aunt of Chris, and one of Mother's closest friends, used to say, "You'd be better off marrying a doctor or a lawyer, or a plumber or an electrician. They have better hours than musicians." Helen was an exceptional person in my life, really a second mother. After my mother died in 1977, I'd talk on the phone with Helen for hours. We had dinner together at least once a week. She was so enthusiastic and kind. I just adored her. Helen filled in the gaps left by my mother; it was sad and wonderful at the same time. A lot of people don't have significant others stepping in and picking up the pieces.

According to my mother, I did everything wrong; according to Helen, I did everything right. One time, when Michael was in his first term, I was painting the house and appropriately garbed in an old shirt and jeans and had a bandanna wrapped around my head. I ran out of paint and whizzed over to the hardware store. My luck, I bumped into Mother and Helen. Mother was beside herself: "How dare you go out looking like this, you're the governor's wife." Helen said I looked adorable. She thought it was sweet and unaffected for me to go out that way. Mother viewed it as a breach of etiquette. All in all, Helen Krips was every child's wish for an exceptional somebody. There was nobody else like her in my life, nobody. She died in 1983 and I still think of her and miss her. People like Helen made me a whole person.

It was because of the Boston Symphony that I knew Helen, but then, I was a symphony brat, and I knew 100 percent of that orchestra. I knew all the men—at that time there were no female members of the symphony— and I knew their wives. (I even knew which of the men had mistresses.) And of course I knew their children, and what they were like.

Many orchestra members were good cooks; some were even great, positively professional. It's not surprising; food and music do go together. The blending was very evident at our house. My mother was an extraordinary cook, really phenomenal. She mastered every aspect of cooking. She could cook any style—French, Italian, German—and the results were mouth-watering. When musicians like Jascha Heifetz and Isaac Stern gave concerts in Boston, Dad would bring them home and Mother prepared feasts. She was courageous about her cooking, very daring. One night Charles Munch and Pierre Monteux came for dinner. Munch was then the conductor of the Boston Symphony and Monteux was a frequent guest conductor. In essence, I'm talking about the boss(es) coming for dinner. Mother refused to take the easy way out by preparing conventional fare. She cooked leg of lamb, bloody, the way the French like it. This was the pre–Julia Child era, and leg of lamb normally was presented thoroughly cooked, the inevitable dryness relieved by gravy. Mother's dish had no need of sauce; it swam in its own rare juices. Munch and Monteux were beside themselves with delight. As chef and chatelaine, Mother could handle any situation, whether it was a last-minute call for a quick snack, or a banquet.

There was a dark side to this, something I always saw, but didn't recognize at the time. My mother never cooked a meal—indeed, never worked in the kitchen—without a glass of vermouth sitting on the counter next to her. It was continuously refilled. I'm not saying my mother was an alcoholic; truthfully, I can recall only one occasion when she had too much to drink. I am saying, however, that based on what I've experienced and learned, my mother was dependent on diet pills and may have been dependent on alcohol as well.

I don't think my dad realized Mother drank her way through the meal preparations. He was so proud of her and delighted in bringing people home. Mother received everybody cordially, if a bit coldly. She did have reservations about some of the guests, and in particular a frequent visitor named Danny Kaye. Danny conducted the Boston Symphony for fund-raisers, struck up a friendship with my dad, and became a regular at our dining table. Danny was a madman. He was also a superb cook, and his specialty was Chinese food. Sometimes Mother would allow him to use her kitchen to prepare an after-symphony supper. He made great meals and even greater messes. No one could believe the fanatically clean Jane Dickson allowed Danny Kaye to leave her precious kitchen in chaos. Mother put up with Danny's antics because she thought he was a nice man and amusing, too. The one thing she found hard to tolerate, however, was the way he talked. In those days, foul language was rarely heard. I don't think my mother ever swore. Even my dad was circumspect about language; his jokes and stories did not depend on four-letter words.

In performance, Danny was scrub clean and never off-color. He never said "damn" or "hell" on stage. Away from the screen or the theatre, though, his language was rough. Mother positively winced at his every word. One weekend, after he left the house, she shook her head saying, "Danny's a nice man, but his language is outrageous." The next morning my father was getting dressed. It was easy for him to prepare for the day since Mother arranged every closet and drawer, lining up his clothes in military order. This morning, there was an unaccustomed snag. Mother was in the kitchen preparing breakfast when Dad called out, "Jane, where are my socks? Come and help me, I can't find my socks."

Mother paused a minute. Memories of Danny Kaye were vivid. She took a cigarette out of her mouth and shouted back to my father, "Harry, I'm busy. Get your own f——ing socks."

I wonder whether Mother would mind my telling that story. I like it because it shows a different side of her. She didn't have a great sense of humor, but, once in a while, she rose to the occasion. Now and then, she blundered into a funny remark. I remember once we were driving in Massachusetts' beautiful Berkshire Hills; Mother and Luca Lehner, one of Mother's best friends, were in the front seat, and I was in the back. The two women were discussing their respective husbands. Mother was describing my father and I heard her say, "Harry's a handsome man, but, really, the best part of him is from the waist down." Though I knew she meant Dad had good legs, I couldn't resist calling out "Mother!" She got the picture and laughed at herself.

For the most part, however, all her life Mother remained a bit self-conscious about enjoying herself. She'd sit with my kids and watch shows like "I Love Lucy" and laugh hysterically. Then, when the show was over, she'd say, "Oh, that wasn't so funny." It was as though she was embarrassed by being amused.

While she wasn't a humorous person, she did have a fine aesthetic sense. She could go out, pick a bunch of flowers, put them in a vase, and the result was a still life, a virtual Monet painting. She was very artistic, too. When I was in the fifth grade she was the leader of my Campfire troop. We started making things with pipe cleaners at Campfire meetings. Mother fashioned marvels with those silly pieces of woolly wire. Later, when I was in high school, she took up sculpting, and everything she touched had something special about it. She had talent to spare and yet, whatever her skills and gifts, basically my mother's life centered around her husband and her children, and, perforce, the Boston Symphony Orchestra.

For our generation, Serge Koussevitsky *was* the Boston Symphony. No matter what his status, everyone at Symphony Hall was overwhelmed by the maestro. That's why my initial encounter at the age of six with Serge Koussevitsky had such significance.

Mother prepared me for the event by taking me to Best & Co. in Brookline, considered the place to outfit proper young ladies and gentlemen. I was no stranger to the store. The minute Dad left on a symphony trip, Mother would take me shopping. She was like someone let out of a cage. I'd ask, "Mommy, why are we doing this when Daddy's away?" She'd shush me and we'd buy. When my father came home, they'd have these terrible fights about money. (Mother had a small trust fund, which gave her a measure of independence; still, she always overspent. And, Mabel always bailed her out.)

Actually, Mother wasn't a spendthrift, she just wasn't good at handling money, and she did like to have nice things. Once, she wanted to buy something for the house, and rather than ask Dad or Grammy for money, she went to a loan shark. She wasn't too swift with the payments, either.

My father found out and hit the roof. "Why didn't you come to me!" he screamed.

"Because you wouldn't have approved," answered Mother.

Dad paid off the debt and she never borrowed money like that again. There was always a tug-of-war over funds in our house; to spend or not to spend, that was the question. (Listen, I go through the same thing myself. My husband is convinced I spend too much and I'm equally convinced he doesn't spend enough!)

At Best & Co., Mother took an outrageously expensive aqua-colored wool suit off the rack. The minute I put on the jacket and skirt, I felt like a princess. I should have. Only a princess could have afforded the outfit. My mother was undeterred. The Koussevitsky encounter was a major occasion, and mother wanted perfection. Whatever else happened, her daughter would be impeccably attired.

She bought the suit, and justified the cost by telling me, "You don't need anything else in your closet when you have an outfit like this. Very wealthy people don't need a lot of clothing and you don't, either. Just one or two good things." (I know Mother was right. However, though I buy good things, I don't limit myself to one or two.)

Once I had my outfit for the Koussevitsky reception,

I needed coaching in the correct way to behave. The Dicksons were to be part of a receiving line and would have the honor of shaking hands with the maestro. Mother rehearsed me at home. I had to make a good impression and I diligently tried to do everything right. I don't think there could have been any more preparation had I been anticipating a presentation at the Court of St. James. We went through some preliminary steps, and all went smoothly until I referred to the conductor as "Koussie," just as Dad did. Mother admonished me: "Never say Koussie again. You are to call him Maestro Koussevitsky. When we meet him, you look him directly in the eye, and take his hand."

Mother assumed the role of Koussevitsky and made me go through the routine. I would enter the living room on Beaconsfield Road, walk over to her, and say, "How do you do, Maestro Koussevitsky," and put out my hand.

At the first attempt, I was looking at my toes. Mother stopped the procedure. "Kitty, lift your head up. You've got to look him directly in the eyes," she said sharply.

I stepped away, composed myself, and repeated the process. This time I looked Mother straight in the eye, took her hand, and said something like, "How do you do, Mr. Koussie." Two strikes.

We continued to rehearse for days. Sometimes our drill took place under Jinny's baleful eye. Mother said my sister couldn't go to the reception because she was too young. Jinny says they didn't take her because she was an ugly duckling and difficult to control.

The day of the reception came and participants gathered in the Green Room at Symphony Hall. My knees were shaking, my heart was pounding. I was a bundle of quivering nerves enclosed in an expensive aqua wool suit. The line moved along and the next thing I knew, I was in front of the *monstre sacré* himself—the great Koussevitsky. He wasn't really tall, but I was a little girl and when he looked down at me, I felt like an ant being regarded by a giant. I saw a huge blue vein on his forehead; it scared me.

My father was on one side of me and my mother on the other. Dad gave me a push. I stumbled forward, looked up, and said, "How do you do, Mr. Koussevitsky."

He took my hand, shook it, and said in his thick Russian accent, "Kwat a preety leetle garrl." He patted me on the head and turned his attention to my father and mother. They exchanged brief pleasantries, and then we moved off as the next family group took their place. The audience was over; another episode in the life of the symphony orchestra player's family had ended.

While it was exciting and fun to be part of this incredible world, it did set me apart. My friends and classmates weren't involved in the esoteric doings of a symphony orchestra. Their fathers had real jobs, in real places like department stores or offices. And while this distinction made me very proud, a part of me wished my life could be more like everyone else's.

THREE

In toto, my childhood memories are positive. Sure, I cried a lot—I was definitely a weeper—but I cried about happy as well as sad things. I was not a particularly good student in school. I wasn't motivated. Not until I returned to college for the second time around did I really put effort into my studies. In grammar school and high school, I was more interested in the world around me.

I was always very popular and had lots of girlfriends and boyfriends. Even as a young kid, however, I wanted to help people. I was a kind of Lilliputian social worker, keeping an eye out for those less favored than I. One of the kids in Runkle was much put upon, the butt of jokes because he was cross-eyed and wore thick glasses. I immediately brought him home to play, introducing him to my mother as "my best friend." She looked askance; he was a total stranger. Ah, but once he was identified as my friend, once he had been endorsed by me, the other kids figured he had something to offer and brought him into the fold. All he needed was the imprimatur from a member of the "in" group.

I have a tendency to reach out first and figure out later what I'm doing. I know that about myself. There are a few other things I know about myself. I know when I say I'm going to do something, I'll follow through. I think I'm a good leader because I don't have to do everything myself; I can delegate work. I'm a kind of female Tom Sawyer. It's okay as long as I don't get too controlling. That's not an attribute, that's a defect and something I need to work on. I have to accept the fact there are some things in life I can't control. When I was young, I wanted to be good to everybody. It's almost the same today. I desperately want the state to bring in more money to help the homeless, and though I see ways of doing it, I can't make them happen; I don't have control over revenue and taxes. I used to get very frustrated over situations that I felt strongly should go one way, but that went the other. I've had to face the fact that I'm not omnipotent.

In fifth grade, I started ballroom dancing classes. They were taught by a young couple in the basement of a classmate's home. Dancing classes for young people were de rigueur in the Boston social scene. Generations of debutantes and their future escorts were trained in exclusive groups that met in country clubs, church auditoriums, and similar settings. In those formal classes children were exposed to the social graces, not just dance steps. Ultimately, the participants blossomed at the various presentation cotillions.

Since most of those dancing classes were restricted,

Jewish debutantes were nipped in the bud. We countered by creating our own classes in places like basements. There were about twenty kids in my dancing group, ten boys and ten girls. I learned how to jitterbug, foxtrot, waltz, and rhumba, and won a lot of prizes. I loved the classes, but then most of the girls enjoyed the classes, and most of the boys hated them.

I had reached that stage in my adolescence where the opposite sex began to take on a hitherto unnoticed aura of importance. Slowly, inevitably, I moved away from an exclusively female coterie of friends. I dated a lot. As a sophomore, I was seeing Harvard men. Imagine, four-teen years old and attending dances at Dunster House! It sounds racier than it was, since like most girls of the fifties, I was a prude.

Mother really got into the swing of my social life. She was totally fascinated by the dating game. Nothing like it had existed in Europe where she was raised. When I started going out, she reveled in my popularity. She would lay my things out before I left and wait up for me to return. I'd sit down and tell her everything that hap-pened. She was living through my experiences.

"You know, Kitty," she commented, "some people might think you are promiscuous because you date so much, and so many older boys. But, I know you're not."

Mother was right. I *was* innocent. As we used to say, I "knew from nothing." Of course, my ignorance didn't prevent me from talking as though I knew everything. I was told a girl I knew was sleeping with a guy at Dart-mouth. I was sixteen or seventeen at the time. I came home and repeated the story to my mother.

"What does that mean, Kitty?" she queried.

"Well, I don't know exactly, but I think it means they slept in the same bed together." I had no idea what I was talking about. I didn't know what intercourse was. I was a mental as well as physical virgin. My sexual ignorance was typical of the day and I think it's why, in part, so many marriages in my era failed. We were in the dark about too many basic facts. And when we *were* informed, it was usually through the worst possible channels.

I was in the third grade when the girl next door told me about menstruation. I went to Mother and repeated what I had heard. Her reply? Her classic, "Now you know."

But, I didn't know, not really. I knew what was coming, thanks to the girl next door; still, I was terrified and totally unprepared when I got my first period. I was in the eighth grade and came home from school distraught and frightened. Mother showed me the sanitary products I was to use and that was it. Though Mother wasn't acting that differently from a lot of mothers of that generation, she should have been sensitive as well as clinical.

Once my sister and I reached puberty, all the warning flags were hoisted. Jinny and I knew you couldn't fool around with boys because you could get in trouble, aka *pregnant*. We didn't actually know *how*. Everything was so vague. Whatever sex education we had filtered in through the whispers of school chums, or came from my dad. He did talk to Jinny and me. I was thirteen and Jinny was twelve when he sat us down for a serious discussion concerning the birds and the bees. Dad ended by saying, "If you ever should get in trouble, you can come to me." Jinny answered fervently, "Of course I'd come to you, Daddy; who do you think is going to pay for it?"

Dumb as we were about the sexual side of life, we

were smart enough to go through the initial rituals. I received my first kiss when I was in the sixth grade during a game of Spin the Bottle. Post Office and Spin the Bottle were the parlor games par excellence of childhood erotica. I didn't like either game, however, because I didn't particularly like kissing. I much preferred jitterbugging.

When I was seventeen, I dated six different boys at the same time. Mother had strong ideas about dating and men. She adhered to the principle of the "weaker sex," whereby girls were to be willowy and slightly helpless, thus encouraging men to take care of them. By her rules I was never to compete with men at sports and certainly never to make the mistake of winning. Whether it was tennis, racquetball, horseshoes, or table games, Mother was adamant: "You have to lose, Kitty. If you win the game you lose the man."

Mother never had much truck with feminism. She hated anything to do with the women's movement and was violently opposed to my involvement. When I became active in the early seventies, she'd go on about how awful "those women" were: "How can you stand them, they're disgusting." She never reconciled herself to the goals of the movement, either. On some front, I think she still was fighting her mother, Mabel.

I was really hot stuff in high school, but sexually I remained a goody-two-shoes. Mother continued to be both proud and aghast at the number of boys I was seeing. They telephoned me all day long and there'd be lists of callers waiting for me when I got home. Mother still believed people thought of me as "fast," though she remained equally sure I wasn't. I wasn't. I dated lots and lots of fellows and remained a virgin until I married.

Growing up and staying in the same town has its rewards. To this day, I keep bumping into men I knew way back when. These encounters occur with amazing frequency, enough to convince Michael that I dated everybody. (Maybe I did. I know I dated my sister's first husband; Jinny says she always got my rejects.)

I may not have been a great student, but I was enterprising. At the end of my freshman year at Brookline High, I applied to Filene's Department Store's Fashion Board. The board, essentially a clever promotional deal, was composed of young people from the Boston area who modeled clothes and represented the store at different functions. I won a seat on the board as the representative of Brookline High. I was fifteen years old, a skinny kid with big, brown eyes. We modeled in fashion shows all over Massachusetts.

As a result of my association with the fashion board, I began to work weekends for Filene's at the Chestnut Hill Mall. On Saturdays, when the store closed, I'd usually go to a friend's house and spend the night. One Saturday I was going to my friend Dotty Edwards's house. I was starving when I got there, and we had the biggest supper you can imagine, consisting of a huge steak, blimp-proportioned baked potatoes, and gigantic hot fudge sundaes for dessert.

I polished off the meal and about one hour later began to have violent pains in my stomach. The Edwardses called the doctor. He came to the house, examined me, and said I probably had appendicitis. I was taken home and Mother called our doctor, John Sears. He came and said I had to go to the hospital. He thought the appendix would have to be removed.

I was taken to the Beth Israel Hospital and within sixty minutes was on the operating table. Mother was in the operating room with me. Later, when I woke up she was still sitting beside me. She told me the doctors had to cut through layers of fat to get to the appendix because I had a stomach full of steak, potatoes, ice cream, and hot fudge sauce. My dad had a concert that evening and came to the hospital direct from the Symphony Hall, still dressed in his white tie and tails. He fell asleep on a bench in the emergency room, and someone thought he was a drunk sleeping it off and tried to get him out.

Both my mother and my father were there with me, but to be honest, I remember Mother being short-tempered rather than sympathetic. The relentless dichotomy of our relationship persisted. Whatever the crisis, she was there when I needed her, especially if I was ill. However, there was an edge to her ministering.

After my appendectomy, on the second or third day of my hospital stay, I was still in discomfort. Wilma Greenfield, who has remained my closest friend from childhood, came to visit me, arriving the same time as the lunch tray. On it were cheese blintzes, one of my favorite dishes. I still couldn't eat anything, however, so after carefully checking to see that no one was watching, Wilma gobbled up the blintzes. She looked so funny stuffing them in her mouth, I started laughing. I laughed so hard, it hurt. After that, I told Wilma to stay away from me until I recovered.

Although I worked for Filene's, I still never had any money. The store gave employees a healthy discount, and I turned my pay right back into merchandise. Fortunately, in my senior year, I left the temptations of the clothing store and went to work for the Beecher Hobbs record shop. My dad had a lot of fun with me during this work stint. Once he called me at Beecher Hobbs and asked me to find a recording of Beethoven's Tenth Symphony. I went through all the shelves and called him back. "Daddy, I can't find Beethoven's Tenth. Do you want me to order it?"

"You dimwit," laughed my dad, "Beethoven only wrote nine symphonies."

Dad pulled stunts like that on me the whole time I worked there. He always liked to make people laugh. At the dinner table, Dad regaled us with stories. Occasionally, he'd tell a slightly off-color tale that went right over his daughters' heads. Nonetheless, Mother would say, "Harry, *nicht für der kindern*." She used the same expression over and over. Eventually, Jinny and I figured out it meant, "Harry, not in front of the children."

A lot of our friends' parents spoke Yiddish when they wanted to exclude their children from the conversation, and while my dad spoke Yiddish fluently, Mother's version of the language wasn't very good. Generally, when they wanted to exchange parental secrets, they used German.

While Mother and Dad did have their secrets, they also shared things with us. I recall that one evening when Dad came home from an orchestra tour in the South, he was furious. "Would you believe it, Jane," he said to Mother, "Marian Anderson and Roland Hayes were singing a concert with us and they couldn't find a decent place to stay." Dad was incensed at the prejudice shown toward black performers. Neither he nor Mother could abide any form of prejudice. Because of their broad acceptance of people, I was taught a tolerance of others, and more than that, a respect for others, no matter what their race, religion, or sexual preference. The older I get, the sounder those teachings have proved.

· · ·

In my senior year at Brookline High, I started putting on a bit of weight and went from a size six or eight to a size ten. Mother had an eagle eye out for any excess weight gain, whether on herself or her children. She subscribed to the adage: You can never be too thin or too rich. I don't think there is generally anything abnormal about a teenager gaining some weight, although there can be special circumstances that can cause such changes. In my case, it happened when I learned about my mother's birth. It was a miserable period in my life; I became very confused and turned to food. While my sister handled the situation with her usual equanimity, I questioned my own authenticity. I became convinced *I* was adopted. Dad calmed me down, as always, but Mother wouldn't address the issue. Solace can sometimes be disguised as food. I gobbled it up.

Mother, too, began to fight her own battles against the pounds, and went up and down on the scales, from rail thin to heavy and back again. Mother took a lot of pills; amphetamines were prescribed for her to lose weight. Mother's weight problem could have been genetic; Margaret, her birth mother, was heavy. Even so, it might have been better controlled had Mother exercised. Unlike my generation, women of her era rarely worked out. Oh, she went on walks, and she gardened, but that wasn't enough. Today's women are aware of the importance of physical fitness. I belong to an exercise class and try to work out at least three times a week and I take power walks at least as many times. It makes a difference.

When I was a senior, I had the honor of meeting one of my all-time idols, and one of the most outstanding women of this century, Eleanor Roosevelt. I adored her, much of my admiration having rubbed off from Grammy Mabel, who revered her. Mrs. Roosevelt was giving an address at Beaver Country Day School in Brookline, and each of the area high schools elected two young women to represent their school. Wilma Greenfield and I were chosen to represent Brookline High. I was in seventh heaven at the prospect of being in Eleanor Roosevelt's presence.

It's funny, I had met all kinds of famous people, had grown up with celebrities sitting at our dinner table, cooking in our kitchen, and sleeping in our beds, yet this was different. Eleanor Roosevelt went beyond mere celebrity. When she walked into the auditorium, it was electrifying. I felt I was the only one in the room and that she was talking to me. She began to speak and I knew what she sounded like because I had heard her on the radio. While the quality of her speaking voice was not great, what she said transcended how she sounded. I remember thinking, if this woman can do it, there's hope for all kinds of women. Combined with that long-ago awakening in the Roxbury shul balcony, I think the Eleanor Roosevelt speech propelled me into feminism.

She talked about women and how we could be anything we wanted. This was thirty-five years ago, 1954, and the truth was, we couldn't be anything we wanted. Not then. Yet she made it sound possible. She spoke of fairness and opportunity. It was an extraordinary lecture. I remember going home and trying to tell my parents what had happened. I simply couldn't express what I felt. Hours later, indeed, the morning after, I still felt tongue-tied and couldn't articulate my emotions. Years later, I read the Lash books about Mrs. Roosevelt's life and learned that she came from an anti-Semitic, racist family; it elevated her even higher in my view. As a true humanist, she was able to rise above her narrow background.

In 1954, my senior year, I was seeing Steven Endler, a junior at Harvard. We dated for about a year and I took him to my senior prom. He had been a counselor at Takajo, a boys' camp in Naples, Maine. Steve drove me to my camp, Newfound, which was down the road from Takajo. I'd been at Camp Newfound for nine summers and was now a full-fledged counselor myself. Before we reached Newfound, Steven stopped at Takajo and pulled up near the tennis courts.

Steven said, "I want you to meet John Chaffetz, the tennis instructor. He's going to be a sophomore at Penn State." Steven called out and John Chaffetz walked toward us. He had two weeks' growth of beard on his face and was very good-looking. We talked for a while and then Steven and I drove off to Camp Newfound.

I don't remember if I thought a lot about John Chaffetz after our meeting. I was pretty busy with all my activities. John and I would meet again, though.

When the time came to apply to colleges, Dad wanted me to go to the University of Michigan. He'd been out there for concerts and thought it was an excellent school. I applied, but I also applied to Penn State. I wanted to go there because a woman I had met at Camp Newfound had a modern dance studio in the college town and ran a dance program that really intrigued me. When Michigan turned me down, I immediately signed up for the Pennsylvania school.

I was as popular at Penn State as I had been in high school. I was dating lots of people including an assistant instructor of physics. Nothing was serious; everything was amusing.

Within the first week of my arrival, John Chaffetz called me. He had come up early because he was an assistant manager of the football team. I have to laugh. Everything was so innocent in those days. I was dating everyone and I was still a prude. I just didn't think about sex. Sure, you kissed and did a little simple petting, perhaps, but nothing more. We had to rely on other things.

I was attractive. I had a good personality and was fun to be with. John joined my retinue of cavaliers, although our relationship was a bit more intense than the others. John took me home with him for Thanksgiving to meet his parents, Mac and Rhoda Chaffetz, who lived in the Germantown section of Philadelphia. They couldn't have been nicer to me. They thought I was the best thing since sliced bread and showered me with attention. It was heady to be so totally appreciated. John was an only child, and I was his chosen girlfriend, so obviously I must be the sweetest, the loveliest, the most terrific this and that. I ate it up. John pinned me that spring and we dated throughout my sophomore year.

I immersed myself in college life. Jinny likes to remind me that I carried on in my accustomed fashion even though I was no longer living on Amory Street. I still never did my laundry regularly, and now I didn't have Jinny's clean clothes to raid. So I did the obvious: When a blouse got too soiled, I went out and bought another. At the end of my first year, I returned home with thirty-two blouses in my wardrobe.

I could afford a little extravagance because I had a weekly allowance, and then some. The "then some" came from my dad. I would write home to both parents, and then also drop letters to him alone at Symphony Hall. The theme of those epistles was invariably money, and just as invariably Dad would come through, sending me checks. I also made money teaching dance, assisting my friend Betty Jane Dittmar at her studio and running some classes on my own.

My first semester I was elected a freshman senator. Alas, when second semester came, my marks weren't good enough and I could not remain in college government. I had to drop out.

I was rushed by sororities and was the first Jewish woman to be accepted by Kappa Alpha Theta. I was also elected "Engineer Girl of the Month," and in the spring of my freshman year was my class's choice for "May Queen Attendant." The latter honor appealed to my mother. I had fulfilled her predictions and was being lauded for my looks. She put a picture of me as May Queen Attendant inside a locket and kept it for years.

Busy on all fronts, I still managed to gain weight during the first year, reaching 130 pounds, which, at five feet six inches, seemed like one ton. I was in good physical shape, though, what with teaching dance classes and taking them, too. Nonetheless, I went up to a size twelve, even fourteen! At college, no one noticed my weight except me. The situation was different at home where my severest critic waited.

I'd fly back to Boston during vacations and breaks, dressing casually for the trip in a shirt, jeans, and sneakers. My appearance drove Mother bonkers. She'd pick me up at the airport, take one look, and say, "Kitty, you get fatter and fatter." Then, as we walked toward the car, she'd throw in little statements like, "Why do you wear those awful sneakers? Are your fingernails clean?"

I sometimes felt as though I were coming home for inspection rather than vacation.

I went back to work at Camp Newfound between freshman and sophomore years. When I returned to college, the pattern of my life continued much the same: academic classes, dance classes, and John Chaffetz. By the summer after my sophomore year, I decided I didn't love John, and told him I needed space. I wanted to start seeing other men.

He was wild. He called me every other minute, saying he was miserable. He was desperate and talked madly, even threatening suicide. (I'd finally found someone more melodramatic than I!)

Nonetheless, relieved of the burden of my exclusive commitment to John, I spent a wonderful summer between sophomore and junior years at Camp Newfound dating lots of guys. I saw a fellow who was head of the navy chorus in Pensacola. He really pursued me.

In the fall, when I returned to college, I had no trouble finding beaus, and while I was getting by scholastically, I was tired of academic life. I loved school, and I was very active, a student leader, but still I was bored, restless. I was looking for a way to bolt.

One evening, John Chaffetz came to see me. He walked in the door carrying a diamond engagement ring and asked me to marry him.

I accepted.

My only excuse is, I was nineteen years old. John was only thirteen months older than I. Certainly neither of us deserved a medal for maturity. He was in the ROTC at the time and would be going into military service. I think he just wanted desperately to have someone with him in the service, and I was the top candidate.

My consent to his proposal was absolutely a dumb

move, and hindsight doesn't make it any smarter. Recently, I tried to put things together, to analyze why I had accepted a ring from a man I didn't really love, a man I'd actually stopped seeing! I came up with a significant event in my life, something that might have triggered my action. The previous summer I had been told of my mother's adoption. It really was a bombshell, and my willingness to marry John Chaffetz might have been a result of shell shock. Who knows?

Another factor was that I wanted to get out of school and there were no other options. I couldn't take a leave of absence (they were practically unheard of then) and I couldn't just quit for no reason. Marriage was the only out.

John's parents were ecstatic about our engagement; my parents were not. They did not voice any objections when I announced my plans, but later I discovered they had reservations. Dad questioned certain qualities in John. Mother saw we had nothing in common. John was very jealous of my relationship with my parents, mostly my dad, but Mother, too. His relationship with his parents was very different from mine; he had real issues of conflict with them that he had never resolved.

John and I decided to marry in March and then we would go off together so he could fulfill his military commitment. We had a big engagement party at Christmas. It was a joint affair since my sister, Jinny, became engaged at the same time. I planned to go back to school in January to take my exams. Although I was under no pressure from my parents, I wanted to finish up the semester. That December while I was at home, I was studying and eating and had become concerned about my weight. Mother had noticed too, and kept commenting on my growing figure.

I had seen pills in her dressing room and asked her what they were. "Diet pills, Kitty," she answered. "The doctor prescribed them for me." My mother took amphetamines; indeed, she took a lot of pills including mood-altering ones. She used Darvon and Darvocet like aspirin. We simply weren't aware, then, of the inherent dangers in such drugs. Much as she wanted me to lose weight, Mother didn't offer me any of her store of tablets. The truth is, I went into her dressing room one morning and took a pill. I liked the way I felt. The following morning, I repeated the process. It was the season to be jolly, and thanks to those little pills, no one was more spirited than Katharine Dickson. In December of 1956, I started using.

I went back to Penn State, took my exams, and returned home. Mother had begun planning the wedding. I bought a wedding gown. Meanwhile, I had begun to lose weight. Eventually I dropped to under 115 pounds. I was a size six again.

I also had boundless energy. Mother noticed the physical and emotional changes. "What's going on Kitty?" she asked me. "You're acting silly."

"I've been taking those diet pills, Mother, and I love them," I answered truthfully. There was no reason to hide what I was doing. I had asked the gynecologist to prescribe the amphetamines for me.

Mother was concerned, but only about my behavior. "Stop taking them, Kitty," she warned, "you're talking too much."

Ah. How could I listen to advice from someone who was doing what she told me not to? Why didn't I look at the results? Why didn't I see that my mother's battle against weight was a losing one? Pills didn't really work. I couldn't see the truth. I had turned twenty; no use to talk to me. Besides, I only took one little pill every morning. That was it. Oh, on few isolated occasions I took more, but I never escalated. Later, at Hazelden, others were amazed my dosage never increased. They found it hard to believe. It is very unusual not to escalate.

I was married in a beautiful and lavish ceremony on St. Patrick's Day, March 17, 1957. There were 120 guests attending. After the ceremony, John and I flew off to Philadelphia to spend the night. We planned to drive from there to Texas via Florida in a full-size silver station wagon we had been given by his parents.

At the hotel we were shown to a tiny room. I went into the bathroom and put on my nightgown and peignoir. I was terrified. I had never seen a man's body, a full, naked body. I was barely twenty years old, a virgin, and shaking in my peignoir. I got through the night. I'm sure it was no worse than a lot of other wedding nights, but from that night on while in this marriage, I looked upon sex as something to get over, to close my eyes through and think about other things. Of course, I had lots of headaches.

The next morning we arose, got dressed, had breakfast, got into the car, and started off toward Florida. I had all new luggage, and neatly hidden in my shiny cosmetic case was a full bottle of Dexedrine. My married life had begun. I was united with a man I really did not understand, and in fact, John Chaffetz wasn't an easy person to get to know. His main interest in life was sports, while I was more interested in dance, theatre, art, etc. Except for the fact that we looked amazingly alike—people mistook us for brother and sister—we had nothing in common. If I had lived with him for one week,

I wouldn't have married him; he probably wouldn't have married me, either. Alas, you didn't do that kind of thing in 1957, and, consequently, there was a wide margin for error. Marry in haste, repent at leisure—another old truism. I did just what the adage said. My first marriage was doomed by a total absence of compatibility.

FOUR

In the pre–birth control pill, pre-awareness era in which I came of age, many women married because, by assuming the role of wife, they could experience a full sexual life. I wasn't driven to marry on sexual grounds. As I've said, I was bored with school, and the only way to get out was marriage.

I'd been raised to get married and have children; I wasn't supposed to have a big career. Mentally, I wasn't equipped to be anything but a housewife. Ironically, in practical terms I really wasn't prepared for that pursuit, either. Except for cleaning bathrooms and making my bed, I didn't know the first thing about running a household. I didn't even know how to cook. Mother never let me in her kitchen. The workings of the stove were a mystery to me. I couldn't boil an egg. What am I saying? I didn't know how to boil *water*.

I went from my parent's house to my husband's house

without ever being on my own. Insanity. None of this seemed particularly important at the time. In fact, I wasn't terribly different from many young brides of my era. I would learn to be a housewife through hands-on experience.

The car ride from Philadelphia to Florida was pleasant enough. I had never been farther south than Pennsylvania and was fascinated by the scenery and terrain. I remember going over a big bridge in Virginia, the longest I had ever traversed. I also remember the thrill of seeing palm trees growing along the side of the road. We stopped the first night in one of the Carolinas, spent the next evening in Daytona Beach, and arrived in Miami the following evening. I don't remember the name of the hotel where we stayed; I do recall it was dingy and crummy. The second night in Miami, I got violent pains in my stomach, really fierce stabs. John called a doctor and I was given a shot. I was in agony. John was solicitous; still, I was one frightened young bride. There was good reason to be apprehensive, only it didn't have to do with stomach pains. A pressing case of food poisoning allowed me to divert my real fears away from the enormity of what I had done.

From Miami we set out for San Antonio, Texas, where John would be stationed. We drove up the west coast of Florida, stopping, at John's suggestion, to see a couple of spring training baseball games. I liked baseball, but not as much as my husband. In time, I discovered he had what amounted to a passion for athletics. John Chaffetz lived and breathed sports and the atmosphere proved too rarefied for me. I wasn't anti-sports; I'd been rooting for the Red Sox, Celtics, and Bruins all my life. I did, however, believe there were other things in life, and more important things, at that.

Eventually, John's sports obsession overwhelmed the "other things" and helped pull us apart. Our problem wasn't unique. The term "sports widow" is widely used, although you don't get the full meaning unless you are one. I know of a couple whose marriage was floundering because the husband spent every moment of the season following major league baseball. After fifteen years of her husband's single-minded devotion to the baseball diamond, his wife threatened to leave him. They went to a marriage counselor. He told them they needed to spend some time together, just the two of them, and suggested they take a second honeymoon. The husband agreed and made arrangements for their trip. Do you know where he took his wife? To Cooperstown, New York, to visit the Baseball Hall of Fame. I don't know if their marriage held together; I doubt it.

We arrived in San Antonio at the end of March. It was hot as hell. I had never known such heat in my life. We moved into a small, adequate apartment in military housing, and my married life began.

I vividly recall the first dinner I cooked. My instructions at the ready, I began the meal and immediately faced the impossible. "Boil water," said the recipe. I didn't know how. I had to go into the index and ferret out the information. I hung over the pot waiting for "a succession of rapid bubbles" to appear. What a triumph when they actually did burst forth! I needed the water to make rice, and in addition I prepared fried chicken, biscuits, and salad. I was proud as punch that I, personally, had created a meal. I'm sure the fried chicken left much to be desired. I had a hard time freeing it from the skillet; indeed, most of the skin and meat slipped off the bone and remained in the pan. In my first attempt at cooking, I learned the fine art of scraping. I pieced the de-skinned bird together as best as I could and bolstered it with mounds of sticky rice. It wasn't a particularly dainty dish to set before my husband; however, John ate the meal and survived. Never underestimate the intricacies of cooking for the first time! In the category of "nerve-racking," preparing that initial dinner was right up there with the wedding night.

Military life is fairly predictable; you're always under the protection of the service. The Boston Symphony had provided a base for my childhood; the air force did the same for my early married years. We were in San Antonio for six weeks. We made friends and entertained at each other's homes. Some evenings, we'd go to the officers' club to dine and dance. There were movies and parties, and of course televised sports events. I kept busy, yet I can't say I was ecstatically happy. It was interesting to be in a new place and a part of the military life; still, I felt my husband was not really with me. And, to be fair, he probably felt the same.

After basic training, John was assigned to Harlingen Air Force Base in Harlingen, Texas. I had thought San Antonio was hot, but it was nothing compared to Harlingen. To help pass the time and to find some relief from the unbearable heat, I began teaching in a swimming program at the base.

Our life in Harlingen was similar to what we'd experienced in San Antonio. We made friends with fellow officers and their wives and used the officers' club. However, there wasn't much to do in Harlingen, and since we weren't far from Mexico, I made plans with two other couples from the base to spend a day in Matamoros, a town just over the border. (Matamoros recently made headlines as the locale of a vicious voodoo cult.)

John wouldn't join us that day. He wanted to watch football games on television. I wasn't going to sit around all afternoon glued to the TV, so I told John I'd go with the others by myself. He was perfectly amenable, though he did make me promise one thing: "Don't eat while you're in Mexico," he cautioned. "Promise you'll stay away from the food." He knew about the lack of sanitary conditions below the border and was worried I'd get sick. I promised him, and to be safe, we packed lunches.

The five of us drove for about two hours. There was no air-conditioning in the car and by the time we arrived in Matamoros, I was dying of thirst. We went into a bar and I had a drink called a zombie. I hadn't eaten all day, and I drank this zombie in one slurp. You can imagine the results. I threw up all the way home. My friends had to stop the car every half hour. This was about the third time in my life that I'd gotten sick from drinking. I was frantic because I didn't want John to know. I bought some mouthwash at one stop and gargled the whole bottle. I guess it wasn't enough. I walked in the house, John took one look at me, and said, "What happened?" I told him the truth. He was so mad I had disobeyed, he didn't talk to me for hours, or maybe he didn't talk because the game was still on.

We were in Harlingen from the end of May to the end of August. Then John was transferred to Panama City, Florida, a place on the west coast of the state about an hour away from Pensacola. I couldn't stand it. First the heat of Harlingen, now the awful moisture and humidity of Panama City.

I caught the Asian flu and was sick as a dog for three weeks. I threw up every single morning. I didn't realize I was pregnant; it turned out my upheavals were due to morning sickness as well as the flu. Early in September, I went home for my sister's wedding, still unaware of my condition. I was very uncomfortable the entire trip. My breasts were unbelievably sore and I didn't know why. I didn't think of pregnancy because I had had my period in the first month.

In October, John was ordered to a mountain base in Almaden, California, just outside of San Jose. We left Panama City, drove to Boston to see my folks, then to Philly to see his, and from there we crossed the country to California. A memorable trip. First of all, I had run out of diet pills. I can't remember why I ran out of pills, or even if I was smart enough to lay off them because of the pregnancy. I had skipped a period and by then believed myself to be pregnant. I figured I was about six weeks along and would check with an obstetrician when we reached California.

While I had been on the base, the military doctors had prescribed the diet pills. They were easy enough to get and I was always supplied. But now, I had none. Consequently, I got into the car and fell asleep, dozing the entire way from Pennsylvania to California. I don't remember anything of that journey except waking up and dozing off. Perhaps it's just as well.

We arrived in San Jose and found an apartment within a couple of days. I needed to get a physical checkup. I also needed to lay in a supply of amphetamines. I went to an obstetrician. After he examined me, he said I was nearly three months pregnant! I was dumbfounded. I told the doctor I was concerned about putting on weight and asked for diet pills, which he gave me. Even so, I gained thirty-five pounds. All along, the doctor cautioned me about putting on too much weight. One day he even threatened to throw me into the hospital if I didn't control my eating.

"I'll watch it, Doctor, don't worry. I'll be very careful," I said solemnly. I left his office and went across the street to a drugstore. I sat down at the counter and ordered a hot fudge sundae. I was happily lapping it up when I felt a tap on my shoulder. I turned around and looked into the scathing eyes of my obstetrician. Promises, promises.

Lieutenant John Chaffetz was a radar specialist and was finally officially assigned to the Almaden base. Again our lives took on the familiar military sheen. We made friends, we entertained in each other's houses, and went out together to parties and movies. The pattern was remarkably steady. And boring.

I became friends with a wonderful woman named Sally Lucas. She was pregnant, too, and we could share our experiences. I introduced John to Sally's husband, Don, and they got along swimmingly. In fact, John would later go to work for Don at a used-car lot he owned called The House of Hard Tops. Eventually, John went into business and they were partners for almost ten years.

On June 8, 1958, John and I went to the movies. I cannot recall the film because, during it, my water broke. We called the doctor and he told us to get over to the hospital. I entered O'Connor Hospital in San Jose that evening. I experienced no other signs and was put to bed for the night. The next morning John and I were playing gin rummy on my bed when I had my first labor pain.

I was about as much prepared to give birth as I had been to get married and to cook dinner. I was given no pain medication; I hadn't had any breathing training. When things got rough, they gave me gas. The nurse came in and said, "Well, honey, you might as well get used to it, because you're going to be in labor for a long time." This angel of mercy scared me out of my wits. I honestly thought I was going to die. John stayed with me and I was clutching at him. Like most fathers-to-be, he hung on for dear life. The labor lasted for four hours, and at 3:03 in the afternoon, my son was born.

John weighed six and a half pounds. He was a wonderful little baby. I was crazy about him even though I had the most awful headaches for five days. They had given me a spinal and made me sit up too soon after the delivery. The headaches were the result, and they took a lot out of me. I couldn't do much but nurse the baby and try to sleep. I didn't have to worry about seeing anybody, since the hospital didn't allow any visitors. I talked to my folks and the Chaffetzes on the phone. I received lots of flowers. At the end of the week, I went home with a baby nurse. I was twenty-one years old now, and a mother as well as a wife. And, I was still using.

Sally Lucas had her baby two weeks after John was born. She and her husband lived in an apartment next door to us. Sally's mother and my mother came to attend their respective daughters and arrived at the same time. They became friendly. Mother was just terrific with little John. She stayed for about a month and I was really sorry to see her leave. Dad came out that September. I cooked steak the first night he was there and John, half-jokingly, complained that I gave my father a bigger piece. It was a dumb remark and didn't sit well with either my dad or me. Dad stayed for about two weeks. Though they adored their grandson, I don't think either of my parents were totally pleased with my married life. Mother, particularly, noticed the uneasy atmosphere. I spent Christmas with Sally, Don, and our babies at Sally's parent's house in San Gabriel, California. I was so happy to have someone like her as a friend. I was so far away from family and old acquaintances, it was a relief to make a strong new attachment. In military life, you are constantly making new friends because you're moved around so much.

In November, John was reassigned once more, this time to Santa Rosa Island, so we moved to Port Hueneme, California. We lived in housing on a navy base for eighteen months. I should say *I* lived there because John came home one weekend a month. The rest of the time, he was on Santa Rosa.

It was during this period that I realized my marriage was in deep trouble. Each time John came home, I couldn't wait for him to leave. I looked forward to his not being there. Whenever he was home, he did what he always did—watched football, baseball, basketball, any ball at all, on television. He focused in on the sports to the exclusion of everything else. It was unbearably boring for me, although I was as much at fault as he. I was immature. We were unsuited for each other. I went through the motions of living. I was like a robot programmed to do the right things. Alas, aside from little John, I didn't take much joy in what was going on. I taught swimming to a group of hulking Seabees at the naval base. I'd take the baby to the pool and put him with his toys while I worked with the men. I also taught children's swimming classes and dance classes, but I dropped them when I became pregnant again. I lost the baby in the third month. I conceived again and this time the pregnancy lasted only six weeks. I felt cut off, isolated. I had no visits from my parents while we were in Port Hueneme and was alone most of the time. Little John had one ear infection after another and I had all the responsibility of his care. I was still taking my morning pill. Syndrox, I think.

One weekend, my husband took me over to Santa Rosa Island to see his living quarters. It was ghastly. I couldn't believe they had to live under such difficult conditions. I felt guilty that I wished him to be there rather than with me. John brought home one of the fellows from a nearby naval air station, and I became friendly with his wife. She had three children and we would get together at each other's homes. Her little girl and John were two-year-olds.

One afternoon, John and I were visiting at her house. While the mothers sat and talked in the living room, the two-year-olds meandered around. I had a bladder infection at the time and was taking Gantrisin. I had put the bottle on a shelf in my friend's kitchen when I arrived. John and his playmate wandered into the kitchen, climbed up to the shelf, found the medicine bottle, and ate the entire contents. They walked into the living room with their mouths stained from the pills. Whenever I read those warnings, *keep out of reach of children*, I want to add: and don't let your children out of your sight! We rushed the kids to the hospital. The doctors were furious. They tended to the children and screamed at me and my friend, calling us unfit mothers. They wrapped the kids in blankets and pumped their stomachs. Oh God, it was awful. "I ought to be pumping *your* stomach!" one doctor shouted to me. Once I knew the children were safe, I wanted to die of shame. I vowed to never ever allow such a thing to happen again. It's one promise I kept.

Although John had signed up for three years of service, he would be let off after two and a half. Toward the end of his stint, he looked for work in San Jose, where we had decided to settle. It was then that our friend Don Lucas offered him a partnership in used-car sales and John signed on with The House of Hard Tops.

Finally John was discharged and we could experience a more normal life. We rented a duplex up the street from the Lucases. Our children played together. We had settled down permanently; no more moving around from base to base. On the surface, everything seemed fine. On the contrary, I was actually miserable. I didn't love my husband. It was a chore getting into bed at night. My distaste and dissatisfaction were obvious.

I had already expressed my doubts about my marriage to my mother when I'd gone home to Brookline for a visit with my two-year-old son. "Mother, I'm going to try to make it work, but I don't know what's going to happen." On this issue, my mother was supportive, more so even than my dad. She understood divorce, it was part of her growing up; my father viewed it as anathema.

Soon after I returned to San Jose, John and I moved into our own home, a house on a dead-end street. A brook ran behind our property, and there was a lemon tree and an avocado tree in the yard. I remember the big family room with a brick fireplace. The house was a dream setting for what had become a nightmare marriage. We were in the house for only three months. On New Year's Eve 1960, John and I agreed to split. We were both filled with sadness at the failure of our marriage. We were simply incompatible; John moved out on New Year's Day.

I called home to break the news. My mother and sister weren't surprised; my father was stunned. "How can you do this?" he argued. "It's a disgrace. There's never been a divorce in our family." How quickly he forgot my grandparents' divorce. Eventually, he calmed down and realized the rightness of what I was doing.

A great weight had been lifted from my life, one that would have dragged me into depths from which I don't think I could have risen. I stayed on in the house and tried to live as normal an existence as possible for little John's sake as well as mine. I did not have the comfort of Sally Lucas's friendship. Once her husband heard John and I were separated, he forbade Sally to see me. She was so upset, they almost got a divorce over our divorce. There was nothing she could do, John and Don were partners and she had to stand by her husband.

Mother came out in February to stay with me. She was horrified by my spartan existence. The furnishings comprised a couch in the living room, a table in the kitchen, and a bed in the bedroom. She immediately went out and ordered furniture—for a house I would be vacating as soon as my divorce came through. John's attitude changed when mother arrived; he got angry and decided he didn't want a divorce. One afternoon he came over to discuss a possible reconciliation. Mother excused herself and went into the bedroom. While John was speaking to me, she made all sorts of noises, harrumphing and sighing so audibly that I had to go into the bedroom to silence her. "Please, Mother, be quiet, I can handle this myself," I told her. She was worried I'd capitulate; I never did.

Mother stayed a month. Johnny came down with measles while she was there and Mother assumed her familiar role as nurse. Then, she had to return to Dad. Three weeks after she left, my sister arrived with her eighteen-month-old son, Robbie, and stayed with me for the month of March. Back in Boston, Mother looked after Jinny's infant, Mikie. I had to remain in California until my divorce went through, and my family would not let me stay by myself. I had a good lawyer in San Francisco and would go to see him regularly. My friends sustained me, too. Even dear Danny Kaye showed up. Danny kept telling me that John was going to need psychiatric counseling. "He's only two and a half, Kitty, but this is a traumatic experience and could have repercussions if it isn't handled properly." Danny was so dear. What a true, caring friend.

And I needed every ounce of friendship I could get. This was really a rough time for me. I was painfully thin. I weighed about 110 and looked drawn and haggard. Though I took no particular pleasure in my skinny state, I still kept taking my pills.

I went to court on the thirteenth of July. Wilma Greenfield was my witness. Wilma reported to the judge that I called her many times and cried on the phone, saying that my husband had told me he wasn't sure he wanted to stay married. It was true. The divorce was granted and I made arrangements to leave for Boston. Before I departed, John Chaffetz came to the house to say good-bye and became hysterical. He started banging his head against the fireplace. I'd been through this scene before, too. This new display was futile. John left, and my neighbors drove me to a hotel next to the San Francisco airport. My son and I stayed there overnight, and the next morning we boarded the plane for Boston.

It had been four years since I married John Chaffetz. It seemed like fifty. I was twenty-four years old, divorced, the mother of a three-year-old son, and on my way back to Boston to start over again. Only one thing had remained constant throughout those four years, my addiction.

FIVE

In late July of 1961 I returned to Boston. Mother met me at the airport and asked if I wanted to go immediately to the Berkshires and join Dad, or stay in town for the evening and drive up the following day. I decided to remain in Boston; I'd had enough traveling for a while. Danny Kaye was performing at a theatre club in Framingham, and Mother and I decided to take John and go see the show. The visit with Danny was a great way to unwind. Watching him perform always had salutary effects. After the performance, Danny joined us for dinner.

The following morning, John, Mother, and I drove to Tanglewood, the performing arts center in the Berkshire Hills of western Massachusetts, where the Boston Symphony Orchestra makes its summer home. When we arrived, my father was waiting for us. Anxiety was written all over his face; my divorce had taken its toll. He was very upset.

The first thing I said when I saw him was, "Daddy,
I'm fine. I don't want you to cry. Everything's going to
be okay." Sometimes I feel I have to protect my father,
he gets so emotional. John and I moved into a small
studio cottage on the estate where my parents lived. The
summer proved to be exactly what my son and I needed.
He was free to romp under the loving eyes of his grandparents; I could relax and think about my future rather
than dwell on the past.

At the end of the summer we moved to Cambridge. I
enrolled at Lesley College and John started at Lesley-
Ellis nursery school. I chose to go to Lesley because I
felt I had two career choices—teaching or nursing. My
mother was the nurse in the family, so I would try teaching. Financially, John and I were okay only because my
parents helped out. Though I received alimony and child
support, it didn't amount to very much—$25 a week for
John, and a couple of hundred a month for me. My rent
alone was $150. Though I took part-time employment,
we stayed solvent thanks to Mother and Dad. Johnny
blossomed. He had all sorts of friends and activities to
keep him busy. I was busy, too. Now, finally, I was
serious about education and worked hard. I gradually
began to date again, too. Nothing serious, though; my
energies were directed toward my son and my studies.

And, then, as the saying goes, fate stepped in. Fate,
in the person of Sandy Cohen Bakalar.

I had known Sandy in high school. She had graduated
three years before me, in 1951, and by this time, 1961,
she was married, pregnant, and had moved into a top-
floor apartment at 126 Amory Street, right next to my
parents. They had become very friendly; Sandy was especially drawn to Mother's taste and sense of order.

While Sandy and I were contemporaries, we became
friendly through my parents. I'd see her when I went to

visit Mother and Dad. One day Sandy broached a subject with my dad: "Harry, I have a friend, a really neat guy, who'd like to call Kitty for a date. What do you think?"

"Forget it," Dad said, "she's not interested." Dad was trying to protect me; he wanted me to get my education and prepare for my future without detours. He felt I should put men on hold until after I'd gotten my degree and a position.

Despite Dad's rejoinder, Sandy's friend did call me. His name was Michael Dukakis and I knew exactly who he was.

I'd met Michael at Brookline High in 1951 when I was a freshman. At the time I was dating Alvin Sommers, a senior, and I was very proud of myself since it was coup to be seeing an upperclassman. One spring morning Alvin and I went into either the yearbook or newspaper room at school, where Alvin introduced me to his classmate, Michael Dukakis. I was dazzled. Michael was a senior and big man on campus. He was active in class politics, played trumpet in the orchestra, had earned his "B" in sports, and was voted "Most Brilliant" in the yearbook. A hello from him meant something—to me at least; Michael still claims he doesn't remember our first meeting. I guess I didn't make that much of an impression on him.

I saw him again four years later, in 1955, when I was a freshman at Penn State. He was a senior at Swarthmore College. I was standing in line at Symphony Hall getting rush tickets with my cousin, Albert Marcus, and some of his buddies from medical school. Michael was in line with a high school classmate of mine, David Silber. David said hello to me and Michael said, "Who is that?" "Kitty Dickson," David answered. He brought Michael over to meet me. We said hello, again, and that was the end of that . . . until Sandy Bakalar gave him my phone number.

I was busy the first time Michael asked me out. We had a nice chat over the phone. I was no longer a starry-eyed high school freshman, though, and viewed his call as pleasant rather than earth-shattering. He called for the second time a few weeks later, and on October 20, 1961, we had our first date. My son's behavior that evening would have scared off a lesser man. John was at the age where he cried whenever I left the apartment. Michael came and shook hands with John and the babysitter and chatted for a few minutes. Together, we walked out into the hall. Immediately, John began to scream. We heard his sobs as we went down to the street. We got outside and looked upstairs. John ran from window to window, flattening his nose against the glass and shrieking his head off.

"Is he okay?" Michael asked.

"I think so," I answered. "Why don't we just wait underneath here, and see what happens." We huddled out of John's sight beneath the living room window. Within a minute, Johnny stopped. "Okay, the sirens are off," I said to my date, "it's all clear." Michael and I got into his car and drove away. Wonderful beginning for a night out.

We went for dinner at Maitre Jacques. I should have realized Michael liked me; Maitre Jacques was one of the better restaurants in town. Afterwards we went to see a foreign movie at the Exeter, an art-house cinema lodged in an old church. We watched an Italian movie, *Rocco and His Brothers*. About halfway through the film we looked at each other, nodded in agreement, and left. I don't know whether it was because we didn't like the movie, or because we wanted to talk to each other. As we walked out of the theatre, a woman came up to us, gave me the once-over, and said, "Hey, Michael, what a surprise! I didn't know you had a social life." I thought it was a bitchy remark. I found out later that the woman, a conservative Republican, had her eye on my date.

Actually, Michael *was* a very busy man and did not do much socializing. He practiced law with Hill and Barlow and planned to run for the state legislature. I didn't know about his crowded schedule, and the woman's gibe in the lobby of the Exeter caught me off guard. It was our first date and it made me uncomfortable. Lord knows, I have a quick tongue; there's a difference, though, between being blunt and being snide. I learned the value of good manners long before I was involved in politics. It's fine to be outspoken; derisiveness is another story.

Michael and I left the Exeter and went back to my apartment on Everett Street for tea. He was good company and I looked forward to seeing him again. I loved talking to Michael, and listening to him, too. We shared a great many interests. On our second date we went to the symphony; on our third date we went to see the musical *Fiorello*. And on our fourth we saw *The Fantasticks* at the Charles Playhouse. We began dating in October, and by the time we sat in the audience at *The Fantasticks*, I knew I had found a man I could love and respect. I've been asked what attracted me most about Michael. He has many exceptional qualities, including intelligence, kindness, and humor. He's also good-looking and I found him physically attractive. All things considered, I might have been most drawn to him for his unswerving steadiness. He's always known where he's going, and I've never been like that. I have such a volatile personality, I think I could be borne by the wind.

How compelling to meet and fall in love with someone who brought to the relationship a quality I lacked.

Michael is my anchor. He's never threatened by what I do, or how much attention I get, and it's been that way since we met. We have ground rules, particularly concerning the children; even so, he gives me room. Though we agree on most things, when we don't, he doesn't make me feel guilty. I don't believe "guilt" is one of the vital signs. My childhood was stacked with remorse; most of the time I walked around feeling I'd done something wrong. I lived under a Damoclean sword of accusation, and at any given moment it could drop and cut off, if not my head, my confidence.

Michael has given me a new perspective on behavior and responsibility. I've helped him, too. Michael always was enthusiastic; he just wasn't effusive. No question, he's a controlled person. He's not restrained on purpose —that's just the way he is. I believe Michael's reserve is part of the first generation syndrome. Whether it's Greeks, or Jews, or any immigrant group, you work very hard to become Americanized and one of the first things you learn is to hold back, to be reserved, formal. Be a pilgrim, a Puritan—an American. Curb thyself. Michael was raised to keep things close to his chest.

When we married, I played Pandora and helped Michael to open up by enabling him to recognize his passions and deal with them. He didn't "change" over the course of the presidential campaign as the media would have it; he changed after we married. He didn't bubble over and stumble around starry-eyed, but I knew he cared about me because of the way he treated me and my son. He was attentive and loving toward John from the beginning. He'd even baby-sit when I had exams or classes.

I remember a particular exam period when John suddenly spiked a fever and broke into a rash. I thought it was German measles, but it proved to be scarlet fever. I was frantic because I was in the middle of studying. I couldn't put my books on the shelf, but I also couldn't shelve my child. I called Michael and he came over and took care of John while I prepared for the tests. I crammed while Michael steered Johnny right through the straits of illness back into good health. What a guy!

My parents adored Michael, and the feeling was mutual. He got along extremely well with my mother; he saw her strengths and recognized certain attributes that were obscured for me because I was her daughter. Michael could be objective. He always referred to Mother as that "good, good person." He loved her laugh, and, indeed, her laughter was wonderful to hear. She'd been conditioned for years by Dad. He would stoke the fires of humor and Mother would respond with total delight. Michael noticed how attentive and protective she was toward my father. "Your mother really looked after your dad," he's commented to me, a bit wistfully, perhaps.

Michael also appreciated Mother's intellectual qualities. She loved books. I remember when I moved into one of my little houses in California, Mother came to visit and took me shopping. We went into a bookstore and she proceeded to order a thousand dollars' worth of merchandise at one fell swoop. She told the clerk to deliver everything to my house. I couldn't believe it. When I protested, Mother said, "Kitty, a home without books is like a house without windows." Some of the books she bought were not your average selections and had titles like *Snow Goose Hunting, Delta Trips, Rare and Unusual Rocks*. When you're buying in bulk, you don't necessarily pull in just the best-sellers. I don't think I ever read one of them.

Knowing how my mother and I clashed, Michael observed recently that our relationship, besides being a standard mother-daughter one, was hyperactivated by pill-taking and mood swings. Our alliance was tainted by addiction. We were both users.

My dad thought Michael was terrific from the first time he laid eyes on him, and Michael and my father continue to share a very special relationship. Everything that was wrong with my first union was right with the second.

In the early days of our courtship, the rose-colored hue enveloping the Dicksons did not extend to the senior Dukakises. Michael's parents were less enthusiastic about me, and when you consider the circumstances, it was understandable. Their objections weren't for the obvious reason of my being Jewish. The Dukakises were Greek Orthodox, and, though they might have preferred Michael choose a nice Greek girl, I'm sure they'd have accepted the right non-Hellene. The problem was not just that I was a non-Greek—I was also a divorcée with a three-year-old child. Michael met my family pretty early on in our relationship, but he still lived with his parents and I didn't meet them until February, when we went to an Americans for Democratic Action dinner. There had been opportunities for us to meet earlier, but it never happened. I remember that once we were going out on Christmas Eve and Michael's car wouldn't start. We went back to his house so he could call a friend and borrow another vehicle. I was pretty sure Michael's parents were home, yet they never appeared.

Euterpe and Panos Dukakis were a formidable couple; it was not easy for me to get through to them. They had immigrated to America at nine and fifteen years of age, respectively, and worked in factories and struggled to survive. They did more than survive, however; they flourished. She received her college degree and became a teacher. He was the first Greek to graduate Harvard Medical School and became a general practitioner in Boston and Brookline. Though he was a successful doctor and quite comfortable financially, they never forgot their early travails, and lived prudently. My mother-in-law is in her eighties and really has no financial worries; still, she carries on in the same manner as she has all her life. Nothing in excess. In classical mythology, Euterpe is the muse of lyric poetry and music and there is something indeed Olympian about my mother-in-law. I greatly admire her—she has incredible energy and an insatiable appetite for learning—but most of all, I esteem her independent nature. I think she probably was a feminist long before me, though she might not have used that term. She's still living in the same house in Brookline not far from my dad's place.

Panos Dukakis was an honest, forthright gentleman. His integrity was unquestionable though he could be somewhat rigid, and, hardest for me, didn't have much humor. He and Euterpe had two sons, Stelian and Michael. Their family circle was as tight as the Dicksons, maybe tighter.

When my children were little, Panos wanted to be their doctor. He simply could not understand why I refused. "I want you to be their 'Papou' [their grandfather], not someone who sees them when they feel miserable and sticks them with needles," I argued. He couldn't fathom my reasoning. Why should I be paying a stranger to do what he, the grandfather, could do, maybe better and, for sure, for nothing? We had lots of arguments on that theme. Panos Dukakis was far less formidable with his grandchildren themselves. He was very affectionate and warm with them and the kids loved to be in his presence. They'd climb all over him calling "Papou! Papou!" (That's what Michael's going to be called by our grandchildren. I don't think I'll opt for Bubbe, though I'll settle for Grammy.) As wonderful as he was with the children, Panos couldn't take it if they misbehaved. Squabbling upset him because he simply couldn't tolerate a situation that was out of control.

In the winter of 1962, the situation between Michael Dukakis and Kitty Dickson was very much *in* control. We were seeing each other steadily and had declared our love for each other, all without his parents' approval. They were not receptive to our relationship. This was a whole new ball game for me. My first marriage had been accelerated by my in-laws. This time, the situation was different. Michael was determined, however, and finally Euterpe accepted the inevitable and gradually embraced me. I think she was relieved when she met me at the ADA banquet. I'm sure she thought I was going to be some sort of bohemian wild thing because my father was a musician. She was pleased to see me conservatively dressed in a red plaid outfit I'd bought in Harvard Square. She told me she thought I was attractive. Panos, on the other hand, hardly looked at me.

After the ADA dinner, Michael went to Puerto Rico with a friend and came back with mononucleosis. He was in bed for three weeks. He called me two or three times a day. Finally, I went over to see him, but he couldn't stay awake and dozed off within moments of my arrival. After that I didn't see him for nearly a month. It was the pits. And I didn't see the Dukakises again until the fall. From time to time, Michael would take John and me over to visit Euterpe, but Panos was never around. It was a long time before I felt comfortable in their home.

During the summer, Michael joined us in the Berkshires. There was a small mountain near my parents' place and John kept talking about climbing it with Michael. He talked a lot about Michael; they had become real pals. Michael bought John a baseball mitt and the two of them spent hours tossing a ball back and forth. Men can relate to each other on a level as simple as a game of catch.

I cannot remember when Michael and I literally began to speak of marriage. Michael claims he was reading the *New York Times* one day when I reached over, pulled the paper down, and said, "When are we getting married?" That's his version. I know I told him I wanted to wait until I was graduated from Lesley.

When Michael told his father we were getting married, the elder Dukakis roared and ran the gamut of patriarchal wrath. Michael listened and then cut him off. He said, slowly and deliberately, with no hostility, "You have a choice, Dad, you either accept Kitty, or you lose me." Panos backed off. He would never give up his son and he knew Michael meant business. Panos remained aloof toward me for a long time.

I knew I could weather Panos's attitude toward *me*, but I was more sensitive about his reaction to my child. Michael's father was apprehensive about little John; basically, he tried to ignore his existence. When I brought John over to their house, Euterpe was lovely with him. She played games and talked to him in the most grandmotherly way. Panos, that austere gentleman, couldn't face my son and would usually absent himself. Michael and I sympathized with Panos's feelings. We decided not to have John at our wedding; we thought it would add an unnecessary strain. John, of course, couldn't have cared less. He went over to my sister's house and played with his cousins while I took on a new husband for me and a new father for him. Eventually, my father-in-law came around. John, an ingratiating child, found his way right into his grandfather's heart. Panos Dukakis was a loving, caring Papou to all my children.

SIX

I was graduated from Lesley College on June 13, 1963. One week later, on June 20, Michael Dukakis and I were married. Our wedding was small, far different from the Cecil B. DeMille production I'd gone through six years before. Mother and Dad, Jinny and her husband, Euterpe and Panos, and Stelian were in attendance. We were married in my parents' apartment on Amory Street by a Unitarian minister. I was very, very happy. Michael and I spent a brief honeymoon in Nantucket. I am certainly not going into the details of my second honeymoon. I will say that I didn't begin my marriage nervously adorning myself with expensive silk nightwear and anticipating the worst. Michael and I have had a healthy relationship from the beginning. We thoroughly enjoyed Nantucket, and it has remained a favorite vacation place.

We returned after five days and moved into a big nine-room apartment on Perry Street in Brookline. Within the year, we made a down payment of three thousand dollars and bought the entire building, which included five additional units. We were landlords as well as tenants. Seven years later, in 1971, we sold the building as condominiums for $13,500 a unit, and made enough money to buy half of the house next door. We're still there. I don't think I could get Michael out with dynamite! During the presidential campaign when the Secret Service men came to guard our house, they said it was almost impossible to make it secure. One of the men commented, "If the governor makes it to the White House, he's going to have to get another residence. This place will never do." The problem never arose. I tell you, though, if I had to put money on where the "other" White House might have been had we made it to Washington, I've no doubt we'd have stayed right on Perry Street, secure or not.

It had taken the movers a full day to transfer John and me from Cambridge to Brookline. It took Michael half a minute to make the switch from his parents' house to ours. I couldn't believe it. He arrived with all his worldly possessions neatly arranged in a fairly large, but by no means huge, cardboard box; he carried his one suit on a hanger. I had to laugh. "You're really making a major contribution to our household," I said, "one box and one suit." Twenty-six years later, things hardly have altered. He has a few more suits but not much else. Michael is the most unmaterialistic person I know, and this indifference to material things is fine, as long as he doesn't expect me to be like him. From the day we married, I've told him, "I have a very different attitude from yours and your way isn't necessarily right." He's respected my position, too, though I've had to go through some slight subterfuge here and there to keep my closets primed. Frankly, on this particular issue, I don't think either one of us has changed that much, although I do think we're more tolerant of each other than we were at the beginning.

I realized he was Mr. Frugal on our first date, having been forewarned by Sandy Bakalar that he leaned heavily toward the economical. She knew from experience because she had dated Michael in high school. In fact, they had a major falling out when he took her to a well-known jazz club on a date. They were shown to a table, seated, and Sandy was ready to listen to the music, when Michael announced they were leaving. He made her get up and walk out because he discovered there was a cover charge. Michael couldn't justify paying the extra money. To this day, he honestly cannot understand how I can spend money on clothes. He loves to see me looking good, and comments on my appearance, yet he'll always counter with, "Yes, it's a pretty outfit, Katharine, but what about all the other ones in the closet? They're nice, too." Sometimes, he'll use ploys like reminding me of my feminist leanings; considering my stance, he'll muse, why would I have need of frills? I've been trying to teach him that there is nothing inconsistent about being a feminist and being feminine, but he hasn't quite gotten it yet.

When I went to Edgehill Newport, I asked him to bring me some clothes. This meant he had to go through my dresser and closets to pick them out. It was just too much for him. At least he didn't have to ascend to the infamous third floor of our house. I think my entire life could be written based on what I have stored on that third floor. What's up there? In a word, everything! I don't throw things away, I put them upstairs. Mother was the only one to brave the garment garret. Periodically, she'd go on safari to the third floor and prune and weed my possessions. I'd hear her thrashing around and muttering statements like, "What's this? Oh no! Dear God." In the end, she'd storm down the stairs carrying loads of solid memories and out they'd go. Since her death, I haven't given the attic much thought. Lord knows what's lurking there. I haven't curtailed my shopping expeditions, although I have to confess, I will sometimes ship my purchases to my dad's house and store things with him. Considering that my husband will be reading this book, I know I'm blowing my cover. Oh well, it's about time, and I have a sneaky suspicion Michael will accept the news with a smile and shrug of his shoulders.

Not long after I returned from Edgehill Newport we were sitting at the breakfast table discussing the events of the past two years and what had happened to me. "Michael," I asked, "do you sometimes feel you married secondhand goods?"

"Sweetie," my husband answered quickly, "no way are you secondhand goods. If anything, I'd call you 'First Quality . . . Irregular.' "

I settled into married life on Perry Street and a new kind of partnership. Michael the private person was also Michael the social activist. He did not enjoy sitting in an office and practicing law. It was only a means to an end, and the end he wanted from the beginning was public service. It started in the state legislature; I'd worked on his campaign in the fall.

My husband and I are both social activists, but our approaches are different. Michael enjoys doing public service in a fairly relaxed way. Though there is nothing low-key about his zeal, he simply prefers to do things without a lot of fanfare. He takes every responsibility seriously, whether it's being a politician or a husband and father. Michael says that professionally you do much better at what you choose to do if you have a strong, stable family behind you; in order to have that backing, you have to help create it. I think whatever else we've done, Michael and I did build a secure family life. Sure, there are special obligations built in. Michael, however, has never viewed these duties as a burden. There's a pervasive attitude in America that says, "If you're going to be in politics, you have to do it seven days a week." Michael would never subscribe to that precept. He gives his all to his work, but not at the expense of his home life. Living in Massachusetts made it possible for him to balance work and home. When he became governor, he could visit the farthest reaches of our state and still be back for the evening meal, because Massachusetts is small enough to get around. Had we lived in Texas or California, it might have been a different story. During the presidential campaign Michael knew he couldn't be home for dinner, and it was hard on him. He still insisted on family time, only then it was one night a week rather than every evening. He was willing to make the concession because it was for a limited period of time; after the election, his life would become structured again. "Sure I'd be home for dinner if I were president," Michael said. "Hell, you live over the store."

While Michael was willing to compromise for the campaign, he would never make that frenetic pace a way of life. You can't run full speed, twenty-four hours of every day, and drop back into the domestic fold for instant comfort. This is as true in business, entertainment, or banking, but especially true in politics. I knew when we married that I had allied myself with a caring partner, not someone who'd desert me. I had done time as a sports widow; I never would have walked into a deal where I'd be a political widow.

I think it was Michael's attitude toward John that tipped me off. He always had time for him, even before we were married. He'd come over and take Johnny out to play. They would walk down Everett Street, through Harvard Yard and into the square. Johnny was about four and his main objective in life was to get his "fumb" into his mouth. I'd look out the window and gaze at the two of them going hand-in-hand down the street. I felt so relieved and grateful. Michael went directly to John and gave him exactly the kind of masculine strength and example he needed. It was like a personal Big Brother program.

As a single parent, I felt strongly that John should remain in contact with his father and his father's family. I stayed close to Rhoda and Mac Chaffetz. Why not? They were my son's grandparents. When Johnny was little and unable to fly out alone to visit his father in California, the Chaffetzes would come to Boston and take him with them. After his wife died, Mr. Chaffetz would come and stay with us and play with John and his sisters.

John Chaffetz remarried, had two sons, and *they* would come and stay with us. We were a living example of a family extended by divorce long before such situations became commonplace. We were in the vanguard.

Even though John's natural father did not live with him, he always had a true father in Michael, who put all the children's needs ahead of everything else. The truth is, he never would have run for the presidency if any of our children had been in high school; they had to be grown up enough to handle his absence. The pursuit of success was never the be-all and end-all of Michael Dukakis's life and I think that's what makes him special. When he says, "My best times in this life are those with my family," he really means it.

Five months after we were married, I became pregnant. I had been through three pregnancies already and I knew some of the telltale signs of a bad one. Once again I suspected something was wrong. I was seven and a half months along and positively huge. I went to the doctor and had X rays taken. My weight was pure water and he decided to induce labor rather than take any more chances. My parents took care of John and I went into the hospital. They started my labor; it was really rough. My water broke and I lost twenty-two pounds; the baby, a little girl, lived for twenty minutes.

My father-in-law was there and he was crushed. This would have been his first grandchild. Michael was miserable also. He never said a word, and neither did I, but we both knew this was my third miscarriage. Would we be able to have children together? We ordered a pathology report to find out why I'd lost the baby. Five months later, I became pregnant again. Because there hadn't been any rush, the pathologist's report on the previous miscarriage had not been done. We still didn't know what had gone wrong. Now we needed to know. Michael made a phone call to the lab, and within twenty-four hours we received a report. There had been a German measles epidemic; I had been infected without realizing it. We were relieved to learn the miscarriage was due to a specific outside cause and not some genetic flaw. Nevertheless, I was a nervous wreck during the entire pregnancy. Little John came down with the German measles during my first trimester, and though I knew I was immune, it gave me uneasy moments.

Just before Andrea was born, an incident occurred in my son's life that had repercussions on his future. John was in second grade and used the Chaffetz name. Though Michael treated John as his own son, John, Sr., remained his legal father. I knew John would not allow his son to drop his birth name and I never pushed it. When young John asked why he wasn't a Dukakis, I explained that John Chaffetz was his father and that's why he had that name. But then I noticed that the papers my son brought home from school were marked "Dukakis" at the top. He had made his own decision. John was around eight when his father found out he was using the Dukakis name. He was furious and threatened to take me to court. He wrote a very strong letter informing me that he would call and settle the matter over the phone. I called my dad, who advised me not to get into a fight. "Just tell John the most important thing in the boy's life is his happiness. If little John is happier using Michael's name, then he should let him." I did what my father suggested. John Chaffetz listened and agreed. Thank heaven, he could put his child's happiness above his own objections.

On November 9 (a week after my "due" date) I took a walk with John, and when I came back, I had a bloody show. I immediately called Michael at the State House. "I'll be right there," he said.

Michael sprinted down the steps of the State House, across the Boston Common, and into the Park Street subway station. He was halfway home, when suddenly, without any warning, the streetcar went dead . . . the lights went out . . . power stopped. This was the Big Blackout of 1965 and the exact moment our child decided to come into the world. Michael got off the streetcar and ran the rest of the way home. Meanwhile, I thought the world was coming to an end, and called a downstairs neighbor and my mother. Both my neighbor and I were relieved when Mother arrived; she at least was a nurse.

Michael arrived home exhausted from his sprint. When the pains became regular, we drove over to the hospital. I arrived at midnight and went into labor just as the lights went on again. Andrea was born five hours later.

She was colicky and skinny and cried a lot at first, but Michael was absolutely wonderful with her. He'd get up in the morning and feed her and change her and amuse her. John was delighted with his sister and paid her the highest compliment, asking if he could bring her to school for show-and-tell. The request was so ingenuous, I couldn't refuse. Ten days after her birth, I wrapped Andrea Dukakis up in a blanket and brought her to the classroom. John carried her in and proudly presented his baby sister as his contribution to show-and-tell. The children in the second grade wrote me letters saying they were very sad that the lights went out, but very happy that Andrea was born. So was I.

Within five months, I was pregnant again. I sensed something was wrong and, indeed, lost the baby six weeks later. In all, I've had four miscarriages. I cannot help but wonder if the pills had anything to do with them. It's a troubling thought.

For the next couple of years, I was busy with my family, but I also had time to take an active part in Michael's campaigns. Michael ran every two years for the legislature and it required a good deal of my time to assist him. I loved working with him and for the good of the community; my special interest was housing.

I became pregnant again in 1968, and this time I was sure it would be a boy. I even went out and bought all boy's clothing. On November 4, 1968, the day after Michael's birthday and the evening before his last election to the legislature, Kara was born. She was a beautiful baby with a big, full face. I called John on the telephone and told him he had a baby sister.

"Oh no," he cried and burst into sobs. Poor John wanted a baby brother more than anything in the world.

When Michael got home, John came into the bedroom, still shedding bitter tears of disappointment. Michael spent the evening comforting him. "Don't you understand, John, you're the special one, you're the boy. It's you and me together," he reassured him. They have stuck together; there's a singular bond between Michael and John.

John was politically sophisticated at an early age; when most kids were talking about superheroes and media idols, John held forth on senators and representatives. His fifth-grade teacher confessed that her pupil knew more about politics than she ever did. No wonder. John was right there when Michael's friends and colleagues gathered at the house. The topic of conversation was politics and he wasn't excluded.

John was also very musical as a child. He played the trumpet in third grade and went to the symphony regularly. I remember him singing around the house all the time. When John got to Brookline High, he auditioned for a special singing group. He made it, and sang with them for three years. In his junior year, he was in a musical production and decided he liked acting better than singing. He went right into a straight play. In order to learn his part, he had Andrea and Kara read lines with him. John was seventeen, the girls were ten and seven. He rehearsed over and over, and his sisters were delighted to participate. The night of the performance, John came on stage and began to speak.

"I helped him with that line," Kara said.

"I helped him with that one," said Andrea.

I tried to hush them. My daughters, however, were so delighted with their contributions, they spent the entire play identifying the lines for which they felt responsible.

Our family was complete. Michael, John, Andrea, Kara, and I formed a solid unit. Every day brought some new challenge, new adventure, new delight. And every morning I took a pill.

SEVEN

Mythology tells us Zeus was overcome with a terrific headache one day. He sat down, put his hand over his eyes, and lo, from his brow out popped the goddess Athena, full-grown and in full armor. What an entrance! Only in legend does someone spring full-blown into the public eye. That certainly isn't the case in politics. You don't leap on to the scene fully prepared and fully armed. You spend years and years girding yourself for the main political arena, and during the first years of our marriage, that's exactly what my husband did.

Michael had been an active member of the Massachusetts House of Representatives from 1962 to 1970, and slowly and surely he built his reputation. Like many political spouses, I was active, too. When your husband is a politician, if you're even the least bit interested, you become a kind of administrative assistant, a distaff éminence grise. By the time Michael was in his second term in the legislature, I was committed to a number of his causes, and a few of my own as well. I was active in all his campaigns and went out with him on the streets and in the assembly halls. I went to house parties and fund-raisers and all sorts of neighborhood functions. On various occasions, when Michael was away or unavailable, crises arose and I felt confident stepping in for him. He welcomed my participation right from the start, and I participated enthusiastically. I did volunteer work at Children's Hospital, taught dance to mentally retarded children, sat on the executive board of the Council for Public Schools, was a trustee of the Boston Children's Museum, and was active in the PTA. Though it was in its early stages, I was involved with the women's liberation movement. Women desperately needed more part-time jobs and more day-care centers. Equal pay and equal opportunity for qualified women is worth fighting for, and I did fight for it. I still do! The situation is better today, though still not ideal.

Michael had immersed himself in the political pool long before we married and he continued to do his laps. He supported people he admired and respected; among others, he'd worked hard for Jock Saltonstall's congressional campaign in the late fifties. In 1966, Michael ran for attorney general and finished second in the Democratic Convention. Frank Bellotti, the opposition, was too tough. In 1970, Michael decided to run in the primary for lieutenant governor of Massachusetts. This was the first year the governor and lieutenant governor would be running together in the general election; previously, they had run separately.

In the Massachusetts Democratic primary, Kevin White received the nomination for governor and Michael

Dukakis got the nod for lieutenant governor. Kevin had been mayor of Boston for years and was a very charismatic man. There was, however, some doubt as to how strong he was as a candidate for governor. We plunged into the campaign and worked hard to get voter support. I was interviewed in the papers, on television and radio, and appeared everywhere from supermarket malls to hotel ballrooms. In one newspaper interview I was asked to name my secret desire. My answer was, "To see my husband elected lieutenant governor." In many pursuits, you can get so caught up in what you're doing, you can't see what's happening. Politics is different. I don't think it holds many surprises. Sure there are occasional upsets like Harry Truman over Tom Dewey; in the main, however, the handwriting on the wall is legible early on.

About a month before the election, I knew the White-Dukakis ticket was in deep trouble. My first inkling came during a parade in Springfield. Michael and I were marching with Kevin and Kathryn White down the main street, and while people lined our route, they weren't very receptive. Cool is the word, and although they were waving signs, most of the banners read Sargent-Dwight, not White-Dukakis. Frank Sargent and Donald Dwight were the Republican candidates. I got the picture and was prepared for the defeat that came in November.

There's a saying from Confucius, "Our greatest triumph lies not in never failing, but in rising each time we fall." Michael was ready to put Confucius to the test, and not for the last time. He had run and lost in a statewide election, and now he was an experienced candidate. He had gone through his trial by fire, and though defeated, had become a recognizable name all over the state. Immediately after that election, Michael began to organize his forces. He wanted to run for governor. Many friends joined in his support from the beginning. For the next four years, bit by bit, every day, the organization strengthened and expanded.

Michael kept practicing law half-time and working with his organization. Then he was asked to participate in a public television program called "The Advocates." Each week the show addressed a significant social issue with advocates representing both sides, conservative and progressive/liberal. Michael acted as moderator and thoroughly enjoyed himself; he was also a natural and quite comfortable with the camera. He stayed with "The Advocates" for three years, leaving finally to devote his full energies to the gubernatorial race.

I had already been in campaigns in 1966 and 1970 and, though this was for higher stakes, it was still a political race. We had just moved from sprint to mile. I enjoyed what I was doing, but I was still a bit stiff and not terribly polished. I gave a lot of interviews, and I look back at those interviews and accompanying pictures and laugh. It was a different era. Candidates' wives were not asked about important concerns. The reporters questioned the candidate on issues and then, almost as though someone had announced, "The brain stops here," they would turn to the spouse and ask her to name her favorite color. Such questions were leveled at me; I answered them because it was expected of me.

In 1974, I was asked if I ever felt like an appendage. I never did. I've never felt like a decoration because I've always had my own agenda. Michael's campaigns were part of my life, a big part, but they were not everything. I had my own priorities, like my dancing. I danced and taught almost continuously up till 1982. Then, too, I was

busy raising a family. My children were reared in a political household. As I've said, John became "aware" at
an early age, and the girls were born while their father
was in the state legislature.

I had been brought up in a certain way by my mother,
and I was determined to do things differently with my
children. Sound familiar? With my son, the job was a bit
easier. Raising a boy was new territory, no precedent
had been set, and, once Michael came into his life, John
had a role model. Andrea and Kara presented certain
problems. Unlike me, I wanted my girls to be independent from the start. My dependence on my parents
helped propel me into an early marriage because I mis-
takenly believed marriage would endow me with self-
determination. I wanted my children to make their own
decisions whenever possible, right from the beginning.
At two years of age, Andrea Dukakis chose her own
wardrobe. My mother would come over to the house and
go nuts watching her pint-sized granddaughter standing
in front of the closet deciding what she would put on for
the day.

"How can you let a two-year-old pick out her clothes?"
Mother demanded.

"Because I want her to; it's good for her," I answered.

For a stretch of her young life, Andrea Dukakis wore
the most outlandish getups. Plaids, stripes, polka dots
—everything came together on my little girl's form. If
she had had to meet the conductor of the Boston Symphony, it wouldn't have been in a perfect aqua blue suit
from Best & Co., of that I'm certain. It wasn't that I
was too lazy to pick out the proper outfit for my daughter; I'd love to have gotten in my two cents because I
wanted her to look smart. More than that, though, I
wanted her to be strong, to have a mind of her own.

Letting her make her own decisions on simple matters like clothing would help establish a sense of independence. I do feel my kids have ego strengths I lacked when I was their age, and some of it comes from confidence in their own judgment. I consciously tried to guide rather than control my children even when they were little. I wasn't always successful. Still, while I grew into independence only at a late stage, my kids were brought up to stand on their own.

When the children were younger, I found Andrea most difficult to handle. Michael picked up on it and favored her, though not at Kara's expense. My darling Andrea was one tough little cookie to raise, and why not? She was bred for independence. Andrea was the problem eater. Except for corn-on-the-cob, a cooked vegetable never passed her lips. She never ate salad. I once calculated there were about seven things she *would* eat. When she went to Princeton, however, she underwent a culinary revolution. Suddenly, her favorite food was sushi. Now she's a vegetarian. Things change.

Scholastically, my children were way ahead of me. John, Andrea, and Kara all attended Lawrence School and Brookline High. The three of them bent over backwards trying to be regular kids. They didn't want judgments made either for or against them because their father was an important political figure. They were a lot more sensitive than I ever was about Michael's position. In those instances, my children were more like their dad.

Michael has his own exacting standards. Of all the politicians I have ever met, in every corner of this world, my husband is probably the most careful officeholder. He's totally uncomfortable with perks. He never has gotten in the habit of relying on his office to get him places. To this day, he often uses public transportation and carries his own tokens. He reminds me of Harry Truman. Truman was proud of the fact he never used stamps from his Oval Office for his personal mail. I think Harry Truman and Michael would have hit it off. Michael is so concerned about the "favoritism" label, he will take absolutely, positively nothing from anyone. In my opinion, he can carry it to an extreme. After his first election to the governorship he did not reward all his campaign workers with appointments and jobs, something that is standard procedure in the political game. Some of them complained they were being punished for their efforts on his behalf. I could understand their feelings. At times, I get weary of being Caesar's wife. There should be a happy medium even in politics.

I didn't want the children to think everything would come their way because of their dad's position, nor did I want them to be suspicious of every little thing. I tried, and so did Michael, to raise them with the understanding that most privileges should be earned. From the time she could toddle, I took Kara with me to the corner drugstore. On every visit, the woman behind the counter, Mrs. Levine, would give Kara a lollipop. I wasn't too crazy about Mrs. Levine's present because I don't approve of giving sweets to children, but I didn't interfere, and watched as my daughter took her treat and politely thanked Mrs. Levine. The ritual was well established by the time Kara was six.

Two days after Michael's election as governor, we went into the drugstore and, true to form, Mrs. Levine handed Kara her candy. We left the store and got into the car. Kara began unwrapping her treat and turned to me saying, "Mom, would Mrs. Levine have given me a lollipop if Daddy wasn't elected governor?"

"What are you talking about?" I answered, "Mrs. Levine has been giving you lollipops since you were a year old!"

Whenever you are in a position of power, the question of people's motives comes into play. Mrs. Levine was doing what she had been doing; Kara's perception was colored by her father's new office. I don't know if people realize how sensitive you can become to even the slightest attentions. Are they doing this because they like me, or because my father is the governor? You cannot help having these thoughts and you cannot help being a bit guarded. In public life, after a while, you can figure out which people are coming on too strong. I think it's important, though, not to become too cynical. There are decent people out there and if you get too suspicious, you're finished.

Some people, however, will try to curry favor by offering favors. I have developed a sixth sense about these situations and know when to back off. Michael didn't need a sense removed to the sixth power; he'd never allow it to happen in the first place. I am not as noble as my husband. There are some advantages I like and, as long as they have absolutely no taint, I'll accept them. Do you want to know what kind of perks I mean? Suppose I drive up to a parking lot and it's full. The attendant comes to the car to tell me the bad news, looks in and sees it's the governor's wife, and suddenly there's a parking space. Or, when a hotel or a theatre is sold out, my office will call up and I'll often get in because of my name. Mind you, I pay for the tickets and the rooms and the parking space! I don't think it is bad to accept such favors as long as I'm not hurting anyone else or getting myself in a position of owing favors. Michael and I, however, are worlds apart on this subject.

I don't think "perks" is a dirty word, far from it. And there are many positive perks. For me, the outstanding benefit has been the number of exceptional people I've met and the beautiful friendships formed from purely political connections. I'm thinking particularly of Bob Farmer, one of my dearest and closest friends. He's like a brother. Bob became finance chairman of Michael's second run for the governorship, and in the process he also became part of our family. He handled the finances for Michael's presidential bid and is now treasurer of the Democratic National Committee. Indeed, he's the most successful fund-raiser in the United States, and, like all fund-raisers, has a bit of malarkey in him. Bob has got a big ego, which I love to tease him about, yet he's also one of the most giving human beings I've ever known. What I love most about Bob is that I can say anything to him, and he knows he can do the same with me. We're not afraid to disagree, a sure sign of friendship. Meeting Bob Farmer was a perk—knowing him is a treasure. Outside of my husband, father, and son, Bob Farmer is my closest male friend.

Because Michael and I are of different faiths, I'm often asked how we handled the religious question. How did we raise our children? Except for my Dickson grandparents' influence, I wasn't brought up in a religious manner, and, though Michael was raised in the Greek Orthodox tradition, he did not have a strong formal identification with religion, either. It wasn't an issue when we married and it still isn't, although, admittedly, my views have changed.

After Michael and I married, we alternated going to temples and churches, though we didn't do much of either. He would accompany me to bar mitzvahs and weddings and an occasional high holy day service. On the other side, I went with Michael to church. Actually, I love the chanting and the liturgy of the Greek Orthodox ceremony, and have been equally attentive to both services.

My attitude toward my religion changed in 1976, when I went to Israel. From that visit I began to feel strongly about who I was and where I came from. I hate to sound corny, but I had a spiritual awakening. My first trip to Israel "converted" me. I had a very strong identification with the country, and felt I belonged there, that I had someplace to go if anything happened. I've since learned I'm not the only one to feel this way. Many Jews, religious and otherwise, have been similarly affected.

Soon after I returned from Israel, I took a single membership at Temple Israel on the Riverway in Boston, a temple my mother's family had helped to found. I go there on the high holidays, sometimes with Sandy Bakalar or my dad. The kids have come with me a few times, though I've never forced them. I don't take my being Jewish for granted, nor do I proselytize. My feelings about being Jewish relate to me; I did not try to influence my husband or my children.

At first, John was exposed to the Jewish tradition because both John Chaffetz and I were Jewish. I sent him to Sunday school for two or three years. Then, he came home and started talking about being a chosen person. I went crazy. I didn't like the context in which he was talking about being "chosen." I took him out of the school. At the Lawrence School, he was especially close to six or seven boys, most of whom were Jewish. The time came for bar mitzvahs, and the majority of the boys did not go through the rite. I gave John the choice and he deferred. To this day, I don't know why he chose not to be bar mitzvahed. I have a feeling he felt it might be an awkward situation for his father. Someday, I'll ask him.

Neither Andrea nor Kara was raised in any formal religion. When Andrea was younger she used to say, "I'm half-Greek, half-Jewish, and all-American." Her answer changed after she took a course in religion at Princeton. Today, if you ask what her ethnic roots are, she'll still answer, she's half-Jewish and half-Greek. Ask about her religious beliefs and she'll answer wistfully, "I don't know what I am."

It was always a mixed bag in the house. As a family we celebrated Passover and Hanukkah and Greek Easter and Christmas. I observed Rosh Hashanah and Yom Kippur on my own. Since 1964, we have been having Passover seders with three other families. We alternate playing host with Don and Merna Lipsitt, Paul and Judy Kantrowitz, and Susan Leeman. I remember taking Andrea in an infant seat to the Lipsitts' for the first seder—that's how long we've been at it. Though our base is the four families, in the tradition of the Passover, we welcome honored guests and have entertained parents and other relatives.

In 1987, it was my turn to do the seder. If you think running for the presidency is a big job, try preparing the Passover meal! It's a soup-to-nuts affair, and the ceremony is intrinsic to the dining, so you have to match the food to the religious text. We have a large group to accommodate, anywhere from eighteen to twenty-four people—banquet proportions. That year I happened to be leaving on a trip to Japan at six o'clock the morning after the first night of Passover. It was late when everyone left, too late to do anything more than put one load of dirty dishes in the dishwasher.

Since none of us has enough dishes, we borrow from each other. This year Merna Lipsitt had lent me some of her china, and had arranged to pick it up the next evening. At seven o'clock that night, Merna arrived at Perry Street and found Michael in the kitchen cleaning up. He'd returned from work and was busily putting things in order.

"Can you beat it?" he said to Merna. "Here's a guy who could be president of the United States washing Passover dishes."

When I returned from Japan, the first words out of my husband's mouth were, "You are never leaving me with the Passover dishes again!"

Funny. We tried to do the right thing by not pressuring the kids toward one religion or the other, and now we receive occasional flak because we didn't take a stand. From time to time, my girls will complain they didn't have a religious upbringing. I tell them we did the best we could. Furthermore, they're morally and ethically fine upstanding human beings and that's what's important. I can't say whether a laissez-faire attitude toward religion will work or not. I think it's totally up to the couple how they handle it. If either Michael or I had felt strongly about our religion at the beginning of our marriage, it might have been a different story.

I must add, after I returned from Israel, Michael teased me by saying, "What's going on, Katharine? You weren't religious when I married you."

I just answered him right back, "I wasn't then, dear, but I am now."

I'm happy to report that during the presidential campaign, though my religion was mentioned in the media, anti-Semitic attacks were at a minimum. The Arab press was upset with my involvement with Israel and took occasional snipes. I received a few sick letters; most were unsigned. I try to answer all my mail; it doesn't matter whether the sender is positive or negative toward me as long as the letter is reasonable. I have a rule, though: I throw out any hate mail that doesn't include a return address. Nine times out of ten, if a person isn't willing to identify him- or herself, the remarks don't deserve to be read.

As I mentioned, the Jewish issue *was* raised during the campaign. Again and again, I was asked about my beliefs—and Michael's. I don't remember anyone asking Barbara Bush her religion; I didn't find out till after the election that the Bushes were Episcopalians. I was as outspoken about my religion as I am about most everything. Jews reacted strongly: Some of them thought I was too Jewish, others said I wasn't Jewish enough. Toward the end, every article about me mentioned my Jewishness, my drug addiction, and the neck surgery I eventually had to undergo, like they were three prerequisites for being the first lady. I used to say, I have other qualities, why don't you write about them?

What I remember about Michael's first gubernatorial campaign has more to do with family crises than political maneuvering. Three months before the primary, I took the girls up to Maine to visit with friends, and while there we did a lot of swimming. We were driving home when Andrea started complaining about pains in her leg. Andrea wasn't a complainer; I knew she must be hurting, and decided to take her to the doctor when we got home. We were leaving for the Berkshires the next day and I wanted to be certain she was okay.

The doctor examined her and found she had a slight fever, but he wasn't worried. "Take her on up to Tanglewood; she'll recuperate there just as easily as she will at home," he advised.

We drove to the Berkshires with Andrea asleep in the backseat during the ride. When we arrived, my dad took one look at Andrea and immediately put his hand to her forehead. "Kitty, she's burning up. This child's sick."

We took her temperature; the thermometer registered 105 degrees. We rushed to the Berkshire Medical Center in Stockbridge, where the examining physician said he thought Andrea had one of three things: the flu, a strep that hadn't presented itself, or osteomyelitis, a bone infection. "I haven't seen a case of osteomyelitis in twenty years," he added. He told me to take her home, record her temperature every hour, and call him in three hours with a report.

In three hours, her temperature went back and forth from 105 to 99 to 105. That evening they put her in the hospital in Pittsfield and began giving her massive doses of oxacillin. The next morning I called my doctor back east and she said to get Andrea to Children's Hospital in Boston. My nephew, Rob Shain, had come on the trip with us, and we put him in the backseat of the car between both girls. What a ride we had! Kara threw up the entire trip. Andrea screamed every twenty minutes because of the pain that seared through her thigh to her hip. She said it was like being burned with fire.

You can imagine what it was like at the wheel of this car. I drove between eighty and ninety miles an hour. When we reached Children's, Andrea was immediately given a bone scan. There were doctors all over the place, interns, residents, and senior staff. When I heard the word "surgery" mentioned, I called Art Pappas, an outstanding orthopedic surgeon and the staff physician for the Boston Red Sox. He came over and reviewed Andrea's case. Within twenty-four hours, they decided against surgery. Andrea was confined to her bed or wheelchair for a month, and was on crutches for the next six weeks. After that, she was fine and has had no reoccurrence. Nobody knows how it happened. Osteomyelitis usually develops when there's a trauma to a particular area. Why it happened to Andrea is still a mystery.

When it happened, however, my involvement with Michael's campaign was over. I spent my days with Andrea at Children's while my husband continued stumping. Every moment he could spare, he came to the hospital. My sister took Kara. John was out in California with his dad. A week before her father won the primary, Andrea Dukakis came home.

Michael was inaugurated for his first term as governor in January 1975. I was so proud standing there with him. And to think, a few short years ago, my secret desire was to see him elected lieutenant governor. Well, I got more than I secretly desired.

I enjoyed being the governor's wife. There were so many things I could do for people just because I was married to the the man in the State House. When I said, "This is Kitty Dukakis," I knew it carried weight. Weight, however, doesn't mean anything unless it's being used to push forward worthy things. During Michael's first term, I had an agenda of my own. As first lady of Massachusetts, I had responsibilities and needed adequate help to get things done.

In the seventies, most governors' wives were not working in the private sector. I, however, was teaching fourteen dance classes a week at Lesley College and the Brookline Art Center, and continued teaching while Michael was governor. I also had an "office" in the State House, and I hired a small staff to assist me. All in all, I was one busy lady.

I was one addicted lady, too. Still on those pills and still subject to those incredible mood swings. One thing had changed, though; someone found out I was taking amphetamines. In 1974, Michael discovered a store of pills in my bureau drawer. I don't know what he was looking for; I'm sure it was perfectly reasonable. What he found was totally unreasonable. He immediately came to me and asked what I was taking. Was anything the matter? Was I okay? I assured him they were diet pills to control my weight. I said I'd stop taking them if it bothered him. Later I thought about this moment when all the uncomplimentary stuff was printed about Michael: How could a man live with an addicted person and not know that she was using? Why didn't he recognize my behavior was out of the ordinary?

Why should he? I behaved as I did when we met and married. Michael had never known me any other way. He saw I was volatile and full of boundless energy. Certainly there are people with these traits who don't take pills. Michael accepted my volcanic nature. My mood swings were part of my personality. Furthermore, he wasn't 100 percent in love with my behavior. We had some tough moments, times when I would fly off the handle to such an extent that Michael would wind up not speaking to me. Of course he didn't know it was the pills talking. Even when he found out the first time, I don't think the full weight of the addictive curse hit him.

In 1974, at Michael's urging, I went to see Gerald Plotkin, our family doctor at the Harvard Community Health Plan. For a few months, I actually did stop taking pills. What started me taking them again? I don't remember. It doesn't matter. Anything could have sent me back. I was a walking time bomb. My fuse was snuffed, and then relit. I never asked for—and, consequently, never received—help from any support group. I was back on pills and hiding them from my husband. If you think that's hard to do, then you don't know how crafty addicts are; I could have fooled Sherlock Holmes. I returned to the pattern of my morning pick-me-up, and for eight more years I abused myself and deceived my husband. My behavior was the same as it had always been. When I went off-the-wall, Michael and everyone else believed it was just Kitty being Kitty.

EIGHT

Michael took office as governor in 1975. Meanwhile I continued teaching modern dance. I loved my work; still, I was eager to broaden my activities. During Michael's first term, opportunities came my way that allowed me to expand my interests and pursuits. I was asked to appear on a local television program to do weekly commentaries and reviews on the arts in Boston. I did it, but I wasn't particularly good. Some people go before the camera and are immediately at home. Not I! I wasn't a natural and I hadn't had any training. The red light went on and I turned off. I would tighten up and sputter. I was a flop. I lasted for about a year and, mercifully, was released. I've learned a lot since that time; the presidential campaign proved to be a crash course in media appearances. I think I've improved. At least, the television camera doesn't hold terror for me anymore.

Putting my initial video fiasco behind me, I looked around for another work area—and got into the travel business. For three years, working almost full time, I helped with a convention service business, and then briefly worked with another outfit in a similar capacity.

I liked working as a professional in the travel field. Indeed, I liked it so much, I used my experience to do a bit of private travel planning. I got together a group of interested persons; more as a joke, the group was called Kitty's Litter and the name stuck. I put the litter together as a result of my preoccupation with Israel. By 1979, I'd been to the Holy Land three times. I wanted to take a mixed company of Christians and Jews there because I felt they could see things differently through each other's eyes. Nearly forty people were on the initial trip, most of whom I knew through the political world; the rest were friends or relatives. The majority came from Massachusetts. They were affluent people; many had traveled extensively on their own, and in style. Luxury wasn't my objective, though; I wanted to provide a quality trip with cultural, educational, and political activities. To that end, I set up an itinerary that would expose the group to important aspects of the country as well as the scenery. On our first journey, I carefully matched every couple or single person in Kitty's Litter with a compatible family in Israel. Details are important —I've learned that in politics and travel. The trip was a smashing success. Though I hadn't thought of making it a permanent travel corps, I was asked to do it again, and again, and again. Thus, Kitty's Litter became a viable entity. In 1981, we went to Greece; in 1983, Italy; and in 1987, we visited Japan. In preparing for the sojourns, I take "pre-trips" to smooth the way for my companions. We've been together for ten years now and real friendships have been forged. The basis of all good relationships is coming together for a mutual purpose and learning to live with one another. I take full credit for establishing the litter and I consider it a real accomplishment.

In 1976, my mother underwent surgery for stomach cancer. After the operation, the surgeon came in and told us sadly, "I hoped I could remove everything. I couldn't." Until shortly before she died, Mother never let on that she knew. She went with us on a trip to Greece in September of 1976 and for the last year and a half of her life continued the established pattern of her existence. She gardened and cooked and read. She continued to look after my father, and kept a caring eye on her grandchildren. She still preferred the refuge of privacy. Indeed, as the years passed, she had become more reclusive. Mother grew especially sensitive when Michael became governor. Her only complaint about my husband was his elected position. She loathed politics. She hated being out in public. Only her great affection and admiration for her son-in-law could overcome her aversion to the limelight.

She bristled when I was quoted in the papers or shown on the television. She told me a million times I was too outspoken. Only once did she acknowledge there might be something worthwhile in being married to the governor. During the Bicentennial celebration, Massachusetts was visited by six reigning monarchs including the queen of England, the king of Sweden, and the queen of Belgium. Mother called me and made a suggestion. "You know, Kitty, this is an historic and important time, you really ought to keep a diary or use a tape recorder." That call was her only positive reaction; there were endless negative ones. Whenever political difficulties were exposed in an uncomplimentary press, Mother would call Michael at the State House and tell him to resign.

She told him to quit his job, and yet, she would never quit hers. Until the last few weeks of her life, she went about putting her husband's day in order. Those were trying and sad times. At first we all tried to keep things going as normally as possible. Mother started radiation never believing it would help. Part of battling cancer is fighting it and Mother just wouldn't. The doctor said she could have lived a quality life for a while longer, but she gave up. She refused to eat anything. She wandered silently around the house like a ghost of herself.

One morning I was seated across from her at the breakfast table when she began to cry. "What is it, Mother?" I asked.

"I just don't know how Daddy's going to manage," she sobbed softly.

"Don't worry," I answered, "Jinny and I will be here to help him." I wanted to say, "Don't worry, Mother, you'll be all right." I couldn't.

I had to accept what she said because she was so matter of fact. It would have been foolish to argue. Mother wouldn't talk about her condition beyond those few words and I knew enough not to push her. Until she went into a coma, she stayed in control. She prepared Dad's breakfast every morning. At the last, she would come down the stairs barely able to move, holding on to Jinny or me to balance herself. Toward the end, Mother could hardly talk. She asked for morphine and that was about all.

One afternoon I was watching over Mother when her breathing became irregular. She'd stop for ten or fifteen seconds. I called my sister and she came rushing over. I had panicked; Mother was not dying, not yet. I remember sitting in the living room with Dad and Jinny. Panos was there, too. I started crying. My father-in-law said, "Don't cry." I answered back, "Don't tell me not to cry, Dad. It's okay to cry." He was of the old school; you're supposed to hold everything inside. He and my mother were alike in some very basic ways. They shared that incredible need for order. During the long weeks of dying, I had to get something from the medicine chest. I opened the door and saw every vial, every bottle, every tube scrubbed clean and lined up. Within two weeks of Mother's death, the cabinet was a mess.

On December fifteenth, a feeling came over me; I knew my mother was going to die. About six hours before it actually happened, Jinny, Dad, and I got into a terrible fight. I was upset because I could hear my mother moaning when the nurses turned her around. I didn't think they were being gentle enough. Dad and Jinny thought I was being hysterical and told me to calm down and keep quiet. I got angrier.

Fortunately, a psychiatrist and friend of the family, Don Lipsitt, came over that night and helped clear the air. Family strife often occurs around a death. You deal with your own pain and don't realize how others are suffering.

Dad kept asking, "Why are you letting this bother you? Mother doesn't know what's happening."

Jinny said the same thing. Why did I let it bother me? Every time I heard my mother cry out, it was like a dagger piercing me. Part of my agony was not being able to get rid of my own pain. Don Lipsitt legitimized my feelings. He was able to connect with me, Dad, and Jinny and left us at peace with each other. A short time later, everybody went to bed.

Acting on my premonition, I decided to stay at Mother's side. I was there for hours. Looking at her, I realized I would never be able to talk to her again, never be able to express the things I wanted so desperately to say. During those last hours, I said good-bye to my mother, but not to my resentments, not yet.

Mother's breathing became sporadic. She'd breathe for a minute and then stop. About three o'clock on the morning of December 16, she drew her last breath. It was over. I ran for Dad and Jinny.

After she was gone, I couldn't look at her again. Jinny stayed with Mother until the undertakers came. The rabbi arrived at five in the morning to talk to us. Mother had been dying for weeks and weeks and weeks, and now the death watch was over. Dad cried, but only a bit. He couldn't believe she was gone. I'm sure he thought she never would leave him.

I went to the florist to order flowers for the memorial service. I wanted them to be as perfect as she would have wanted. I had such an awful tightness in my throat and chest, I could barely talk. Dad got the musicians together and the memorial service was held at Temple Ohabei Shalom in Brookline. We got through it okay.

Ten days later, on my birthday, Dad, Jinny, and I went up to the house in the Berkshires. As we walked in the door, I heard my father let out a great sob. I couldn't bear to hear his pain. That spring, we buried Mother's ashes under a tree near the Berkshire home she loved so very much.

The next ordeal was less than a year away.

On September 19, 1978, something unexpected happened at the voting polls. After four good solid years of governing, Michael lost his bid for reelection in the primaries. He had been too busy administering to take time to really campaign, and was stunned by the results. I was stricken but not as surprised. I had a feeling Michael was in trouble, but most of our friends were as convinced as Michael that everything was hunky-dory. Michael expected his record to speak for itself. He had served honorably and successfully for four years, surely he would be reinstalled.

He might have been, too, had not Edward King, his opponent in the Democratic primary, waged a vicious campaign marked by rumor and hate. The maneuverings were idiotic, almost laughable, and yet they defeated my husband. He did not pay enough attention to what was going on because the mudslinging was so low and so far afield. When the filth was hurled, he turned his back. Nevertheless, his strategists were able to convince the voters that Michael was an aloof and indifferent leader more interested in the general right and wrong than the actual needs of Massachusetts residents. Big Ed King, a former football player, they presented as a warmhearted, caring man. Who needed an austere pedagogue in the State House when you could have a Santa Claus?

The afternoon of the primaries, Michael was taking a nap when he received a call from a local television reporter. "I'm sorry to tell you this, but you should know, the exit polls are showing Ed King as the winner." I barely remember the events that followed. I was sick with bronchitis and had a fever of 102. I dragged myself to the 57 Hotel in Boston where Michael gave his concession speech. I was in a daze emotionally, and physically spent. I looked like a zombie. Later, I called the whole rotten business "a public death." That's still my opinion. Typically, Michael took full blame for his unseating. For the next two or three months he was quite down; he

KITTY DUKAKIS

couldn't believe he'd lost to someone whom he had dismissed as not worthy. Four years later, he had the opportunity to seek redress.

They say bad things happen in threes. In 1977, Mother died. Michael was defeated in 1978, and in 1979, Panos Dukakis succumbed to several strokes. Up until his eighty-first year, he'd been in remarkable shape. Then, slowly, he began to fail. He died on November 5, 1979. He had lived to see his son elected to the highest office in the state. He died while Michael was attempting a comeback. Anyway, I don't think Panos set much store by the political scene. His pride in his son had more to do with Michael's character. In that respect, Panos Dukakis was a lucky father.

The fact that I continued my own career and activity made the years when Michael was out of office much easier on me. Michael began teaching at the Kennedy School and I was busy with my newest venture. Two weeks before Michael left office, I began classes at Boston University School of Public Communication and received my master's degree in broadcast and film in 1982.

Michael's second campaign for governor was victorious and he took office again in January of 1983. A few months after he resumed the governorship it became crystal clear to me I could no longer work in the private sector. For one thing, politicians' spouses have to be careful, and, for another—an even more compelling reason—there were too many important matters in the area of human services crying for attention. I didn't want to be in private business anymore, I wanted to do something of consequence.

I had two "bees" in my bonnet. I met with Graham Allison, the dean of the Kennedy School of Government at Harvard, and told him of my ideas: to do a seminar

149

for the spouses of governors. There are numerous instances where a spouse can assist the governor and even do things on her/his own, but there weren't any real guidelines. Spouses' programs were always determined and overseen by the governors; we never had enough backing or time to do our own things. Since many spouses actively worked for the state, I believed we should have an itinerary tailored for us. Dean Allison was receptive, and, along with the staff at the Kennedy School, I helped organize the first Spouses Seminar at Harvard in the spring of 1983. Heather Campion, who was in charge of special events at the Kennedy School, did a superb job in putting the seminar together. I didn't know where the seminars would lead but I knew they were a step forward.

At the same time the seminars were getting off the ground, I met with a group from the Kennedy School to activate my other idea: I wanted to unite the public and private sectors with the common goal of improving open spaces. This became the Public Space Partnerships Program. We met every couple of weeks and got rolling by June of 1984. Though the idea was mine, I could not take on the full responsibility for the program; I could only be at the Kennedy School three days a week. After interviewing a number of candidates, I hired Renee Robin as executive director. Over the past half-decade, the Public Space Partnerships Program has been responsible for some very positive changes. One of the first was the transformation and renaissance of a park in Chelsea, Massachusetts, long abandoned to the drug trade. The neighborhood consisted of older people who'd been there for generations and younger people who had just moved in. Many of the inhabitants were refugees or immigrants. This was a poor community and they felt powerless over the doings in the park. With the cooperation of the mayor's office, city hall, the police, the recreation department, and the state offices of community and development, the PSP went to work. Four master's candidates in landscape architecture from the University of Massachusetts took the Chelsea park project as their theses. However, before anything could be done, we had to get rid of the drug dealers. They were bold as brass. They'd pick up the stuff at one end of the park, drive to the other end, and sell it. I remember going there and watching them myself as they went about their business. They knew damn well I was the governor's wife and it didn't slow the trade down one second. For about three months, the police put the area under close surveillance. Eventually, the traffic flow broke down, the dealers dispersed, and the park was ready for rejuvenation. It was dedicated in June 1988 and still thrives. We also restored Winthrop Park near Harvard Square and created a trust that takes care of the maintenance. We originated a program in Malden with a bank, city hall, and the Massachusetts Bay Transit Authority. And so it continues. I'm proud to have brought people together in these mutually beneficial projects.

Separate from the Harvard ventures, and also very dear to my heart, was the beautification program I began with state agencies. The idea wasn't original. I was inspired by the wonderful woman who did so much to glorify this country, Lady Bird Johnson. I knew Lynda Johnson Robb before I met her mother. Her husband, Chuck, was governor of Virginia and we had become acquainted with them at the conferences Lady Bird had initiated her beautification program from the White House and never lost interest. She carried on after President Johnson left office and still participates from her home in Texas. I visited the LBJ ranch twice and brought people from various Massachusetts departments with me. The ranch is magnificent and reflects the loving attention of Lady Bird. In her domain, I saw firsthand what could be done to restore the natural beauty of the land.

Following her example, we started an award banquet in Massachusetts. Instead of cash prizes, trips were donated by hotels and agencies to honor and reward those who perform above and beyond the call of duty to keep our state beautiful. The trips proved to be incentives as well as bonuses. Thanks to Lady Bird Johnson, we were able to transplant a good idea from Texas to Massachusetts.

Of all my endeavors in the public interest, human services is closest to my heart. My involvement began in the mid-seventies when I started my Holocaust studies. I began reading up on the Holocaust on my own and then became active with a project in Brookline called "Facing History and Ourselves." Upon returning from my second trip to Israel in 1977, I spoke at a local United Jewish Appeal dinner. I told the group I had visited Yad Vashem, the Holocaust Memorial, on both my visits to Israel. After my UJA speech a constituent from Brookline came up to talk to Michael and me. We had been receiving compliments and I expected to hear more kudos. This man, however, spoke right from the hip. "If you really care about the Holocaust, Kitty, then you should get involved. If you would act as a liaison with the department of education, it would help the cause immeasurably." I accepted the challenge. I convened a meeting with the superintendent of schools in Brookline and the program directors of the Facing History project. That was the beginning. We did not limit ourselves to the Holocaust. We investigated other examples of man's inhumanity to man like the forgotten genocide of the Armenians. We raised money for an Armenian component to the Holocaust program.

For me, awareness breeds a desire to take positive action: The more I learned, the more I wanted to do. In 1979, I was appointed to the United States Holocaust Commission by President Jimmy Carter. Later, when the commission became the United States Holocaust Memorial Council, I was appointed a full-fledged member to that body. In 1979 I went with the council to Poland. I have never worn religious symbols; however, on this trip I had a Star of David around my neck. Isaac Goodfried, a Holocaust survivor and the cantor of Atlanta's largest synagogue, was also on the Polish journey.

We had just taken off when one of the committee members said, loud enough for me to hear, "What's that shiksa doing with a Star of David around her neck?"

Isaac responded, "She's not a shiksa, she's Jewish."

For a moment I thought I was back in the balcony in the Roxbury shul!

That major goal of the Holocaust Council is to erect a museum in Washington, D.C. To that end, land between Thirteenth and Fourteenth streets in the shadow of the Washington Monument was given to the council and construction is under way. At the time of my appointment, there were only two women on the commission, myself and Hadassah Rosenstadt, a survivor of Auschwitz. She and I roomed together on the trip to Israel, Russia, and Poland. Hadassah was terrific, but I was unhappy with the committee. Though women were on the advisory board, there were only two females on the council of nearly fifty men. Women as well as men were victimized in the Holocaust, so why not equal representation? I made a few enemies by calling attention to the chauvinist, sexist bias.

After nearly eight years of work, my association with the council was curtailed. I was dropped. Ostensibly, the reason goes back to the initial appointments. President Jimmy Carter erred by naming mostly Democrats to the commission. As a result, when Ronald Reagan became president, he appointed a conservative Republican as chairman and compounded that situation by selecting mostly Republican males to take the place of Democrats. I was caught in the middle. I was a Democrat; I was a woman. I was also outspoken. Alas, the council was politicized.

As my interest in human services became more publicized, I was approached by many organizations eager for my support. In January of 1980, I started working with the Lutheran Service Association and under its auspices helped to get children out of refugee camps and into foster homes in the United States. One particular case came to symbolize, for me, the importance of not merely becoming involved but of seeing things through to the end. When it was announced in the newspapers that I was going to Thailand on another refugee mission, Saroum Tang, a young Cambodian woman living in Lynnfield, Massachusetts, wrote to me. In the letter she told a tragic—and, unfortunately, all too typical—war story. Her family had been caught in the terrible Pol Pot massacres, but she somehow had escaped and been brought to the United States. For some time she had believed she was the only surviving member of her immediate family, but recently she had learned that the youngest sibling, her brother Pich (pronounced "Bike"), had also come through the slaughter, and was now in a refugee camp on the Thai border. Saroum begged me to contact officials and get her brother to the United States. Her plea was a moving and direct challenge. I vowed to do my utmost to make this reunion possible.

When I arrived in Thailand, I contacted various members of the Lutheran Service Association and eventually found myself in the refugee camp, face to face with Pich Tang. I promised him I would do my best to get him out. Actually getting to the boy had been difficult enough, but it proved to be easy compared with the task of then bringing him to the United States. I spoke to anyone and everyone who might help, including the United States ambassador to Thailand, members of Congress, and representatives of the Immigration and Naturalization Service. I spoke to the press too; I never underestimate the power of the media.

Over a month of pleading and haggling, there were times I became so frustrated I wanted to turn the whole business over to someone else. I couldn't do it, however, because I knew, deep down, that turning it over to someone else meant risking that it might never happen.

After endless conversations, countless telephone calls, and many letters and telegrams, Pich Tang was brought to America and reunited with his sister. They're together now, building a new life, and I'm so proud that I was able to assist them. Pich is now a full scholarship student at Brandeis in Waltham, Massachusetts. Unfortunately, there are hundreds—thousands!—of war victims like Pich and Saroum Tang. Most of their stories do not end as happily, however, and it's not because people don't care or even try to help; they do!

I learned from my experience that no matter how fervid your conviction, you can never let up in actual efforts. When you're dealing with bureaucracies, you don't take "no" for an answer. Lip service doesn't count. You have to be totally committed and absolutely determined. I have applied these principles in all my dealings with human services issues, from the global problem of refugees to the rights of women in Massachusetts prisons. I have discovered that, more often than not, the best way to get things done is to do it yourself.

While Michael was in his first term, our country celebrated its bicentennial. As governor of one of the thirteen original colonies, he had to preside over innumerable ceremonies as well as receive and make welcome an inordinate number of visitors from overseas. These were not simple tourists, either; the list of callers included presidents, prime ministers, sheiks, chiefs, kings, and queens. Ceremony is important, and complicated; "protocol" is the operative word.

Before these dignitaries arrived, Michael and I attended numerous meetings at which we discussed delicate matters of protocol and decorum with people skilled in international diplomacy. We spent many hours going over the appropriate methods; we wanted to give our best. Generally, we greeted the guests together. On the few occasions Michael was unable to attend, I had to meet dignitaries, like the king of Sweden, solo. Though I handled the formalities pretty well, I was happy Michael was there to share the moment at our most meaningful arrival, the appearance of the queen of England. Before she and Prince Philip arrived, Michael and I took a kind of crash course in royal "dos and don'ts." By the end, we had mastered the most significant "don't"— never hold out your hand or touch the queen unless she holds out her hand first.

I'm a fairly down-to-earth person; still, I had butterflies in my stomach when we went to meet Their Royal

Highnesses. As governor and first lady of the Commonwealth of Massachusetts, we were the first people in line
when the royal yacht *Britannia* docked in Boston Harbor; thus, we were the first Americans to greet the royal
couple on their historic visit.

The harbor was teeming with boats, banners, and cir-
cling aircraft, accompanied by shrieks of whistles and
horns—really a remarkable mixture of sight and sound.
The *Britannia's* gangplank was lowered and a carpet
rolled down from the top. I looked up and there was the
queen of England standing at the ship's rail. Prince
Philip stood behind her. They looked magnificent.

The queen stepped onto the gangplank. The carpet
was slick, however, and with her first step she began to
slide down the gangplank toward us. Miraculously, when
she reached the bottom, she managed to catch herself
and land on her feet, as erect and regal as if she had just
stepped from her throne. As a dancer, I was in awe of
her absolute and utter control; she willed her body not
to betray her. She stood on the pier, gazing serenely at
us with the most beautiful blue eyes, and smiling a most
unruffled smile.

For the rest of the day, Michael and Kevin White, the
mayor of Boston, escorted the queen, while Kathryn
White and I had the great pleasure of sharing the company of Prince Philip. What a charming man. What an
exciting day!

The Bicentennial was a magical time. So many wonderful things were happening, and not all of them at home.
We were invited as well to participate in celebratory
activities in Israel, Venezuela, Greece, and Ireland.

My trip to Israel came about unexpectedly, as a sub-
stitute for a planned visit to Cuba. In a United Nations

vote against Israel equating Zionism with racism, Cuba had cast its vote with the majority; I felt I could not in all good conscience go to a country that censured Israel. The decision proved to be fortuitous; it was this trip to Israel that marked the turning point in my spiritual life.

All of the '76 trips were inspiring; each had a special flavor. Israel was my religious awakening, Venezuela was an exciting political venture, and the trip to Greece was interesting on several counts. It was an official visit and Michael and I spent three days in Athens, where we were wined and dined by elected and appointed dignitaries. Then, at the end of our visit, we flew to Michael's father's village on the island of Lesbos (also called Mitilíni). The village, now called Pelopi, was originally named Yelya, which is the Greek word for "laughter." I'm not so crazy about the change; I'd relish having antecedents from a town called Laughter.

In Pelopi we were greeted by cheering people and assorted silent livestock. Following the exuberant welcome, we went into the town hall to get Michael's father's birth certificate and other related material. Finally we were brought into a taverna for an official banquet. We were seated at long tables, and as I looked down the wooden lengths, I realized I was the only woman present. Twenty-five men and no other females. I turned to our host and asked, "Where are the women?" He laughed nervously and brushed aside my question. "Please, please, do you want to start a revolution?"

It was tempting. I was not happy to see women enjoined from participating in *all* the festivities, and I said so. I'll *always* say so. I said it as recently as April of 1989, when I spoke before a group of businessmen in downtown Boston. When I looked about, I saw there were very few women in the group. And this was Bos-

My mother was a
beautiful young woman.
This picture with me was
taken in 1937.

2

This is a family picture taken at
34 Beaconsfield Road. My
father, my mother, Jinny, and
me.

3

I must have been twelve when this picture was taken at Camp Newfound in Harrison, Maine. My mother had gone to the camp when she was young. I spent ten wonderful summers there.

4

My early modeling career, with other members of the Filene's Fashion Board and a sailor in Westfield, Massachusetts, in 1952. I'm second from right.

My high school graduation picture, 1954.

5

The infamous evening with my dad, associate conductor of the Boston Pops Orchestra.

6

7

My freshman college picture in 1955, taken at Penn State when I was in the May Queen's court.

Shadow dancing with Betty Jane Dittmar, my first dance teacher. I taught dance for Betty Jane during my years at Penn State.

8

Wedding to Michael on June 20, 1963.

9

Our honeymoon on Nantucket.

10

Morning has never been my favorite time of day. However, our family always tried to eat breakfast together.

11

In front of our house before Michael's inauguration as governor in January 1975.

12

13

*Right after Michael was inaugurated. Here we are with his
parents, Panos and Euterpe Dukakis.*

With Michael in Bermuda, 1975.

14

15

With Dad and Danny Kaye at a UNICEF event in Boston.

Teaching dance in the mid-seventies.

16

17

With Queen Elizabeth,
Prince Philip, Elliot
Richardson, and Michael
at the Bicentennial
Celebration in 1976.

Leaving Michael on my
first trip to Israel,
January 1976.

18

19

With Mother, Dad, and Michael on our arrival in Greece,
sixteen months before Mother passed away.

November 1982—the happy faces of victory, with Andrea (left)
and Kara (right).

20

21

Intermission at the Hatch Shell, where Dad was conducting. Also with us are my sister, Jinny Peters, and her husband, Dr. Al Peters.

Staff and plane crew in Sky Heaven. Notice the pandas ("Panda" was my Secret Service code name). With me are John Schley, pilot; Tom Bona, co-pilot; John Keller, issues and speechwriter; Paul Costello, press secretary; Bonnie Shershow, my special assistant;
23   *and Marlene Dunneman.*

22

With John McMahon, Sandy Bakalar, and Andrew Savitz, on the steps leading to the infamous "Love Nest."

On the night of the New Hampshire primary, February 1988.

Doing a blanket dance with the Klinket Indians in Alaska.

With Bob Farmer—a superb fund-raiser, a great friend.   26

With Michael the night he won the Democratic nomination.

27

The family together during the campaign.   28

*At a New York fund-raiser with Harry and Shari Belafonte,
and two good friends, Nadine Hack and Ruthie Goldmuntz.*
                                                              29

With Michael's delightful cousin Olympia Dukakis, at the Democratic Convention.

With members of staff and Secret Service during a one-day rest in Maui.

32

June 1989, meeting cousin Michael Byrne at his home in County Clare.

A recent picture of John, Lisa, and Alexandra Jane at the beach.

33

Dancing with Michael at a street fair during the National Governors Association meeting in Chicago, July 1989.

34

Three first ladies. With me are Bea Rohmer (left), wife of the present governor of Colorado, and Dottie Lamm (right), wife of that state's former governor.

35

ton, not a tiny Greek village formerly called Laughter. I stood in a luxurious hotel banquet room, addressing leaders of the Democratic party, yet the situation was similar. I had to ask the same question: "Where are the women?" Frankly, unless we keep asking, nothing will change.

I had looked forward to the Irish portion of our Bicentennial travels for many reasons. I was eager to visit a new country, especially one where I had roots. The mystery of my mother's ancestry haunted me, since I am the kind of person who has to know as much as can be known, and being in the dark about even a small portion of my family bothered me. At the time, I knew my mother's father was a "Byrne," and that he definitely was Irish. His first name, however, was vaguely recalled as either Edward or James, and it was not clear whether he had immigrated himself or was the child of immigrants. Not much to go on, but once we had made plans to visit Ireland, I became determined to try and locate *my* Byrnes.

When we arrived in Dublin, I placed an inquiry in the County Clare newspaper. My information was admittedly sketchy; Byrne is a common name and, although I wasn't aware of it at the time, I didn't even have the correct first name! No one answered my ingenuous advertisement and the preliminary search was stillborn. I failed to find my roots but the rest of the trip proved most fruitful, despite a mishap in which Michael suffered a broken collarbone, an accident that he took, as was typical, in stride.

I realized later that it was incredibly naive of me to think I could find my ancestry on my own. I went about it like a rank amateur and got the results I might have expected. However, I fell in love with Ireland and looked forward to my return. I knew one day I would determine my mother's origins, and that part of the answer, at least, lay in that lush green land. Thirteen years later, I did go back to Ireland to find my family—only this time I did it right!

II

CENTER
STAGE

2/23/89

Dear Kitty,

Twenty years in the Secret Service have exposed me to numerous personalities in many areas of life. I have worked with many people through six presidential campaigns, not to mention foreign heads of state. Without a doubt you were the most unpretentious, down-to-earth principal I ever had the pleasure of working with.

I had the utmost admiration for you for the personal and political strengths you brought to your husband and his campaign. Your intelligence, insight, and warmth were so refreshing, as was your electrifying personality. I was in a unique position to observe you objectively for several intense weeks during that very trying time in your life. Your efforts towards that noble vision that was shared by many millions were, simply put, superhuman! I was, and will remain forever, very proud to be a small part of that time in your life and will always treasure those memories. You and your beautiful family are in our prayers.

SINCERELY,
JIM KALAFATIS

NINE

Suppose you woke up one day and someone said to you, "Good morning, for the next few years you're going to be cut off from most of your friends and family and sent off to wander all over the country. And, though you'll be living out of a suitcase, you'll have to be impeccably groomed and on your toes at all times. You'll go to bed in the early hours of the morning, and after a bare minimum of sleep, rise before dawn. You'll eat fast food on the run during the day, and, at night, dine on countless chicken dishes in assorted banquet rooms and conference centers. You may be dog-tired, feeling ill, or just plain grumpy; still, you must attempt to charm, court, and capture the support of everyone near you, and always with a smile. You will be briefed and prepared for almost every situation because an army of camera-wielding, microphone-waving reporters will be in constant attendance waiting for you to say something significant, or—even better for their journalistic purposes—to make a slip.

"Eventually, you will be surrounded by protectors. They will be well-meaning and entirely necessary adjuncts, yet, because they must guard you from possible harm, you will be even further distanced from family, old acquaintances, and the very people you are trying to reach.

"You will be praised a bit and damned a lot. Everything you do, every gesture, every blink, every sigh, every move, *everything*, with the possible exception of what you are thinking, will be public knowledge."

Essentially, this is what it's like to be in a presidential campaign. However, the contenders and their families usually don't go public with the inside story; when the race is over, most participants remain quiet. Often, the details are documented by others because the losing contestants are so dejected and depleted, they don't want to go over the events and the winners don't have to. While the strain of participating in a national election is common knowledge, no one can know the absolute physical and mental stress unless he or she has been involved. Intellectually, you can accept what it might be like; until you are physically in a campaign, however, you cannot comprehend the intensity.

I've always been an enterprising person. My pre-presidential campaign days were filled with activities, or so I had thought. They were "idle" compared to what was crammed into an average campaign day. I have over a dozen huge notebooks listing every event of the presidential race from the primaries to election night. Out of curiosity, I recently glanced through those books; I wanted to assure myself I was remembering correctly and not exaggerating. A look at one particular day—

Monday, April 25, 1988—confirmed my memories. It's astonishing to see how much action can be jammed into less than fifteen hours. From a 7:00 A.M. breakfast in Philadelphia, I flew on to four other Pennsylvania cities —Erie, Harrisburg, Pittsburgh, and Scranton—and was back home in Brookline by 10:30 P.M. My Pennsylvania sojourns covered ten major events, ranging from addressing high school students to meeting with factory workers. Virtually every minute was accounted for in the notebook page—even "food" was entered as a topic. I was amused to read that at 1:40 P.M. I was scheduled for sandwiches while flying from Erie to Harrisburg, and at 4:30 P.M., on my way from Harrisburg to Pittsburgh, the timetable called for fruit and yogurt.

Though it's not listed, I somehow feel the fruit and yogurt was topped off by a glass of vodka. Aside from liquor, the only item not registered on my schedule is the actual intake and output of my breathing!

Running for the presidency is exciting, exhilarating, and exhausting. Frankly, I don't know how anyone, except perhaps for an incumbent, could go through the rigors more than once. I assume that winning must be wonderful; I know that losing is devastating. To this day, I believe the 1988 presidential campaign set a new low in common decency.

Once upon a time, there was such a thing as "trust." That sense of confidence made it possible to let down your guard on occasion. Veteran political reporters speak nostalgically of the halcyon days when they were in the business of reporting, not distorting. For the candidates, it must have been a welcome relief, if only for a few minutes, to relax and talk off the record. We never had that kind of comfort in the '88 race. We had to be "on" every minute. There was no repose. However circumspect we tried to be, mistakes were made and minor errors in judgment were magnified into major setbacks. At one point, while visiting a military outpost, my husband was advised by his staff to put a helmet on his head and ride around in a tank—a seemingly harmless venture. Michael should have taken his cue from former presidential aspirants. During one of his campaigns, the Republican candidate firmly advised his staff, "Remember, boys, Nixon doesn't wear hats." Nixon's great adversary, John Kennedy, avoided them too. Both men were aware of how foolish anyone can be made to look in unaccustomed wear or poses. Poor Michael. He was victimized by his own advisers. He put on the helmet and got into the tank. Pictures were taken. The result was a glut of ridiculous shots that the media gleefully put before the public.

It didn't stop at silly pictures, either; traps were set all along the campaign trail. Misinformation about such Massachusetts issues as Boston Harbor pollution, the prisoner furlough plan, and so on, were fed into the journalistic maw by the eager advertising executives who ran the show. If future campaigns are allowed to continue in the same vein of scurrilous attacks, cheap innuendoes, and blatant defamations, our country will suffer the consequences. Furthermore, you cannot hold yourself above what is being done in your name. My husband refused to stoop to the tactics employed by some of his opponents. He thought he could run on his strengths. Because of his convictions, he lost the services of his key adviser and supporter. Michael learned the hard way that the political ring, unlike the boxing ring, sanctions low blows.

How did my husband decide to run for president of the United States? Well, he didn't walk in the front door and say, "Hi, honey, I'm home. How are the kids? I'm going to run for president." In truth, it was an accumulation of events, and not a pat scene like something out of a television sitcom.

From the very beginning, speculation about Michael's seeking the presidency ran far ahead of his even *casually* contemplating the idea. In the late seventies and early eighties—indeed, from the moment Michael lost his bid for reelection as governor of Massachusetts—he had one, and only *one*, political objective in mind—to get back into the office he had been so humiliatingly denied. The 1978 defeat was crushing because it came out of nowhere. The judgment call was based not on the way he was governing but on his "ways" as governor. In the book *The Quest for the Presidency*, authors Peter Goldman and Tony Fuller sum up the overthrow in one telling sentence: "The voters of Massachusetts who had suffered rogues, roués, and scoundrels gladly, could not forgive Dukakis his implacable goodness." I think that's about as reasonable an observation as any. After the ill-fated primary, Michael withdrew into himself and spent endless hours going over what had happened. For a while, no one, not even those of us who loved him most, could reach him—*for a while*. I couldn't bear seeing him languish—it was so unlike him.

The public Michael has always been so different from the private person. He's been described as cool, cautious, brooding, and stubborn; cerebral rather than emotional. At the same time that the press labeled him "cold," I was stamped "hot." I don't care what the media says, my husband is a loving, caring man with a sense of balance about all things. He's a sunny kind of person and I've drawn strength from his natural positivism. The "clouds" gathered on my brow, not his.

Gradually, Michael came out of his postelection doldrums. Over the next three years, while teaching at the Kennedy School of Government, he gathered his forces and planned his return. Friends like Paul Brountas had never left, and there was an important addition to the ranks—John Sasso. Michael and John met for the first time less than a week after the primary upset. Michael showed up for a political event in support of a Sasso-organized property-tax initiative. John was bowled over when Michael appeared. He had assumed a defeated governor would be a no-show. He didn't know that, despite the hurt, Michael is the kind of man who meets all his obligations. They next met at the 1980 Democratic convention. In the interim, John had worked on Ted Kennedy's unsuccessful presidential campaign. John admired Michael's leadership qualities and was keenly interested in my husband's prospects for a return to office. The two men "clicked." In late autumn, John Sasso joined Michael's staff and was named campaign manager. It was a fortuitous appointment.

During the gubernatorial contest, John and Nick Mitroupolos, Michael's head of personnel, began to ponder the possibility of a run for the presidency, and the two of them attempted to interject the idea into Michael's overall strategy. Michael wouldn't hear of it. He cut them off, saying, "Your job is to help me get reelected governor, period!" But, while Michael's tunnel vision homed right in on the gold-domed Bulfinch building on Beacon Street, John Sasso continued to gaze at the distant D.C. horizon. Others, too, embraced the idea of Michael's seeking the presidential nomination. *After* the state election, I became one of them.

Michael campaigned with a vengeance and was reinstalled in the State House for a second term. He had been vindicated and took office a happy and fulfilled man.

If he were looking ahead at that point, it was only toward a third term in exactly the same place. He loved
the job for two basic reasons. He had the opportunity to
govern, to make the changes that could improve the living standards of the people of Massachusetts, and,
equally important, he could do this *and* lead the normal
personal life he demanded. This had been the pattern of
our existence. Whatever else happened, I always knew
Michael was there, for me, and for the children. He was
fanatic about being a parental presence. While the children were growing up, at least one of us had to be at
home every evening. For years I had classes that met
on Thursdays; perforce, it became Michael's night at
Perry Street. He brought the same zeal to his home duty
as he did to the State House and carried out his duties
as husband, father, and governor with equal regard.

In January of 1984, a little older and a lot wiser, we
became the governor's family once again and our daily
lives soon fell into a familiar, comfortable rhythm. One
persistent "off" beat, however, could not be ignored.
Ever since Fritz Mondale mentioned him as a possible
vice-presidential candidate in 1984, Michael's name had
been appearing regularly on the lists of potential presidential candidates. Now that the governorship was in
hand, Sasso and the others who had worked for Michael
could turn their attentions toward the White House. In
December of 1986, we went to Florida for a five-day
vacation. While we were there, we read a memo John
Sasso had sent to us. In it, John set down the reasons he
believed Michael should try for the White House. The
message was convincing and I could see Michael mulling
over the proposal, although, at the time, he didn't choose
to discuss it. After our vacation, however, came the del-
uge. Partisans began contacting Michael, urging him to

get in the race. Suddenly, there was support from all over the country. People wanted Michael to run; some were Democratic regulars, others were classmates from high school and college and former students from the Kennedy School, men and women who had been in class when Michael taught there. A network was growing. These supporters called him in his office and at home. They wrote letters and sent telegrams. They were clamoring for his participation. Michael heard them, our children heard them, and I heard them.

The truth is, I was elated at the prospect of my husband running for the highest office in the land. I expressed the opinion, many times, that he could do a better job in the White House than the present occupant. That's not so unusual. A lot of spouses say that about their mates. The difference was, my husband was in politics. I can't tell you how often I sat with him at the breakfast table, reading the papers, and commenting on the current scene. The Iran-*contra* situation really set me off. "Can you believe what's going on in Washington?" I cried out one morning over the latest revelation of deceit. "It's madness. Honestly, Michael, *you* should be in the White House; you wouldn't allow this to go on."

I don't think Michael took me seriously. In truth, while I was very sincere, I can't say I was particularly serious. It was just talk. Then, when others began to rally around my husband, I took a fresh look and realized what I had been saying was correct—Michael Dukakis should run for president. I was convinced Michael could make a difference and was eager for him to throw his hat in the ring. Typical of our personalities, Michael was just beginning to weigh all the aspects of such a decision, while I was off and running.

Though Michael had proven himself as a governor, he

realized, far more than I, that running for the presidency was much more complicated, demanding, and debilitating than anything our family had previously experienced. He expressed some concerns about carrying out the duties of the office, but was far less worried about "being" president than getting there. As the groundswell of support rose, I rode the wave and was soon joined by my son. After a seven-year career as an actor, John Dukakis had turned to politics and was working for Senator John Kerry in Washington. My son and I called each other daily and discussed the future. We were going out of our minds trying to figure out Michael's position.

One day I'd say, "I don't think Dad's going to run."

The next day, after speaking to his father, John would telephone and tell me, "Gee, it sounds like Dad *is* going to run."

This went on for two months. While John and I were enthusiastic about Michael joining the race, Andrea and Kara were less happy. Though they had been raised in a political climate, and had adjusted to public life, my daughters were wary of the consequences of national exposure. Increasingly, Michael was virtually assaulted by zealous supporters. Three or four times a week, he met with men and women, some of whom flew into Boston from great distances.

I've read innumerable and varied accounts of how and when my husband decided to enter the race. For the record, this is what occurred. On the second Saturday in March 1987, Ellen Goodman, the syndicated columnist of the *Boston Globe*, came to do an interview with the governor and his wife. During the conversation, the subject of the presidency was broached, and though Michael didn't actually make a definitive statement, he didn't cut

off the question immediately. For the first time, he discussed the possibility and actually sounded amenable to
the idea. When the interview was over, Michael showed
Ellen to the door, thanked her, shook hands, and said
good-bye. He closed the door, shrugged his shoulders,
turned and said to me, "Well, Sweetie, I *guess* we're
going to run."

Michael made a preliminary announcement late in
March. In April, I took my Kitty Litter group on a trip
to Japan, returning on April 29, 1987. The next morning,
Michael formally announced his candidacy. That declaration signaled the end of the normal everyday existence
my husband so prized. During the course of the primary
and the general campaigns, our residence shifted from
Perry Street in Brookline to midair anywhere over the
United States. We spent nearly two years poised for
flight, in flight, or on our way to as many areas of the
country as it was possible to reach. Michael made his
announcement in New Hampshire and Massachusetts,
then Georgia, and finally in Iowa. After the Iowa declaration, he went on to New York.

At first, I had to pinch myself. Was this really happening? Then, as the momentum grew, it seemed natural
for Michael to be running, and any initial awkwardness
I experienced faded away. When you're a child, the
president of the United States seems a lofty being—
certainly that's how I viewed Franklin Delano Roosevelt. When you're grown up, and when you've been in
politics for a number of years and have met a few White
House occupants, you realize that the president is an
elected being, not an exalted one. Looking back, trying
to recall how I felt during the early days of the campaign, I can only say, very tritely, it was like a dream.
One minute I was half-jokingly telling my husband he

ought to run for president, and in the next moment, he was. One minute, I was the wife of the governor, and in the next, a potential first lady.

After Michael's announcement, I stayed in Iowa and began campaigning on my own. Things fell into place. I had a car, an advance person, and a staff that included Marilyn Anderson-Chase, Andy Savitz, Michael Lufrano, and Jim Peck-Grey. Marilyn headed the staff, Andy was press representative, and Michael and Jim acted as advance men and schedulers. That first day in Iowa, Andy, my daughter Kara, and I drove from Des Moines through the southwestern part of the state to Ottumwa. I'll never forget the journey. On the way, we had to pass a town called Pella. Pella is the tulip capital of the United States and during our journey every variety of tulip imaginable was in bloom. What an incredible sight. I viewed the fields of beautiful flowers as a good omen. We reached Ottumwa, parked the car, put a nickel in the meter, and walked around the block to our destination. The minute I turned the corner I saw emblazoned on the hotel marquee: WELCOME KITTY DUKAKIS. I was staggered. In the 1953 movie *It Should Happen to You*, Judy Holliday plays Gladys Glover, an unemployed New York model. Gladys decides she wants to be a celebrity. She rents a billboard overlooking Columbus Circle and has her name printed in huge letters on the sign. Overnight, she becomes famous. When I saw the sign on the hotel, I knew exactly how Gladys felt.

I got a kick out of seeing my name up in lights, albeit in Ottumwa. I gave my first speech on the presidential campaign there to some twenty-five people. Anne Forgy, my college roommate, came from Columbia, Missouri, to be with me and it was comforting to look out and see a familiar face. From that inauspicious debut before a handful of people, I went on to address hundreds, even thousands, of people.

Almost without any realizing, the campaign began in earnest. Everything was accelerated. My schedule started out at a fast clip and quickly moved to the frenetic. We'd get up at seven in the morning and be on the road by seven-thirty. It's not a simple procedure to be up and out in less than thirty minutes, not for a woman, anyway. Men have it easy: They get up, shower, shave, comb their hair, get dressed, and leave. Women have a few more things to which they must attend. Getting dressed, for instance, isn't a simple matter of which similar suit to put on; it's much more. An appropriate wardrobe has to be carefully assembled because it's going to be discussed and analyzed. From Jackie Kennedy's pink suits to Nancy Reagan's red dresses, during a campaign women's clothes make the headlines. Then there's the question of hair and makeup.

Regarding the latter, I never used much. I applied a moisturizer and a foundation, and when I had a tan I cut down on the foundation. I've always used a concealer under my eyes because I always have circles under them, always. I'd finish with eyeliner, shadow, and blush. Really basic stuff. The basics had to be augmented when I began appearing on television. The camera is merciless, and makeup becomes de rigueur. Not just for women, either. As for my hair, I went to a beauty salon on a fairly regular basis, though I don't think I was especially fussy. My heavens, there were plenty of occasions when Michael would take up a scissors and trim the edges. He's pretty good, too. As the campaign continued, I started being photographed and televised often, so I had to rely on professionals and, gradually, makeup and hairstyling were incorporated into the agenda. Eventually, my hair had to be done every day, sometimes twice a day. When Rodgers and Hammerstein's *South Pacific* opened on Broadway, Mary Martin received much publicity because she actually shampooed her hair on stage every night, and two afternoons a week. As a youngster, I read newspaper and magazine articles about Ms. Martin's feat and was very impressed with her endurance. Three decades later, I was doing the same thing. In a T. S. Eliot poem, the cautious J. Alfred Prufrock measured out his life in coffee spoons; I measured out the campaign in hairdressers. Years ago, when I was a kid, I'd read in magazines about actresses who traveled with personal hairstylists. I thought that was *the* most extravagant thing any woman could do. Imagine, having someone with you just to do your hair! Well, when you are caught up in a presidential campaign, a hairdresser isn't an extravagance, he or she is a necessity!

Like it or not, when you're appearing in public, before you open your mouth, you are subject to such intense scrutiny it makes an MRI look like a casual glance. As wife of a governor, I was used to public perusal and I think I did okay—sure, I got some bad notices, but mostly they were about what I had said rather than how I looked.

As wife of a presidential candidate, however, I had to be as nearly perfect as possible. You learn as you go along, often by making mistakes. We live in an electronic age measured by sound bites. It's on and then off, with little in between. When you're "on," you've got to be in total command; rarely are second chances provided. Television is the Colosseum, the main arena in which the battles are won and lost, and television is a visual medium. I don't like to talk about presidential campaigns in terms of appearances, but in today's world it's a fact of life. But while my clothes and hairstyles may have changed, my goals and my focus always remained the same—to make the best possible impression in my effort to help my husband in his race for the presidency.

When I was scheduled to appear in a city and needed to have someone do my hair and makeup, my staff would contact the local television stations and ask for recommendations. Each city had its own expert and, as far as I'm concerned, these men and women were the unsung heroes of the campaign. Mind you, there were a few villains, too. In one major city, I had my makeup done by a local person who left me painted like a she-devil. I headed straight for the bathroom sink, scrubbed my face, and applied my own makeup.

Other similar crises occurred, including the failure of a hairdresser to show up, and in Miami—a city where I definitely wanted to look my best, especially since it was one day before the primary—a hairstylist who left me looking like an extraterrestial. Andrea came into the room, took a gander at me, and said, "Mother, you can't go out like that. You can't let Daddy see you."

"There's nothing I can do, Andrea," I answered dejectedly. I walked into the other room.

Michael took one look and said, "Go back in there, you've got to do something. You can't go out like that."

I went back in the bedroom and, with Andrea wielding a brush on one side and me doing the same on the other, we finally smacked the crest down enough to make my hair look halfway decent.

The story isn't over, however. This man in Miami turned out to be a fraud; he wasn't even a hairdresser. (I was living proof of that fact!) He *wanted* to be a hairdresser. What's more, he charged an exorbitant amount for his services. In the end it was all straightened out, but it just goes to prove that there are people who will take advantage of any situation. Of course, as a member of a presidential campaign party, you are a sitting duck; you have to keep your sense of humor or you'll go mad. Fortunately, the majority of people you deal with are good and true. That was certainly the case with those wonderful hairdressers.

Diana Vreeland, the late fashion notable, once wrote, "Whatever the fashion, the important thing is time for upkeep. We take it for granted that a girl [sic] gets the best she can for herself. But, if she doesn't keep it up, if it isn't in beautiful condition, if the shoes aren't cleaned before she wears them every day and her bag isn't cleaned and everything in it cleaned, she'll never look like anything." I learned by experience that "upkeep" is tremendously important for any woman who's on public display and constantly on the move. I become a professional traveler and, parenthetically, a world-class packer. I designated one drawer in my bureau especially for travel. In it, everything I needed—from lingerie to a fully primed cosmetic bag—was carefully prepared, lined up in military order, and ready to go. At a moment's notice, I could transfer the contents from drawer to suitcase. The more I traveled, the more sacrosanct that drawer became. The first thing I did when I returned from a trip was to put the drawer together again. Chaos may have reigned over the rest of my life, but that drawer remained in apple-pie order. A portion of my closet had to be similarly uniform. Dresses, coats, and suits were grouped together according to their prospective use. Going south called for lightweight garments, while heavier clothes were needed for northern climes. Consequently, my clothes were arranged on the rack from light to heavy as well as simple to dressy. I know just by the position in my closet whether a dress was suitable for Altoona or Atlanta. Oh, if all my life were as neat and ordered as my drawer and closet were at that time!

A few days before road trips, I checked to make sure the garments were pressed and clean. I traveled with a spray that takes out wrinkles. I also discovered a neat trick, one I'll share. If you keep your clothes on the hanger, covered in the plastic bags used by dry cleaners, you can fold them into luggage and they won't wrinkle. Truly, by the end of the campaign, my ability to pack a suitcase was down to a science; I think I could have gone to the moon for a month with an overnight bag.

There were a couple of times, however, when even my advanced skills failed me. Late one afternoon, I arrived in Richmond, Virginia, for an evening event . . . without my valise. It had been left behind and was sitting in the front hall on Perry Street. I was beside myself! I wanted a change of clothes. I *needed* a change. You can't imagine how sweaty you are at the end of a day of campaigning. Everything's sticky. The magic perk-up formula is to get out of the dress you've been wearing, leap into a shower or tub, and change into something fresh. I could get out of my dress and leap into a tub, all right, but that's where the formula ended. I had to get back into the same dress. The next morning, Susan Trees, one of my staff members, came by to pick me up for the breakfast meeting. She took one look and, knowing the situation, said casually, "Gee, Kitty, that's a lovely dress you're wearing, you should wear it more often." We both laughed. Laughter is of paramount importance on a campaign; without it, I don't think anyone could survive.

In Iowa, we drove everywhere, making six or seven stops a day in towns that were about fifty miles apart. Around ten o'clock at night, we'd end up in some small city or town, spend the night, and get up the next morning to repeat the process. The routine gets a little boring because you do the same thing day in and day out, week in and week out. Fortunately, the monotony is broken up by moments and events that are truly memorable. I remember going to a state fair with Andrea. The main event, judging steer, took place in a huge pen. Andrea and I were escorted into the ring, where we stood amidst a horde of enormous, lowing beasts as the judges roamed around awarding blue ribbons. No matter where we stood, we seemed to be downwind. It got to be pretty close. You haven't lived till you've been surrounded by prize beef on the hoof.

Attending state fairs was only part of what we were called upon to do. During the campaigns, both primary and general, we were asked to show up at, or perform in, just about every contest, competition, meet, or game known to man. And I did everything, from a blanket dance with the Klinket Indians in Alaska to a hula in Hawaii. By the way, no matter where we went, mainland or islands, invariably we found a Hellenic connection. Each town we visited had at least one Greek family. Often, they were the proprietors of a pizza place or a coffee shop. To a family, they were wonderfully demonstrative and hospitable. It wasn't surprising. The Greek community, in general, was thrilled with Michael's candidacy. As one gentleman said, "We are a proud people and the last Greek in politics was Spiro Agnew. We suffered with that image. Now we can point to someone admirable. It is a wonderful feeling."

. . .

In the first months of the primary, there were eight Democratic candidates: Michael, Jesse Jackson, Joe Biden, Paul Simon, Dick Gephardt, Al Gore, Gary Hart, and Bruce Babbitt. With the possible exceptions of Hart and Jackson, every one of them had to fight for recognition. "Fight" is an apt word.

The fray hadn't even begun when three other possible candidates, Pat Schroeder, Sam Nunn, and Bill Bradley, dropped by the wayside. Of the trio, I knew the most about Pat Schroeder from Colorado. We had met and I had a lot of respect for the stands she had taken on the environment and on women's and family issues. No question, she'd been a good congresswoman. Nevertheless, I was a bit miffed at her for entering the race; I felt she posed a threat to Michael. His candidacy was attractive to women on so many levels because he had supported women's issues. I wasn't happy about a woman taking away the focus he had so rightly earned. Well, I didn't have much time to worry because she was out of the race in the blink of an eye. Nunn and Bradley were never viable competitors.

I was friendly with some of the candidates and their wives, and became particularly close to Bruce Babbitt's wife, Hattie. Bruce was the governor of Arizona and Hattie and I had gotten to know each other earlier through the governors' meetings. Like me, she has her own career—she's a lawyer. Also, like me, Hattie set aside her work to join in her husband's campaign. Unlike me, however, she had young children, and it was tough for her. Sometimes the children would join them, but most of the time they had to be left at home. Tipper Gore and Jane Gephardt had small children, too. I don't think I could have campaigned if my children were little. Actually, I wouldn't have had to; as I've already mentioned, Michael said he never would have run if our children weren't all out of high school.

During the primaries, existing friendships among candidates and their wives are put on a funny kind of "hold." You still like each other, but you're in a fight and you have to keep your guard up or you're going to be knocked out. All the time we were together, there was an underlying feeling, "Don't say anything that might reflect on your husband." The smiles and the hugs were there, but there was an edge to everything. On the simplest level, it's like actors vying for a role. You may like your competition, personally, but you sure as hell think you're the best one for the part. Despite the break in relationships, I felt a kinship with those spouses. I'm happy to say, that feeling survived. After the primaries were over, the ranks closed and everyone worked together. The reunification of erstwhile combatants is part of the formula for presidential campaigns. I still feel close to all of those women; they were there for me in the general election.

As the primaries progressed, our friends at home began to rally around us. From the outset in Iowa, six women friends traveled with me: Sandy Bakalar, Alice Jellin Isenberg, Helen Spaulding, Debbie First, Wendy Minot, and Anne Harney. They paid their own way, and took turns traveling to assist me. It was like a Big Sister program. We had some pretty wild times, too; there's nothing staid about campaigning, especially in the early stages.

Sandy joined me for a trip to Elkader, Iowa. We were scheduled to spend the night in a highway motel on the outskirts of town and arrived in the late afternoon. The main building of the motel was on the highway. To get to my bungalow, I had to walk on wooden steps about three hundred feet up a hillside. Inside was an oversized round bed smothered in a plush velvet coverlet. There was a Jacuzzi in the bathroom. I put a few things away, then decided I was hungry.

Sandy, Andy Savitz (the advance man), John McMahon, and I drove into town to get something to eat. The only place open was a bar. We went in, took a table, and ordered a couple of drinks. There were no other customers except for two men seated at the bar. They got up, went to the jukebox, put some money in, and came over to us.

"Wanna dance?"

Sandy and I looked at each other. We nodded our heads and got up to join the men. Sandy and I don't make it a rule to walk into bars and start dancing with strangers, but we were friendly because they were friendly and I was wearing the protective mantle of the campaigner.

"You visiting Elkader?" my dancing partner asked.

"Yes," I replied.

"Where are you staying?"

"Over at the motel on the highway," I answered.

"You're kidding!" gulped my partner.

"What do you mean?"

"Gosh, lady, you're staying at the 'Love Nest.' "

"What's the 'Love Nest'?"

"They rent that place out by the hour," explained my dancing companion. I couldn't wait to tell Sandy. When I did, she got hysterical. Neither of us could stop laughing. Sure, it was funny, but that night I barricaded the door of my bungalow with every available piece of plastic-covered furniture—just in case.

The primary race was ages ago, and while I don't think there's any need for me to go into the nitty-gritty, some aspects do stand out and merit recognition. The late Milt Kamen was a horn player turned comedian, and one of his favorite stories concerned his days in the orchestra of an opera house. After years of playing, he went to the opera on his night off to see a production of *Carmen*. The next day he came running into the pit and excitedly spoke to his colleagues, "Guess what! You know when we're going, *Oompah, oompah, oompah, oompah*? Well, you'll never believe it, but the guy on stage is singing the 'Toreador Song'!" It's the same in a campaign. You get so carried away playing your part, you can lose track of the whole until something happens to remind you that there is a more important melody being sung. It's not always harmonious. One of the earliest discords was the Gary Hart mess.

I think Gary Hart was one of the most uncomfortable politicians I have ever watched. He seemed ill at ease just being with people and shaking hands. I always felt that way about him. In 1976, Michael and I went to Venezuela, where Gary and Michael had both been asked to speak at a conference in Caracas. During our stay I got to know and like Lee Hart. One afternoon, she and I went for lunch with some other American women. After the others had left, Lee and I decided to do some shopping alone. We were due back around five or six and felt we had plenty of time to browse. Eventually, we found ourselves in a strange part of the city and were unable to find an English-speaking cabdriver to take us back to our hotel on the outskirts of town. We spent hours trying to get back. I told Lee I was really concerned because I knew Michael would be very worried about me. She laughed wryly and said she was certain her husband wouldn't notice she was missing. We reached the hotel and, sure enough, Michael was beside himself with anxiety, greeting me with, "Where were you, what happened?"

Gary Hart didn't even know Lee was missing. I thought that was kind of telling.

The Donna Rice business happened so quickly, I couldn't quite believe it. And yet, looking back, I could see it was entirely possible. Gary was gone from the race in a few days. I felt a sense of sadness for Lee because I liked her so much. On the other hand, I was happy her husband was out of the picture. He had been the front-runner in Iowa, and now there was one less candidate. When he came back into the race in New Hampshire, part of me felt sorry for him, too. It was pathetic. Anyhow, when someone is running for the presidency of the United States, whether one likes it or not, the public wants to know everything there is to know. This was a reality even before Gary Hart was born and is especially true today.

In July, all the spouses of the Democratic candidates were brought together to speak. Each of us was to say a few words about our spouses and ourselves. Hattie Babbitt got up first and disarmed everybody. She's very pretty, and has a sparkling sense of humor. Jeanne Simon was terrific and had her own little cheering group. Most of us were feeling our oats and were enjoying our solos. Except for Jill Biden, none of us had asked our spouses to attend. Jill was so nervous she wanted Joe there, and he was, too.

Right after that event I flew to Traverse City, Michigan, to join Michael for the National Governors' Conference. Both the Republicans and Democrats convened in Traverse City; then we Democrats went off for our conference to Mackinac Island. What are governors' conferences like? As in all conventions, important issues are discussed, some are even resolved, and social activities flourish. Over the years, I have become acquainted with a number of extraordinary people through the governors' conferences.

I also found out about many things at the governors' conferences, some of which had nothing to do with politics. I vividly recall discussing plastic surgery with one of the other wives. I had given the idea a few thoughts, but this woman had taken action and had already undergone quite a bit of surgery, most recently a tummy tuck. She described the process and the excruciating pain. The report was enough to deter me. I'll live with my wrinkles.

Many of the governors bring their families to the summer conferences. Kara had joined us and had a great time at the conference; she eagerly plunged back into the campaign. Whatever their earlier reservations, both my daughters now threw themselves enthusiastically into the race. John, of course, had been actively involved from the beginning. Our children were an integral part of Michael's campaign, something I never anticipated. I didn't even think Andrea would join us. At first, she refused to do anything on her own; she just didn't feel up to it. Six months later she was acting as a surrogate for her father. And she was magnificent. Except for a long stretch in Iowa, Andrea was on the road. Kara worked on the campaign during the spring and summer. In the fall, she returned to Brown and took three-day weekends. A tough schedule. I was particularly happy to see the way Andrea and Kara kept in touch with each other. All three of my children, four including John's wife, Lisa, were in constant communication. The cause took over, and they espoused it as strongly as their father. Though they often were scattered throughout the country, we were in contact and knew exactly where they were at any given moment. Funny, I used to think John was the political animal of my children. The way the girls rose to the occasion, I wouldn't be surprised now if any of my children wound up in government.

Remember the old bit of doggerel, "Ten little Indians sitting in a line, one went home and then there were nine"? The primaries progressed, and to paraphrase the above verse, "Eight little candidates sitting on the wall, and one by one, they began to fall." I was not surprised at the outcome; though each candidate had been qualified, I thought Michael was especially capable. For one reason or another, with the exception of Jesse Jackson, the other candidates faded away from the public consciousness. It didn't surprise me that Jesse remained in the forefront. He wasn't running just for a nomination, he was running for recognition.

I met Jesse Jackson in Iowa in the summer of 1987 at a speaking engagement. A couple of his children accompanied him and I was impressed by them in the way that a parent often is impressed by the children of others. Jesse and I were scheduled to speak on the same program; I was really nervous because of his reputation as an orator—a reputation that is well earned. Thank heaven, I spoke before him; he is not someone I would want to follow. The subject was drugs. I did okay and then Jesse got up and positively wowed the audience. He talked about the malaise in our school systems and what he said made sense. He was eloquent, articulate, and moving.

As often happens with Jesse Jackson, there weren't many specific proposals for change, but that didn't seem to bother his listeners. I watched them as he spoke.

They were mesmerized, and so was I. That first time I heard Jesse Jackson in person all stories of his "charisma" were borne out. The atmosphere around him was charged. It was a dazzling performance. I knew prior to this time that he was a formidable opponent, but I hadn't known the extent of his magnetism until I was in his presence.

Nonetheless, persuasive rhetoric aside, I had real reservations about Jesse Jackson's qualifications to be president of the United States. He was a preacher who had never held an elective office. It seems to me, no matter what the candidate's race, creed, or color, the presidency should not be an entry-level position for politics. In Jackson's case, the actual requirements were overruled by the astounding fact that a black was running for the highest office in the land. We therefore had to be extrasensitive toward him because of the imposed racial double standard. This built-in condescension was unfair to the other candidates; in truth, it was unfair to Jesse himself. I don't like the double standard, but I'm afraid that's the way it will be until there is real equality in this country.

In my mind, there was no question that Jesse Jackson was a bit of a showboat, someone who might stretch the facts to make himself more comfortable. As time went on, I became increasingly concerned because he never espoused specific, definitive proposals for anything— whether the concern was agriculture or foreign policy or education or environment. He could state the problems better than anyone, vividly captioning the current scenes, yet he offered no substantial solutions. Beyond their sound and fury, his speeches lacked significance.

Shortly before the Democratic convention, over the July Fourth weekend, the Jacksons were scheduled to visit Massachusetts. By then, Michael's nomination was pretty secure. He and Jesse had had their problems throughout the campaign, not the least of which was Michael's refusal to kowtow to the Jackson bombast. For Michael, Jesse was just another contender, and he treated him as such. With the nomination fairly certain, Michael wanted to clear the air, to reach out and personalize a relationship that had had more downs than ups.

When Michael was advised that the Jacksons would be in our state for the holiday, he told me to invite them over to our house for dinner. In this instance, he didn't *ask* my opinion; he had made up his mind. I said okay but I was concerned. I feared that Michael's spontaneous gesture, one he would have extended to anyone in the given situation, might be used against him. Jesse promoted himself as "number one." He might use the dinner for his own purposes, particularly in regard to the still unannounced choice for the vice-presidency.

Michael had never said anything to me, yet my instincts told me Jesse was not going to be named to the number-two spot. Why, then, should he be brought into the fold? He easily could interpret the dinner invitation as a "promise," or an indicator. Besides raising his hopes, such a meeting offered him another avenue to the media. Normally I might have put up a fuss; however, it was so soon after I had had neck surgery, I was not focusing sharply. I stifled my vague fears and prepared for the dinner.

Naturally, I wanted things to go off without a hitch and went to work on the details. In the old days, you could call people up, tell them to come on over, and serve just about anything. Eating habits have changed, however; whether it's because of allergy or conviction, people can be extremely fussy about food. A hostess has to be up on her guests' dining preferences and prepare the menu accordingly. I consulted with my Boston staff and we opted for a typical New England dinner featuring chowder and salmon. Before anything was set, I told my staff to get in touch with the Jackson staff to make certain there was nothing on the menu that Jesse or his wife, Jackie Jackson, could not eat. My office called Jackson's headquarters, ran down the menu, and asked if it was acceptable. The Jackson people said they thought it sounded fine. They promised to check with Jesse and get back to us. In the meantime, I heard that Jesse didn't eat fish. I called my office and told them to offer an alternative menu of chicken or whatever. Once again, they telephoned Jackson's office and submitted the revisions. The Jackson staff assured us that Jesse did eat fish; the original menu was fine. I instructed my staff to remain in contact with Jackson's people. Five calls went back and forth between the two headquarters; the last was made a couple of days before the dinner.

When the Jacksons arrived on Perry Street for our small dinner, television cameras, still cameras, reporters, and hundreds of "neighbors" were there to greet them. Until that moment I hadn't realized I lived in such a populous neighborhood! Jesse and Jackie got out of the car and we greeted each other. Jesse took me by the elbow and made a beeline for one of the television groups. I still wore a neck collar from recent surgery, and, I must say, Jesse was quite gentle as he guided me into the television area. As always, his eye was on the media. On the way to the cameras, he greeted the neighbors. We spent about five minutes outside and then went into the house. To keep the occasion as normal and low-key as possible, Michael and I had decided to serve the meal ourselves, while the caterer remained in the kitchen and prepared the food.

In retrospect, we were attempting to make an ordinary evening out of an extraordinary one. First we had hors d'oeuvres—a platter of fish and chicken pieces in a teriyaki sauce—and drinks in the living room. I was pleased to see Jesse take one of the tidbits. As I recall, Jackie and I had drinks, Michael and Jesse didn't. I know Jackie and I smoked; it seems we share the same habit, and our husbands commiserated and briefly lectured the two of us on the evils of tobacco. All of us chatted for about fifteen minutes, mostly about our kids. (Later, Jesse told the press he was exasperated by the small talk; *I* don't consider the subject of my children small talk.)

Jesse was pleasant and talkative, and I remained uncomfortable. Even though the evening had been arranged by us, I couldn't shake the feeling that it was a setup. Michael and Jesse were at opposite ends, running against each other. We were attempting to be together in a positive way, and yet the situation seemed too artificial, too staged.

We finished the preliminaries and went into the dining room. The table was beautifully set and adorned with flowers. I used a combination of the Limoges that had belonged to my mother and some Japanese pieces I had purchased. The sterling silver was my grandmother's. It was definitely a dinner party setting. (Michael and I don't dine grandly; we usually eat in the kitchen.) The meal began with the chowder. Michael, Jackie, and I went right to it, enjoying the soup while Jesse talked. I looked up at one point and noticed he hadn't touched his bowl, not a drop. I decided it would be wiser not to say anything and cleared the plates. I brought them into the kitchen and told the caterers I was worried because the guest of honor hadn't eaten.

What I didn't know at the time, what all that careful

planning and telephoning had not revealed, was that
Jesse Jackson did indeed have an eating idiosyncrasy.
Despite my sincere attempts to do the right thing, no
one thought to inform us that Jesse is lactose-intolerant.
And I served a milk-based chowder! Next, I brought out
the main course and the salad. The salmon was delicious,
under- rather than over-cooked. I looked around the
table to see how my guests were doing. Jackie was eating and commented on the tastiness of the food. Jesse
hadn't picked up his fork. He was waxing eloquent over
his untouched plate.

"Can I get you something else to eat?" I asked him.

He said no and went on with his dialogue. I was really
upset. I couldn't tell if he even noticed he wasn't eating.

Look, I had been on the campaign and I knew the
perils. Sometimes your stomach can go out of sync and
you just can't put anything into it. I had to assume Jesse
was not feeling up to par, though you'd never have
known it by listening to him. I was relieved when one of
Jesse's sons, Jonathan, accompanied by Andrea, John,
and Lisa, came in the dining room. Michael had invited
them to join us for dessert.

Once more I offered some food to Jesse and once again
he declined. He hadn't touched anything, not even the
salad. I was worried. He seemed so affable and yet, by
refusing to eat and offering no reasons, he was insulting
me. Why was he doing it? I didn't have much time to
speculate: As had been prearranged, we had to leave for
the annual Pops Fourth of July concert on the Esplanade
on the banks of the Charles River. We'd been in the
house for less than an hour, and in all that time, Jesse
had eaten maybe one piece of teriyaki chicken. He did
thank me.

We drove to the concert and took our places in chairs

that had been set up in front of the Esplanade's shell. On the ground next to Jesse's seat was a Styrofoam container of take-out chicken. Later, we were told that Jesse ate only chicken. Five phone calls and no one on the Jackson staff had volunteered that pertinent piece of information. Why didn't they tell us? Your guess is as good as mine. We said our good-byes at the end of the concert and Jesse and Jackie went off to their hotel as Michael and I headed home. I told Michael that Jesse didn't eat, and I added that it bothered me. Michael said not to worry, I'd done the best I could. I wasn't surprised when Jesse went to the papers and described the Fourth of July dinner in less than glowing terms. He told the reporters he didn't like fish and couldn't eat the food I served.

In July we traveled to Atlanta for the Democratic convention. I expected my husband to emerge victorious and eagerly anticipated his nomination. Why shouldn't I? I had urged him forward. Furthermore, I never felt I had to make unreasonable sacrifices in order to assist him. On the contrary, I had a very strong sense of myself as a person with her own things to do. If Michael were elected president, he would run this country in a first-rate manner, and as first lady I'd have an even better opportunity to implement the programs and initiatives in which I believed.

The business of running for the presidency—and it *is* a business—is a serious matter and shouldn't be treated with a devil-may-care attitude. The results are too important. At the outset, though, the circus aspects predominate. All the hullabaloo and attention was like a tonic. Initially, I was buoyed by the excitement and the surge, then, suddenly, with no warning, I panicked. Just before New Hampshire, when Michael's chances seemed to be the best, I became petrified, terrified at the prospect of his winning.

It's hard to explain. I wanted him to win, yet I was frightened of the outcome. I would be on campaign trips for three and four days and come home to an empty house because Michael and the children were on the road. I sat at home and waited for them to return, and while I waited, I worried. I was getting a foretaste of what was to come, and my apprehension grew. Michael was good enough to be president, for sure, but was I worthy to be his partner? I had been among those who pressed him to run for what I believed were good reasons. Now I wondered whether I should have been so certain of what my husband ought to do. Should I have raised doubts rather than hopes?

I was desperate, and in my despair, I turned to alcohol. I was exhausted from campaigning and convinced I was going to make mistakes. I couldn't measure up, so I measured out the booze. My low opinion of myself reached a new high. The bottom line was, people wouldn't like me and I would pull my husband down. I just couldn't handle my doubts and was plagued by self-loathing. Part of the panic came from the incredible feeling of inadequacy; the other additive was the terrible loneliness. I returned to Brookline from the New Hampshire primary, a time when everyone else was away. I couldn't bear the emptiness of my own home. Twice, I drank myself into a stupor. I had obligations, speaking dates, and couldn't make them. I canceled two trips before the Ohio primary and told the office I had the flu. People were annoyed at me for being a no-show. I didn't blame them, but I didn't give a damn.

Michael came home and found me in bed—completely

zonked. He was horrified. Still, he didn't gauge the true depths. In Michael's assessment, the drinking was an immediate response to the pressures of the campaign rather than an addiction. He assumed my condition was temporary.

"Kitty, why are you doing this?" he asked me.

I didn't have an answer. I said, "I'll be okay, don't worry." I snapped out of it enough to reassure him.

Indeed, such is the nature of alcoholism that I convinced *myself* that I would be okay. It's part of the denial mechanism; we lie to ourselves. The denial prevents us from seeking the help we need and enables us to lie persuasively to others. Caught up in the throes of an arduous campaign, my husband was easily deceived. I confused him with my artifice. I kept denying I had a real problem, and I was a convincing liar. So convincing, I pulled the same deal again!

Not long after the first episode, my husband came home from days of strenuous road work and found me lying on the bed, the blinds closed and the phone unplugged. This time, Michael called Al Peters. My brother-in-law came over and checked my vital signs. I responded okay, but, Al said outright that I had a real problem.

We were in the middle of a presidential campaign, however, and in such instances personal problems are often tabled. Externals demand immediate attention. We've all had experiences where we put off facing the situation at hand because of the big picture. A perfect example occurred in 1988 after Joe Biden, one of the Democratic presidential candidates in the primaries, withdrew from the race. As it was later revealed, Michael's campaign manager, John Sasso, had released tapes to the press without telling my husband, and, worse, without admitting it to Michael; these tapes were indirectly the cause of Joe Biden's withdrawal. They showed he had used material from another man's speech without ascribing proper credit. In fact, it was subsequently revealed, this was the one and only time Biden had *not* acknowledged the English statesman, Neil Kinnock, as the original source. Knowing the way my husband felt about keeping his campaign free from such maneuvers, John Sasso had acted ill-advisedly. He had to be dismissed.

The incident seriously hampered my husband's campaign. As bad as I felt about the whole business, as far as Joe Biden is concerned, I believe it was a blessing in disguise. Caught up in the exigencies of the race, I'm certain Joe would have ignored certain incipient signs of illness, such as the headaches that plagued him. Freed of the pressures of the campaign, he was able to seek medical help; as it turned out, he had an aneurysm and had to be operated upon . . . twice! If Biden had remained in the running, chances are he'd have taken a few aspirin and gone on to the next event. The presidential race dictates that all one's thoughts and energies be directed toward the goal; everything else falls by the wayside, including health. As far as I'm concerned, Joe Biden is alive today because he dropped out of the primaries.

When I began to exhibit signs of disease, I didn't seek help, did not heed the warnings. I was too busy helping my husband, so I made excuses: I wasn't an alcoholic, I was just distraught and had a bit too much to drink. Besides, I didn't have time to think about being an alcoholic, and, actually, for the rest of the campaign, I never had another major alcoholic incident. All I drank was those one or two cocktails at the end of the day. You're not an alcoholic, I assured myself, you just lost it a couple times. Everything's fine.

My reasoning, as I've learned, was a perfect example of alcoholic thinking. I didn't overindulge; I merely looked forward to that sweet little drink at the end of the day. And, of course, the rigors of campaigning helped keep me in place. The days were structured and there was a sense of moving forward even when sitting still. I woke up every morning charged with excitement about what the day was going to present. I was high enough on activity to curtail my liquid intake.

TEN

My memories of the 1988 presidential race were highly colored by matters of health rather than state. In late April of 1988, I had a tingling sensation down my right arm. I'd been shaking so many hands, I was convinced it was from all the pumping, so I let it go.

In May, on Mother's Day weekend, I was staying at my sister and brother-in-law's house on Cape Cod. I was reading *The Bonfire of the Vanities* by Tom Wolfe when I started getting hot and cold sensations all over my body. Early the next morning, I went for my accustomed fast walk. I had gone only a few yards when I began exhibiting all kinds of crazy symptoms. I returned to the house, but the symptoms did not stop. I had numbness in my left hand, horrible headaches, and a continuous series of hot and cold flashes.

Ah, but I was in a campaign, and I didn't have time to

pause for trivial health problems. I brushed aside my aches and pains, dismissing them as symptomatic of my current crazy life-style. After the Cape weekend, I had a heavy campaign schedule on the West Coast. I was to meet Sandy Bakalar in Los Angeles, campaign in and around L.A., and from there, fly to Santa Fe, New Mexico. Sandy and I planned to wind up our trip at the Canyon Ranch Spa in Tucson, Arizona, where I could get some desperately needed R and R.

I got to Los Angeles, and the first morning went for a fast walk along the deserted streets. My left foot started dragging. I couldn't control it. My head throbbed and the hot and cold flashes washed over me. I remember thinking, "Oh my God, I've got multiple sclerosis." The symptoms would not go away; I had to do something. I called a doctor friend and got a recommendation to a neurologist, Dr. Edward Davis. I went to see Dr. Davis the next morning. He gave me a neurological checkup, the works, including a scratch test with a pin. I couldn't feel it. The doctor told me I was going to have an MRI.

Here we go again, I thought. "What's an MRI?"

"It's magnetic resonance imaging," answered the doctor. "MRIs are invaluable in determining neurological abnormalities. You know," added the doctor, "twenty percent of all patients are claustrophobic and can't take the test. I'm sure you'll be fine."

I was glad someone was sure. I told the doctor I'd take the tests, but events were scheduled in San Diego that afternoon and I had to attend. The doctor said it would be all right to go as long as I returned that evening for the MRI.

What he didn't tell me was that he was extremely concerned. I was manifesting symptoms indicative of one of three possible ailments: multiple sclerosis, a tumor on my spine, or a troubled disc. The doctor hoped the problem was the disc since it was the least serious of the triple bill.

Without knowing the dangers myself, I told Sandy and my staff I had to go in for the MRI. Sandy, Bonnie Shershow, and Jim Peck-Grey were with me. Bonnie was my trip director and executive assistant. She had worked with me on the Open Space program.

My last event on that evening before the MRI was a speech to an audience of Jewish leaders from greater Los Angeles. According to my staff, I gave my best speech of the campaign. Maybe I wanted to be remembered at the peak of my abilities. Certainly I was scared about the test, plus, I just didn't feel I could spare the time to have anything wrong with me. My neck had been bothering me off and on for months and I'd gotten used to it. I had never brought it up because I figured it was due to the stress of traveling; I made excuses because I had to keep going.

That night Dr. Davis took me to a trailer on the grounds of Cedars of Lebanon Hospital. I had to remove all my clothes because I could not have anything on my body that might attract a magnet, even something like a wired bra. I slipped on a thin robe and was helped onto a gurney.

Meanwhile, Sandy, Bonnie, and Jim were taken to the control center, where, along with the doctor, they would be able to see the imaging appear on the screen. The doctor told me I'd be wheeled into the apparatus and left alone for around nine minutes. It was essential for me to be as still as possible, to breathe gently and not move at all. Naturally, I began to feel a little shaky. I was pushed into the apparatus, which was something like being inserted into a capsule. Once I was in the narrow confines, I felt as though I were being lifted off into space.

I lay there thinking about many things, but mostly I

thought about Michael and the children. Within ten minutes the doctor came in and wheeled me out. He had a big smile on his face and reassuring words on his lips. "We have much more to do, but basically the news is good. Your fifth and sixth discs are pressing against your spine and that's been your problem."

I was very grateful to hear a diagnosis applied to my pains, and while I still had no idea how serious my condition might have been, I felt vindicated as well as relieved to hear I had an actual physical problem. I was wheeled back in and "imaged" for another forty minutes. After the tests, I got dressed and went to the doctor's office to see the MRI results. The pictures are very different from X rays. Though I have never been able to read the latter, I took one look at the MRI results and clearly saw a disc protruding.

"What's going to happen now?" I asked.

"You're going to have to have surgery," he answered. This was not what I wanted to hear.

"When?"

"I'm going to let your doctor in Boston decide that," Dr. Davis replied. I told him to call Nick Zervas, an old family friend and the head of neurosurgery at Mass General. I went back to my hotel, had a big dinner, and started to get ready to fly to New Mexico for the next events. I made my appearances in Santa Fe, and flew off to Canyon Ranch Spa, a beautiful and well-run place. Sandy and I arrived that evening. We got to the dining room late. I was starving and Sandy was pretty hungry, too. We ordered lamb chops and were dismayed when these skinny little pieces of meat were put before us. They looked more like lamb "chips." We forgot we were at a spa; everything was calorie controlled. Actually, they weren't trying to starve us; we could have asked for seconds. We ate dinner and returned to our little bungalow. Within a half hour, Sandy pulled out every bit of junk food she'd brought with her and we both hit the Twinkies. The phone rang. It was Nick Zervas and he was brief: "Kitty, I want you to come home."

I laughed. "I'm not coming home, Nick, I can't. I've got to go back to Los Angeles. The primary is next week and I've got to be there."

"You can't be there. You've got a serious condition. I'm waiting to get these tests; in the meantime you should be coming back."

I wouldn't budge. I had to be in L.A. for the primary. Nick realized I was immovable and backed off for the moment. He agreed to wait for the tests and call me in the morning. Sandy and I finished the junk food and went to bed. The next morning, Nick called, telling me to get a cervical collar and to come home immediately. We went through the same routine—he insisting I leave, and I adamantly refusing.

"Listen, Kitty," Nick sighed, "I can't argue with you on the phone all day. Do what I tell you. Go down to the nurses' station and tell them to put you in a cervical collar. I'll call them and give them the procedure. Take a plane tomorrow. Meanwhile, for God's sake, don't do any physical activity."

Here I am at a spa and I'm not supposed to do anything physical. Great!

Nick called the nurses and told them what he wanted. They went to the local hospital in Tucson and got the collar, then made me put it on.

It was Monday of the Memorial Day weekend, so I called Nick: "Listen," I said, "there's no sense in my coming home on the holiday. Let me stay one more day."

He told me I was crazy, but agreed I could stay. I had

to promise to be in Boston by Wednesday. I am stubborn. Here I was, yoked with a huge cervical collar, with nurses constantly checking me because they're terrified I'm going to be paralyzed, and I'm bargaining with the doctor for time. The nurses were wonderful and took very good care of me. I even had a massage and a facial, the most gingerly administered services ever given, I'm sure. I made as much of my time at the spa as possible, although I was in a little pain all the time and the collar was driving me crazy.

Just before I left Canyon Ranch, I had a row with Andy Savitz. He was trying to keep the story out of the papers and didn't want to let the press near me. My instincts told me there was no way to hide. If we didn't tell them the truth, they were certain to believe my condition was more serious than it really was. He read me the press release he had prepared; I found it too evasive.

"I'm sorry, Andy," I said in my most no-uncertain-terms tone, "you're not going to do it that way. You are going to do it the way I want. I want to deal straight and you have to be specific about what's wrong."

Andy made some quick adjustments to the press release and I approved the copy. We headed toward the plane and Andy said, "Look, when we get to Boston, we've arranged to have a car on the tarmac so you don't have to see the press."

I didn't like that plan, either. I didn't see any need to dodge the press. I had a specific, identified problem, and if I slunk around as though there was something to hide, the rumors would begin. "I am going to see the press," I told Andy, "and then I'm going directly to the hospital."

"Directly" was the wrong word. Sandy and I arrived

at the airport in Tucson only to be told our plane had developed mechanical difficulties and couldn't take off. We sat in an operations room at the Tucson airport and waited—and waited. Finally the pilots decided they could take off, and we flew to Chicago, where we changed planes.

By now, I was almost out of it. The cervical collar was unbearable and the pain was unending. When we arrived in Boston, the press was everywhere. I told the reporters and the newscasters what had happened, and, to the best of my ability, I told them what was going to happen. They were wonderfully supportive and understanding. I was whizzed off to Massachusetts General Hospital with a cortege of motorcycle policemen leading the way. Nick Zervas was waiting to greet me. He didn't *ask* how I was, he *told* me.

"The other tests came in, Kitty. As soon as we can arrange it, you're going to have surgery." I was admitted to the hospital and put to bed. I couldn't get over it. My husband was off campaigning for the presidency and I'm lying in a hospital bed contemplating surgery! It was so frustrating.

The following morning, a Thursday, I was given yet another scan test. After this, Nick advised me I would be operated on the next morning. "We can't wait any longer," he said, "there is a risk of paralysis."

The word "paralysis" got me. I'd done everything on my own; now, I wanted my husband. They reached Michael in San Francisco, where he was scheduled to debate Jesse Jackson that evening. Michael immediately called me. "I'll be there by midnight," he promised. He telephoned Jesse and told him the situation. Jesse was completely understanding and wished me the best.

Meanwhile, I wanted someone from my family with

me. My dad was away and my kids were all in California. My sister was the only one around, but she was teaching. When I called the Green Lodge School in Dedham where she teaches, I was told Jinny had just gotten her thirty students on a bus for a trip to see the Big Apple Circus.

When they gave her the message that I had called, she decided to get the kids settled into the circus and then answer my call. I had not used the word "emergency" and she had no idea I was in need. I got a bit hysterical when my sister didn't call back immediately, so I called the State House and asked two of the staff workers to go over to the circus and get my sister. I knew I shouldn't be dealing through the State House— Michael would have a fit if he knew I was sending people on personal errands—but I didn't care, I was frantic.

The men found Jinny sitting in the midst of her kindergarten charges, enjoying the show. They told her to get on the phone to me right away, which she did. I was so irrationally angry at her for not calling right back, I began to scream. "How could you?" Poor Jinny didn't know what I was talking about. I explained, and after she finished work, she came right to the hospital, and stayed with me every single day.

The flowers began to arrive, so many that Massachusetts General Hospital looked like a botanical garden. From all over the country, hundreds and hundreds of floral displays were sent; thousands of letters and cards arrived as well. It was overwhelming and very disruptive for the hospital, especially when word got around that I was there. The crowds began to gather as patients and staff from other floors went up and down the stairs and up and down the hall trying to get a glimpse of yours truly. It was a madhouse.

I can laugh about it now, but at the time the commotion was unnerving. I was sick and facing surgery. I did not want to be an exhibition marked "presidential candidate's ailing wife."

In the early evening of that first day, my friends and family came to visit. Then, around midnight, after my visitors had gone, I heard sirens shrieking. My husband's entourage came roaring into the city and I could hear them all the way down Storrow Drive. At last, Michael was at my side. Did he ever look good to me!

A cot was set up in my room and Michael spent the evening. We talked about a lot of things. My main topic was food, since I couldn't eat anything because I was being operated on in the morning. My stomach growling, I finally fell asleep with Michael's reassuring words ringing in my ears: "It'll be okay, dear, don't worry, everything will be fine." I think it would have been an easier night for Michael Dukakis had he debated Jesse Jackson.

The next morning at six the attendants came for me and I was given an anesthetic. I told Nick Zervas I was chemically dependent and they'd have to be careful about substances. Nick told me he already knew. I remember going to the operating theatre on the gurney and being transferred to the operating table. Then I was out. After four and a half hours of surgery, I was put into a separate recovery room, where there was a bed for Michael next to mine. I woke up and the first thing I gasped was, "I want something to eat."

"I don't believe it," Michael answered. "You can't have anything to eat, you just had surgery."

He was only partly wrong—all afternoon I ate Jell-O.

Before the operation, the orthopedic surgeon had warned me, "You're going to hate me in the morning, Mrs. Dukakis. You're not going to have any pain in your neck; the pain will be in your hip. We're going to take a piece of bone from there to use as a plug in your neck."

That evening, full of gelatin and with a hip that felt like an elephant had stepped on it, I was moved back into my room. It was piled with flowers and looked like a funeral parlor.

My kids called. They were in California for the primary and I insisted they stay there. I could handle things by myself now; the worst was over and Michael and Jinny had seen me through. The nurses got me up and walking, and by the second day, I was picking my way up and down the hall.

My dad returned to the city and came to visit. "How are you feeling, Kitty?" he asked.

"Turn on the television, Dad, they'll tell you. They've been talking about me all day," I answered.

My dad laughed. "You know, Kitty," he said wryly, "you have a talent for making a career out of catastrophe."

On Thursday, the ninth of June, I left the hospital. I was so happy to get home. I walked in the front door and was helped upstairs to the bedroom. It hurt, but I had this stupid smile on my face because I was home. The second I got into bed, the smile was wiped away. I was in agony. The pain was so unbearable, I began to cry. Michael didn't know what to do. I kept moaning because I couldn't get comfortable. There's something so awfully frightening about being sick in your own bed. I felt better at MGH; now, I was miserable.

That night Michael had to go to a fund-raiser. Nick Zervas was at the event and Michael told him about my condition. My medication was barely stronger than Tylenol and didn't help that much. A substance problem comes home to roost when you are in physical pain.

Wretched as I was, I would not take any strong medication. Actually, I *could* not without risking a relapse. No matter what the agony, the danger is in the "first" pill or the "first" drink. There is no way a substance abuser an take just one. It is the first pill that gets us hooked and the first drink that gets us drunk. It was a concerted act of courage for me not to yield, and I don't mind patting myself on the back for standing firm. I was drug-free although I was in denial about alcohol. But oh, it hurt. Nick was a darling. He came back to the house with Michael and showed me how to rearrange the pillows on the bed to get comfortable. It wasn't a painkiller but it did make things more bearable.

Three days later, I took my first walk around the block. Michael was with me and we were followed by the Secret Service. I started walking every day and slowly began to get back into the swing of things. Bonnie gradually began arranging interviews, no more than two or three a day. I don't think the reporters will ever forget those interviews on Perry Street. Boston was in the middle of a terrific heat wave, one of those summer specials that occasionally belie the traditionally temperate New England summer climate, and I would come down to the living room to find the reporters sitting around sweating bullets.

Some of them couldn't believe it. "Mrs. Dukakis, don't you have any air-conditioning?"

Michael makes few concessions to the elements. I'd explain that the only air conditioner was in the bedroom, adding, "And, if you came in the wintertime, you wouldn't stay very long then either, because it's so cold in our house." We keep the temperature at sixty-two degrees in the winter and even lower at night. Michael will say it's sixty-five, but I don't ever remember seeing the thermostat climb that high. It all started with the oil embargo in the early seventies. Michael began conserving and just never went back, even when the embargo was lifted. People came to our house wearing ski jackets and parkas and never took them off. Hot in summer, cold in winter. I was used to the Dukakis brand of climate control; I felt sorry for the reporters and photographers who weren't.

About the third week I was home, Anne Wexler called. Anne was in the Carter White House and runs her own public relations firm in Washington, D.C. The convention was coming up and I needed a press secretary. Anne told me she had found someone interested in the job—Paul Costello, who was working for Marshall Field's in Chicago. Paul was very qualified to serve as press secretary; among other assignments, he'd been a deputy assistant for Rosalynn Carter in the White House. Paul came to our house for an interview. Later, he told me he had come early and walked around the neighborhood. He couldn't get over how simple our environs were; he expected a huge mansion and extensive grounds. Ha! Paul and I clicked right away. He has a wonderful sense of humor, a great gift of gab, and knows everything there is to know about what's appropriate when you're dealing with the press. On July 1, two weeks after our meeting, he began work as my press secretary.

Paul had a list of about eighty-five people who wanted to interview me, including Barbara Walters and Chris Wallace. Meanwhile, I had agreed with Michael not to have the press in the house early in the morning or late at night. Michael was insistent about keeping the privacy of our house sacrosanct during those hours. What I didn't tell my husband was that I arranged to do an early CBS-TV interview with Kathleen Sullivan.

The morning of the interview, the crew and Paul Costello arrived at 6:00 A.M. Michael came downstairs in his pajamas, took one sleepy look at the assemblage, and said, "What's going on?"

"Oh, we're doing an interview with Mrs. Dukakis," a production assistant answered.

Michael was furious. He walked over to the refrigerator, poured himself a glass of juice, and stomped upstairs. I should have told him. I didn't because I didn't want him to get angry. Well, he *was* angry, and poor Paul was caught in the middle. That evening, Michael had a long chat with him. It was a good talk. Michael realized Paul was not responsible for the CBS invasion, that someone else had given the go-ahead. Mr. Costello was off the hook, but I wasn't. I could take it. No more early-morning or late-night interviews were scheduled at our house.

About a week before Paul joined my staff, on June 20, 1988, Michael and I celebrated our twenty-fifth anniversary. Sandy and David Bakalar invited our family and friends to an anniversary brunch at their home in Chestnut Hill, Brookline. They have a beautiful home and lovely grounds. David collects art and is a sculptor, and the gardens are full of his works and those of classic and contemporary artists. I was still encased in my cervical collar, hating every minute of it, but even the clamp around my neck couldn't dampen this wonderful occasion. Twenty-five years! Michael and I arrived at the Bakalars' and were greeted by family and friends. Every one of them was wearing a cervical collar with the number 25 written in the center! Even the statues in the garden were adorned with collars. I remember a Henry Moore piece with a hole in the belly and a collar round the neck. What a sight!

. . .

As hectic and harried as it gets, in one way, being part of a presidential campaign is a rare privilege. To be granted the opportunity to address issues and concerns before audiences all over the country was an honor, and I gave it my very best.

It wasn't an easy adjustment, however. Michael and I said good-bye to our accustomed, normal existence. Our lives became unmanageable, that is to say, we could not manage them alone. I turned myself over to my schedulers and to my staff. They told me what I could and couldn't do. The reasons were always right, and I couldn't argue. I couldn't stand it, either.

At one point I remember thinking, I have lost total control over my life; that was the moment I decided to get back in the driver's seat, or, at least, to have a say in what I was doing. I didn't want my life being run by my staff, I wanted my staff to *help* put things in order. I insisted I be consulted about the scheduling, and once that issue was ironed out, things went more smoothly. Still, I had to make compromises, conscious choices that were difficult yet necessary. I wanted to continue in the Public Space Partnerships Program at the Kennedy School, and for a while I did. I worked two or three days a week in Cambridge, and the other four or five days, I traveled for Michael.

It was crazy. Within a few months, I had to stop my work and devote myself entirely to the campaign. There is absolutely no way to lead a normal life during a presidential race. You have to make up your mind you're going to give yourself totally to the project. Your course is set and you must follow it. Everything else falls by the wayside. I made sacrifices; some of them were difficult. My work life, my home life—both were disrupted; I expected and accepted those aberrations. One concession really got me, though. I could not go out and greet the people with a heavily flavored breath, and so, for one and a half years, I gave up garlic and onions.

A month after my surgery, my left foot began tingling again. This time I took immediate action. I called the doctor and he suggested another MRI. I returned to Mass General with a phalanx of Secret Service men, and once more I was wheeled into an MRI capsule. The MRI is accompanied by loud bangs almost like cymbals and drums crashing. As I lay on the cot, the doctor talked to me through an intercom. After a while, I didn't answer; the doctor could not imagine what had happened. Despite the noise, I had fallen asleep, probably the only patient undergoing the MRI who's ever dozed off. I told the doctor the din in the MRI was nothing compared to the noise and commotion I was used to.

It turned out the tingling was not serious. The imaging showed everything was okay. Nick Zervas said I could continue campaigning, adding that I also should continue to wear my cervical collar.

"When can I take the damn thing off?" I asked him.

"Three days before the convention," he answered.

The collar was miserably uncomfortable; many times I was tempted to ignore the doctor's orders and chuck my yoke. Finally, a week before we left for Atlanta, I ditched it. What a sense of relief.

Someone asked me what was the difference between campaigning for the nomination and campaigning as the candidate. For me, the contrast between the two was made most conspicuous by the acceleration of media attention and the introduction of the Secret Service. Michael wanted his privacy and tried to stave off the Secret Service. When it was obvious he needed protection, staffers and I got on his case. The Secret Service started following him in May. They were terrific, but as wonderful as they were, their presence made my husband uncomfortable. He really never got used to them following him around. He liked them as people; he just couldn't bear having bodyguards.

Traditionally, the Secret Service joins the candidate's wife on the second or third day of the convention. Since I was fragile from my surgery, they started with me about a week or so earlier. I had a good relationship with the Secret Service and got to be very fond of several of them. Nonetheless, the agents were an overwhelming physical presence. They were all around our house, in the front and back and in both driveways. Every time Michael and I went for a walk, four or five of them accompanied us on foot while a carload of them waited in reserve. There is no time they aren't in attendance. Some agents traveled from place to place in advance, and there could be as many as eight or nine men with me in a given place. When I stayed in hotels, they'd take up positions outside my room.

I had two women assigned to me; they would accompany me into ladies' rooms and places like that.

Ironically, the Secret Service is there to help protect your privacy, yet, because of their presence, you have no privacy. Michael thrives on personal contact. Once the Secret Service took over, he lost that precious touch. He couldn't move freely. He was in a cocoon and couldn't reach out. Neither of us had ever experienced anything like this before, and it was very difficult—especially for Michael.

Eventually, you find yourself going from one airport to another, one state to another, one city to another, one rally to another, and the only people you have any real contact with are your staff and the people guarding you.

Not that I didn't want the Secret Service. I appreciated their presence, especially during the last two months of the campaign when shoving, pushing, and shouting hordes enveloped us. The crowds were friendly; still, the sheer force of humanity was frightening. At those times, only the presence of the Secret Service gave me a sense of security. Michael and I definitely were in new territory. At first it was easier for me. I wasn't the candidate, therefore fewer agents were assigned to me. Except when I was with my husband, I could move more freely, and consequently I was more relaxed.

The further we got into the campaign, the more attention I received. My head wasn't turned completely around. In spite of being thrust into the spotlight, I think I remained true to myself. I was the same Kitty I'd always been, only now, a few more red carpets were rolled out. At the beginning, there had been some question about the extent of my role. I was only a spouse and, generally speaking, candidates' spouses are treated like unwanted pregnancies. They're tolerated because they're married to the candidate and not perceived as having any real value of their own.

I could not play the role of the "silent woman," it's just not my style. My staff was larger than the staff of any candidate's wife had ever been, and the quantity helped to ensure quality. I plunged into the fray and really spoke my mind on my husband's qualifications and on the issues. Michael and I worked as a team, and though I received a great deal of attention, there was never any doubt that Michael was the candidate. I was there to do the things my husband found difficult. My passionate nature was needed to set off his more "placid" one. Also, Michael was more obviously "together" when I was along.

No one realized the stress I was under. The constant scrutiny was overwhelming. Toward the end of the race, even I had had enough. A week or so before the election, Michael and I were walking along with our band of agents. Suddenly, I didn't want anyone around me, looking at me, watching me. I turned to my husband and said, "All I want to do is take a walk by myself. I just want to go off in the woods where nobody knows me." At that moment, I needed privacy more than anything else in the world. I quickly put aside my desire to escape and continued walking. For me, it was a matter of that moment and maybe one or two others; Michael yearned to be free of his protective trappings every minute of the campaign.

As we prepared for the Democratic convention in Atlanta, Michael's staff members suggested my staff be expanded. Marilyn Anderson-Chase, Andy Savitz, and Jim Peck-Grey were still with me at the Democratic convention. They left after Atlanta for other campaign assignments. I hired Heather Campion to take charge of my convention staff. Chris Noell, my assistant at the State House, shifted gears and came over to the campaign to do scheduling, and Michael Lufrano became her assistant, and Nancy Kohn (Sandy Bakalar's daughter) was our office manager. They were all terrific. Ten days before the convention, my staff held a meeting at the Park Plaza Hotel. Twenty more advance people were taken on and were assigned to cover me for every event. By this time, everyone was looking forward to the convention. We were on a high.

ELEVEN

We arrived in Atlanta and found the weather a lot chillier than in Boston. The Georgia cold spell was a welcomed, if brief, relief. Michael and I were ensconced in an extraordinary two-bedroom duplex suite on the top floor of the Hyatt Hotel. Put Michael Dukakis in the lap of luxury and he wants to run. Put me in and I get right in the swim. Our suite had a Jacuzzi and a sauna and I had convinced Michael we should try it out. We were happily submerged when we heard a knock at the door. Michael got out of the bath, put on his robe, and went to see what was happening. He opened the door and came face-to-face with a television crew led by Susan Trees; they were ready to do live interviews. Michael started laughing and went back to fish me out of the Jacuzzi.

The royal treatment in the suite never ended. We were inundated with Godiva chocolates, wine, vodka, hors d'oeuvres, everything. Plus we were surrounded by even more Secret Service men. They were everywhere. If I walked out of the room, if I went from one floor of the suite to the other, someone was watching. I was doing eight and nine events a day. By events, I mean anything from having tea with a select group of Democratic supporters to giving a speech in front of thousands of workers, or being interviewed by the press or television. I was exhausted. We were going to bed at one and two in the morning and getting up at 5:30.

It was like one big party: breakfasts, luncheons, dinners, receptions. I gave a breakfast for all the governors' spouses the second day of the convention. Then I did twenty-two satellite feeds, taped interviews that were beamed simultaneously all over the country. Paul Costello briefed me over and over. Everything went wonderfully well. Only one aspect bothered me, and I wasn't alone in my concern.

All the time we were caught up in the eddy of entertainment, there was an undertow of worry. Jesse Jackson was making noises. Based on his performance at our July Fourth dinner, I knew Jesse would find it almost impossible to be a team player. And during the first week of the convention, he certainly attempted to get the spotlight off Michael and onto himself. This time we were anticipating difficulties, and from the moment we arrived, negotiations got under way with Ron Brown and the rest of Jesse's staff. Eventually, Jesse and his faction came around, but not without a final grandstand play.

Michael was preparing to accept the nomination when a call came to our suite about four hours before his speech to the convention. I answered the phone and the gist of the message was, the Jackson people wanted

Jesse and his wife to join us and the Bentsens—Michael had chosen Senator Lloyd Bentsen as his running mate —on the podium before our respective families came out. I lost my temper and said the request was ridiculous. There was no way that would happen. Our children had worked too hard and long on the campaign to yield their places to anyone. I talked to Michael and he agreed. However, there were some very strong discussions going on; there were even people on the Dukakis committee who wanted Jesse on the podium. Finally, at about four o'clock, I said, "If you bring them out before my children, then I won't be there." The suggestion was withdrawn.

I still have mixed feelings about Jesse Jackson. On the one hand, he is an inveterate grandstander and headline seeker. But there is another side to him. Jesse Jackson had been the first to telephone after I announced my diet pill dependency, and he spent nearly a half hour encouraging me. I was very touched by his response. As I said, I have mixed feelings about the man.

Michael had worked hard on his acceptance speech. Two days before he was to deliver it, he came into the bedroom of our suite and asked if I wanted to read it.

"Of course I do," I said, "I was just going to take a little nap. I'll read it before I doze off." I began reading. The speech was wonderful, straight, true, heartfelt, full of hope—and I fell asleep halfway through it. It had nothing to do with the contents; I was exhausted. Michael walked in and found me. He took the papers out of my hand and later told everybody his speech had put me to sleep.

Just about our entire family was with us at the convention. In addition to our children, we were joined by my mother-in-law, my daughter-in-law, and Michael's first cousin Olympia. Olympia Dukakis is another very special woman. Not only is she active on the stage and screen, she's also been busy behind the scenes with her New Jersey–based theatre company. We'll always remember that prescient moment during the 1988 Academy Awards ceremony when Olympia lifted her Oscar in the air and said, "Let's go, Michael!"

The schedule at the Democratic convention was hectic for the entire family. My kids were flying in and out of the hotel suite trying to keep up with their appointments. Funny. Here we are on the threshold of the greatest political moment of their father's life, and Kara and Andrea got into a snit. Shades of Jinny and me. Shades of sisters everywhere. Something came up and my daughters took opposing positions. Kara appeared in our suite, said she wouldn't share a room with her sister, and took over our other bedroom. No matter what the magnitude of the occasion, the small personal side always surfaces. Happily, the girls resolved their differences in time to fully enjoy the convention activities.

Michael gave his acceptance speech; this time I stayed awake. I think it was the proudest and happiest moment of the months that had preceded and the months to come. I was not simply standing on that dais at Michael's side—surrounded by family and looking out at thousands of delegates and loving and supportive friends—I was on top of the world. I still get goosebumps when I recall that moment. I was so very proud of my husband, and proud too of all the people who recognized his extraordinary worth. I was also proud that Lloyd Bentsen was his running mate. I adore him and his wife. B. A. Bentsen and I are very different, yet I find her the personification of the words "lady in grace." As for Lloyd, he's great.

. . .

Why did my husband lose the election? My personal belief is that Michael Dukakis was not identified strongly
enough in terms of any of his attributes before the other
party began to attack him. The venal and devastating
assault began to characterize him before his real persona
had a chance to emerge. He doesn't show his emotions
easily, but, dammit, he has them. I wouldn't be married
to him if he didn't!

Michael is a different kind of political animal. He's
direct and honest. He will not break his own strong feelings about his ethics and belief and alter his personality
to please somebody else. That was one of the problems.
The Michael Dukakis his family and friends know wasn't
the person seen by the rest of the country. They wanted
to see somebody glittering with passion. What they saw
was a very bright, articulate person who did not come
through sufficiently as a caring, sensitive, compassion-
ate person. Roger Ailes and Company were able to paint
a better picture of George Bush.

The race for the presidency is a media game. It's
sixty-second sound bites on the airwaves, and the bottom line is, our advertising was not as good. Consequently, Michael was never able to rise above the
Republicans' definition of what he was and what he stood
for. Compounding the situation was Michael's inability
to respond quickly enough to some of the charges leveled
at him. Most of them were false and could easily have
been diverted, the Willie Horton and Boston Harbor
incidents being two prime examples. The former was
a cheap shot. More than forty states have parole programs similar to that of Massachusetts. The Republican
governor of Texas, Bill Clements, had signed a bill
giving more days of furlough for prisoners than ever
before!

In my opinion, Michael and his staff did not fight back when they should have. In many ways Michael still ran on a state track and the loop had been growing bigger and bigger; he didn't get into national stride. That chilling incident at the second debate was the nail in the coffin. Michael was asked what he would do if I were raped. Michael made a mistake; he answered a question he should have hurled right back into the face of his questioner. I was in the front row and when I saw my husband attempting to deal with the query logically, I was heartsick. After the debate we went to a fund-raiser at Ted and Susie Fields' house in Los Angeles. I spoke to him in the car.

"Michael, what were you thinking when he asked that question about me?"

"I don't know," Michael answered. "It wasn't as though I didn't expect it, either. I've been asked the same kind of thing about twenty times."

"Yes, but this was a debate. You should have known that question might be asked; you should have been prepared for it." An edge had crept into my voice.

Michael shook his head and shrugged his shoulders. "Kitty, I just blew it," he said simply.

He was right, and it wasn't going to help if I kept harping on the subject, so I began talking about other things, positive ones. I tried to stay upbeat. I'm honest with Michael. I don't shield him from the truth, nor do I stab him with it. And while I try not to go for the jugular, I do speak my mind.

During the campaign, the staff often came to me because they didn't want to burden Michael with unpleasant stuff. I absorbed information and tried to maintain a balance. On the one hand, he had to know what was going on; on the other hand, he couldn't be inundated with picayune bits of business. He had bigger worlds to conquer. I couldn't handle him with the extremes of either kid gloves or boxing gloves; I simply had to deal straight. It's not that I treated him differently—he would have noticed if I had, and immediately said something—but I did attempt to be tactical as well as tactful. Sometimes it worked, sometimes it didn't. One of the most precious aspects of our marriage is our honesty with each other. Since the day we met, we've been able to talk to each other. Michael listens to me. He doesn't always follow what I have to say, but he listens. I've learned over the years how to push and how not to push. There are certain buttons I won't press because they're ineffective.

You have to weigh the factors, especially when a candidate is under stress. The game by nature is one in which everyone on your team constantly builds up your ego and says what they think you want to hear. A spouse, a caring one, will tell the person things he or she *doesn't* want to hear. In August, I told Michael he had to be more aggressive and take a tougher stand. Michael didn't want to hear it. He wanted to maintain his accustomed sense of fairness. He said over and over that he didn't want to hit back in the same manner he was being slugged. And there were plenty of opportunities to play their negative game. Ugly rumors were circulated about George Bush's personal as well as political life. Michael would not allow his staff to seize those contemptible suppositions and use them against his rival. In politics, honor is quaint. If you want to rise to the top, it seems you have to stoop a bit first.

Three days before the presidential election on November 8, I was in a hospital in Minnesota with upper respiratory infections. My temperature was 103 degrees, I had nodules on my neck, and my sinuses were inflamed. I consider myself a relatively healthy person, yet I was plagued by ailments during the campaign. I needed to have all my systems on "go," and they began balking.

Admittedly, the pressure and the pace could have killed anyone.

Happily, Paul Costello helped me through those trying last weeks. I did press conferences and one national interview after another, *rat-tat-tat*. Paul helped me prepare by going through some of the possible questions. He didn't give me answers; he did help me collect my thoughts and present them in the best light. You have to be at the ready, yet you don't want to seem "programmed." Paul Costello deserves a great deal of credit for showing me the difference between being a robot and being a real person. He had enough confidence in himself and me to be able to speak the truth. We'd get on a plane and he'd say, "Let me tell you what happened," and would proceed to go over the events, pointing out the mistakes as well as the achievements. I never really had anyone do that before. I had played the adviser role with Michael, and now I had someone who was on my wavelength, doing the same for me. It made a difference being counseled by someone experienced in the field, someone whom the press respected. I respected him, too, and it made a difference.

John Keller joined my staff around the same time as Paul. John did my issue speeches. When you have important things to say, it's important they be said in the best possible manner, whether you're telling people that the only thing they have to fear is fear itself, or advising them not to ask what their country can do for them, but rather to ask what they can do for their country. Good ideas are like diamonds and need to be put in the proper setting. They have to be cut and shaped. A good speech writer is a skilled jeweler. I have a process I've been going through for a long time with whoever is writing my speeches. I meet with the person to discuss the topic and cover all the points I want brought out. The writer prepares a draft, which I read through for corrections and changes. A good speech writer knows how to express what you want to say without imposing his or her personality or opinions on your words. After I've corrected and edited the speech, the writer prepares a finished copy. Even this can be changed. The point is, whatever the language, the ideas expressed must be mine. Otherwise, it isn't my speech. I have had a variety of people work on speeches for me, many were really good; John is extraordinary. There's a chemistry between us; philosophically we're in the same boat. He has learned what I'm comfortable with saying and writes accordingly.

Occasionally, something will slip in that doesn't sit right. In 1989, I appeared before the Massachusetts Democratic party to accept recognition as a 1988 Democrat of the Year. A passage in the draft criticized the legislature on a specific budget matter. Even though I agreed, I crossed it out. I didn't need to take jabs at the people who were honoring me, at least not at that particular time. I could let them know later.

Giving a prepared speech is one thing, extemporizing is another. I learned how to think on my feet, fast, especially during question-and-answer sessions. There are lots of ploys: For example, if a question you can't or don't want to answer is posed, you make up your own question and answer it. You can't make this a rule, however, because you'll seem too evasive. Basically, you have to be prepared for any query and, in a campaign, you rely on your staff to bring you up on material. I had a hard time in Alaska because I had no idea that a particular environmental protection issue was so hot. I did about fifteen interviews and every one of them was torture. Michael's position, and mine, was to protect the environment. Unfortunately, it ran counter to the governor's position. He was a Democrat who had supported Michael's candidacy. There were many points of contention between government officials and environmental protectionists. The tragic oil spill that occurred later dramatically changed opinions.

I also encountered a tough situation in Topeka, Kansas, toward the end of the campaign. We were in an airport hangar for a rally after an event at a local high school. A group of anti-choice demonstrators started jeering and making catcalls. They were right in my line of vision and they were really being ugly. I got rattled and couldn't find my place. It was awful, doubly so because the rally was being televised.

As if being jeered at weren't enough, some of the reporters came at me with verbal rapiers flashing. When you're at the end, and you're obviously "finished," it's like turning over a rock, all these little worms come out and decide they're going to crawl all over you. Usually, there's a wiseass young reporter who thinks he's on the way to becoming an important journalist and can boost himself by making a national figure uncomfortable. My luck, one of these characters appeared after the Topeka High School event.

He couldn't have been much more than twenty-three or -four and he started asking me how I felt now that my husband was going to lose the election and couldn't possibly win. "Aren't you depressed, Mrs. Dukakis?" he said, dripping sincerity.

I wanted to hit him. I mean really slug him. Instead of counting to ten, I was a wiseguy right back at him and gave a sassy answer.

When we got on the plane, Paul Costello started rolling his eyes, an indication I had erred. I should have known better. You can never win battles with the press; you have to understand they've got the final word. And, what purpose was served by my being as rude to someone as he was to me? None.

In truth, I feel that 95 percent of my interviews, both pencil press and television, were positive. More important, I have strong feelings about the First Amendment. I believe there is no alternative to a free press. It has to be accepted, warts and all. Look, members of the press are human too. Some are lazy, some are ambitious, some are cruel, and some are sensitive, kind, and loving. I have made real friends among the press. I was so pleased to hear from many of them when I went into treatment. National people like Marian Burros, Sam Donaldson, Peter Jennings, Tom Oliphant, Diane Sawyer, and Barbara Walters took the time to write and offer me their good wishes.

The last weeks of the campaign were extremely trying. We were advised Michael's efforts were doomed; still, we kept at it. You know, my husband had been a success story from the time he was a little boy. He'd done well at everything he'd attempted. He came back from defeat and was reelected governor; he successfully campaigned in the primaries and became the party's choice. For someone like Michael, the certainty of defeat was difficult to accept. It was the ninth inning, there were two outs, the batter had two strikes, yet he kept swinging. Both of us looked away from the inevitable and focused on the improbable.

The day before the election there were rallies in San Francisco and Los Angeles. Both were wildly successful. I then flew with Michael to Des Moines for a demonstration at two o'clock in the morning; five minutes before we landed my head started banging—I was hit by my first migraine headache of the campaign. After the Des Moines rally, Michael took off on his plane and I flew in mine to Philadelphia. My head was still throbbing. Nothing had changed; everything indicated Michael was going to lose.

I flew into Boston and attended another rally with Michael at Logan airport. Then we went home. I tried to take a nap. I didn't drink anything. I went to bed for a couple of hours and thought more than I slept.

That afternoon, some reports began coming in that indicated the race was winnable. They persisted into the early evening. I had been preparing myself for defeat, and yet you really cannot prepare yourself. No matter how sure you are that you can expect the worst, it's awful. Unfortunately, Michel Benayun, who does my hair in Boston, could not travel with me, so Richard Penna came over in the early evening to do my hair and Louise Miller was there to do my makeup. Thumbs up or down, I had to look good.

We had six television sets in the living room. I had to laugh; I could just see Michael's face when the electric bill came. My dad and my mother-in-law came over, so did Jinny and Al; Lisa, John, Kara, and Andrea were there; Paul Costello and Bonnie Shershow, too. We sat in the living room and watched our hopes die.

I remember Michael was wearing a maroon cardigan sweater. He looked weary, more like Mr. Average American sitting in front of his television screen than a protagonist in the country's premier political battle. A little before 9:30 P.M., Dan Rather appeared on the screen. Michael took my hand as the CBS news commentator announced an electoral landslide for George Bush. We all looked at each other. It was over. Michael had grasped my hand, now he released his grip and went into the kitchen to write his concession speech.

We drove over to the World Trade Center in downtown Boston where all the newscasters had gathered, along with banks and banks of cameras. A group from the television show "Saturday Night Live" had entertained the gathering. My friends told me they were very funny. They used to do the most hilarious imitations of Michael and me on the program.

I remember walking through the crowd. The band was playing and everyone was cheering with tears in their eyes. We stood on the platform and Michael spoke. My mouth was frozen into a smile, but my eyes gave me away—they were dead. After the speech, we went into a side room reserved for family and friends. My dad was wonderful. He spoke to the reporters and joshed with them. Michael met with his workers, thanked them, and then we went home.

The next morning, Michael went back to work at the State House.

I was going someplace, too: downhill.

On January 19, 1989, I had flown to Los Angeles to give a speech for the United Jewish Appeal. The speech was okay and I was moved by the obvious affection my audience showed toward me. The next morning I went to the Los Angeles airport. An airline representative met my car and escorted me into the lounge area. There seemed to be five thousand television sets in that lounge and they were all tuned to one event, the inauguration of the forty-first president of the United States of America. The airline representative apologized because of the on- slaught of coverage. He was sweet, and I appreciated his concern. Realistically, why wouldn't the sets be turned to such an important milestone? Nonetheless, I didn't want to watch it. I moved my seat seven times and still I couldn't get away. I spent the half hour before my plane took off hopping from one chair to another. I knew January 20 was inauguration day and thought I had prepared myself by stuffing all my feelings in the back of my emotional closet. Faced with the actual real- ity of the ceremony, I wilted.

I was flying to Tucson by myself to meet Kara. We were going to spend the week at Canyon Ranch. We were there for five days and had a good enough time. I was happy to be with my daughter, but I was haunted by the spectre of the election. I was sad and in a kind of fog. I wasn't drinking. That control would be short- lived.

III

BACKSTAGE

Dear Kitty,

Eleven years ago this April I went through treatment for alcohol and drug dependency at Long Beach Naval Hospital. Without a doubt that treatment experience was the most positive thing I could have done. It was the beginning of a new quality of life for me and for my family—a deeper understanding and appreciation of the values and trusts I am afforded each day.

Please know my thoughts and prayers are with you as you discover a new you—one I know you will like and accept as the fine person you are. Sobriety is to know a new joy. Congratulations to you and your husband for openly addressing one of our country's greatest problems.

I wish you only the very best in your recovery. Jerry joins me in sending best wishes to you and Mike.

FONDLY,
BETTY

TWELVE

The first time I took an amphetamine from my mother's drawer, I felt terribly guilty. I continued to feel that way each and every day I took a pill. No matter what I did or what I accomplished, a patch of deceit existed at the core of my being and I could not shake it.

In the beginning, it was easy to get pills; doctors prescribed them without any fuss. Even after the initial warnings about the effects of amphetamines appeared, physicians continued to write the necessary paper for me. Over the quarter century that I was using, I learned to ferret out professionals who would prescribe with few or no questions asked. They weren't sleazy men, either; they simply didn't know I was addicted. I didn't give them time to find out and they never tried to unearth my secret.

Still, I shouldn't have been given pills on demand;

there's something wrong with a system in which a patient can receive a potentially harmful medicine so readily. I always went to different drugstores to get the prescriptions filled, trying not to visit any one of them repeatedly. Records are kept by pharmacies and I didn't want my name to be linked to amphetamines. I was covering my tracks. You cannot take this kind of action and not realize you're acting improperly. I knew it was wrong. I followed the routine I thought I needed to get through the day, and those days were affected by my deeds more than I realized.

Michael became aware of my unsettled nature in the summer of 1962. We had gone away for a weekend together for the first time. There had been some problem or other with John, nothing major, and yet I had reacted violently, losing my temper. Michael stood there looking at me as though I were crazy. My anger passed almost as quickly as it arrived and I calmed down. Michael wrote it off as an example of moodiness. Under that heading, I got away with outrageous behavior.

I had a short fuse with everybody, including my children. I think I was a good mother, I certainly intended to be. However, when I was in a temperamental pique, I'd blow the kids away. They, like everyone else, got used to my outbursts and wrote it off as "Mommy in one of her bad moods." In reality, it was "Mommy suffering the effects of substance abuse."

In 1974, when Michael confronted me with the pills, I honestly tried to stop. I saw my doctor and he did the best he could. I stayed clean for three months. But I couldn't keep away. I didn't get the help I needed and I began using again. So for the next eight years I lived a double lie, deceiving my husband as well as myself. I thought I could do it alone. I couldn't. When you are addicted, you need help from those who are recovering. And when you're willing to admit you need that help, you're taking the first step.

I cannot remember the exact moment I made up my mind to try to get off the pills for good; it came as a culmination of incidents. Matters came to a head in 1982 when Michael was in the middle of his campaign for re-election as governor. He was bound and determined to make a comeback after his ignominious defeat four years earlier. I sincerely and desperately wanted to be a good wife and campaigner. I knew my demeanor was important; I also knew my behavior could get out of hand.

Though it had nothing to do with politics, one episode does stand out. I acted terribly at Kara's graduation from Lawrence School. I was talking loudly and snapping. I squirmed in my seat as the eighth grade went through the ceremonies. Michael told me to sit still and I told him to shut up and mind his own business. I had played this scene many times, the impatient, backbiting mother and wife. I looked over and saw my lovely daughter sitting with her classmates. She cast a glance at me and smiled. I thought I detected a glint of apprehension in her eyes. I suddenly got a picture of myself sitting there, tight and grim, my mouth and eyebrows drawn together. I began to think about what was happening. This was my daughter's graduation and I was well on the way to making it a miserable experience for her and the rest of the family. What on earth was I doing? There was no excuse; my conduct was indefensible. I knew I had to do something.

On June 20, 1982, Jinny, Al, Michael, and I went to the Blue Strawberry restaurant in Portsmouth, New Hampshire, for dinner. Michael and I were celebrating our nineteenth wedding anniversary. On the trip back, I spoke to my brother-in-law. I trusted him. He always had been open about his own alcoholism and his subsequent recovery. I spoke directly, very directly: "Al, I've been taking diet pills for twenty-six years. I need help."

Al responded immediately and put me in touch with a doctor friend of his. The doctor, in turn, gave me the name of a woman in New York. I called the woman and arranged to meet her in the city. I was working as a meeting planner then, and took frequent trips to Manhattan. It was so weird. Here I was trying to change my life, yet that very morning I got up and took a pill before flying off to New York. The woman I met had been addicted to diet pills. She had moved from them to alcohol and then entered a recovery program. She was a stranger, and yet I opened up to her immediately. I told her I felt my life had become unmanageable. I acted peculiarly and could not correct myself. I alienated family and friends. Sure, there were good times, but, all in all, I felt the preponderance of negativity; I truly believed my behavior was slightly insane. The woman listened quietly. When I finished, she suggested I enter the treatment program for alcoholism and other drug addictions at Hazelden in Center City, Minnesota. Besides being a first-rate facility, Hazelden was far away from the political arena in Massachusetts where Michael was campaigning.

On the July Fourth weekend of 1982, I finally took the next step. I called Hazelden and made a reservation to enter the clinic on the fourteenth of July. I had told Michael what I planned and he supported me.

On July 14, Michael drove me to the airport. I was a nervous wreck. I wouldn't let Michael come in with me; I didn't want to call attention to him. I slunk into the waiting room, sat down, and buried my head in a book, hoping to remain unnoticed. We had concocted a story for general consumption that ran along the following lines: I had hepatitis and was going to recuperate at the home of my college roommate, Anne Forgy. We kept the story simple to discourage any possible investigative probe. The story was more than simple: Anne Forgy lived in Missouri and I was going to Minnesota. Just in case someone did snoop, I called Anne to inform her of the ruse. She was one of the first to know and never said a word.

As I sat in the airport hiding behind the book, a man I knew entered the waiting area with his two daughters in tow. They sat down not far from where I was trying to seclude myself. I shrank deeper into the pages, pretending one small volume could hide me from the world. I overheard the man speaking to his children My luck, he was putting them on the plane to Minnesota! He left, and the girls went aboard. I waited, and then snuck into my seat. I spent the entire trip bobbing my head in and out of the book to dodge the girls.

When I arrived, I was met by a driver from Hazelden. The clinic was about an hour away. It's a beautiful place, nicely situated on a lake. Immediately, I was put into a detoxification program. I'm told every facility does the same: You arrive, you go into detox. I was very honest with the staff. I told them I had taken a pill during the flight. I could see no reason to lie to people who were trying to help me. Others, I learned, are not so open. They prevaricate; if the deceptions continue they almost certainly drop out, voluntarily or otherwise. My luggage and I were thoroughly examined. Everything was opened, every jar, bottle, tube, pocket, lining, or case—anything that might conceal contraband is subject to perusal. All legitimate medication has to be turned over. I was on thyroid medicine and gave the bottle to the examiners. In turn, my own medicine was given to me by the staff.

At the end of the initial interview, I was assigned a room. I made right for it, passing the recreation area where the other arrivees were watching television and drinking coffee. I did not join them. I didn't want to socialize. I was embarrassed to be in the place. I settled into my room and stayed there, reading. At midnight, a nurse came in and proceeded to give me four Librium. To this day, I am baffled about the amount of medication with which I was detoxed. For three days, I slept almost constantly. I drowsed during lectures, napped in front of the television, and dozed off talking to people. I couldn't stay awake. I have spoken to experts and physicians and many thought the dosage was excessive. Since my stay, methods have changed and improved.

At Hazelden, I was told I was an alcoholic. It made me laugh—I wasn't a heavy or even a steady drinker. Sure, I'd had a couple of isolated incidents of overindulgence, but for heaven's sake, how many people haven't had too much to drink at one time or another?

Had I looked into my history more thoroughly, I would have come up with evidence supporting Hazelden's assessment. In truth, I *was* a daily drinker; I had a hefty shot of vodka almost every night. Moreover, I exhibited other signs. Incidents I considered unimportant were indicative of my condition. For years I attended Boston Pops concerts, watching my dad conduct. At Pops, the orchestra seats are removed and tables are set up on the main floor of Symphony Hall. Light drinks and light refreshments are served while music is played. (Pops got its name from the sound of champagne being uncorked.) I usually would host two tables and took charge of ordering. When the sparkling burgundy was served, I'd finish before anyone else. I remember checking the contents of my guest's glasses. If they contained liquid, I would fume to myself. I wanted to order more bottles and couldn't understand why the others "sipped" at their drinks. Why couldn't they keep up with me? My thinking was alcoholic. I just didn't know it.

At Hazelden I was in a unit with twenty-four other women. I kept busy with homework assignments and meetings. I made friends in the program and remain in touch with some of them to this day. I was helped at Hazelden; I accepted the fact that I was addicted to pills. The problem was my inability to identify in terms of alcoholism. I kept telling myself there was no way I was an alcoholic! I could count my episodes of intoxication on the fingers of one hand and have a couple of digits left over. The chronology of my alleged alcoholism was so brief as to be almost nonexistent.

The first time I had too much was at the end of my senior year at Brookline High. I was chairman of Class Day and had spent the morning and afternoon painting signs and backboards in preparation for the ceremony on the following morning. I was so busy I didn't have anything to eat. That evening my friends and I were going to Brookline Night at Pops, an event that I had organized. First, however, we went to a party where they served a spiked punch. I had two glasses and got sick, not surprising when you consider I was drinking on an empty stomach. Worse than my sickness, however, was my fear at having my father see me in such wretched shape. I fortified myself with strong coffee and sobered up. My friends and I arrived at Pops and took our places at a special table. Pops is famous for playing encores, and, at the time, one of the most performed was LeRoy Anderson's "The Waltzing Cat." Encores are announced by large placards held aloft by the musicians. When it came time for the Anderson piece, the printed announcement was raised and the audience roared at the message. In my honor, Dad had changed the title to read, "The Waltzing Kitty." "The Staggering Kitty" would have been more appropriate.

My second drinking episode occurred during sophomore year at Penn State. I had a few too many at a fraternity party, and once more I threw up. Since seventy zillion coeds had been doing the same thing for generations, I didn't attach any importance to the incident. I didn't repeat it, either. The zombie in Matamoros was the third and last drinking episode of my young life. Aside from a few "giddy" reactions, I'd never had even a minor drinking scene since. This wasn't a boozer's provenance and I refused to budge my position. If Hazelden had to get me off the pills by calling me an alcoholic, fine. I just wouldn't buy it. My stance was fortified by the number of enablers surrounding me at home. An enabler is someone who unwittingly assists the substance abuser in continuing his or her addiction. Most often, an enabler is a loved one. All my family were enablers. None of them—father, husband, sister, or children—believed I was an alcoholic. I was a drug addict pure and simple. I left the clinic twenty-eight days later, and since then have never taken another diet pill, a day at a time.

I returned home on August 20, a month before Michael's primary. Normally, after leaving a rehab center, you attend meetings of the fellowship. At first, I went to a couple of them, but I simply could not identify with other alcoholics. Anyway, I didn't want to show up at the large gatherings for two reasons. One, my husband was running for office; two, I wasn't an alcoholic. Regarding the first excuse, the question of whether I would help or hurt a campaign by admitting my addiction is debatable. Ever since I went public with my problem, I have been deluged with letters and approached by thousands of people who are in recovery. They tell me they are grateful I addressed my problem in the way I did and urge me to keep the public informed. My second defense—I was no alcoholic—reflected my inability to be honest with myself.

Back in Brookline, I went to a psychiatrist who was herself in recovery. Others set up special meetings of a support group in private homes. I attended them for about five months. I would introduce myself by saying, "I'm Kitty and I'm a drug addict." I didn't add, ". . . and I'm an alcoholic." I said those words at Hazelden; I wouldn't say them anymore because I didn't believe it. At Hazelden they talked about having to reach your lowest point before you can help yourself. They were right. I didn't recognize my total chemical dependency until I hit rock bottom; I was seven years away from that nadir.

Gradually, I began to find excuses for not going to the private meetings and, finally, I stopped. One of the difficulties with my disease is thinking you are unique. You feel you can do things your way. Certainly that's how I felt. And I was wrong. The people in recovery who helped me avoid the standard procedure were wrong, too. I don't blame them; it was my mistake. My solicitous friends set up the private meetings because I refused to attend public ones. They deemed it better to keep me in some sort of constructive procedure. My friends were inadvertent enablers. Without a strong armature of fellowship bolstering me, I slipped away. Who needed the group? I was off pills, wasn't drinking, and had recovered nicely from my "hepatitis." I didn't need them because I didn't have a problem.

Michael was reelected governor and inaugurated in January. In April, I began drinking again. It was "controlled." I didn't drink every day, and, for a while, took nothing stronger than wine. You know the old shibboleth, "I'm not drinking, it's only wine." Well, alcohol is alcohol is alcohol, whether it's in wine, liquor, or beer. The body can't tell the difference because there isn't any. My disease couldn't tell the difference, either. I was kidding myself. However much I wished to pretend I was dependency-free, I was not. A few ounces every night, and before you know it, the mental and emotional process sets in.

Something else happened after I left Hazelden. Every year following my treatment, I went through seasonal depressions, starting at the end of August and lasting till March or April. The extended low phases were unbearable. To help deal with them, the doctors prescribed antidepressants.

I did not face hard facts about my dependency problem until after the presidential campaign. On July 5, 1987, when I publicly admitted I had a drug dependency problem and had been to Hazelden, I was not merely trying to forestall any possible trouble for Michael's campaign. One of the tenets in recovery is helping others like yourself. I had five years of not using pills behind me and felt comfortable with that part of my recovery; I wanted to help others. When I told my counselor at Hazelden I planned to reveal my drug addiction, she expressed concern. She had heard I was drinking, and though she didn't think I was in serious trouble at the time, she believed I was an alcoholic and feared there would be an inevitable crisis. How right she was!

I went ahead with my plans. We called a press conference and I talked about my addiction to diet pills. In retrospect, while it may not have been a wise personal move to step forward, I do think my action was a positive one and I don't regret it. By speaking too soon, I left myself wide open for censure and ridicule later, when my alcohol dependency was revealed. Somehow, though, I think people understood what I was trying to do. My heart was in the right place.

In late February and early March of 1988, around the time of the New Hampshire and Ohio primaries, I experienced those two drinking bouts. I canceled several trips to Ohio and stayed home. That's when Michael found me passed out on the bed and called Al Peters. Al brought me around. As I've said, he suspected then that I had a big problem, but there was no time to handle it. There was a campaign going on.

By plunging into the contest, I was able to put a cap on my drinking. As the pace quickened, my drinking lessened. I went on to the regimen of one cocktail in the evening and was able to carry it through—with a few exceptions.

One of those exceptions occurred during the Iowa primary. We stayed at a hotel in Des Moines that had a bar famous for a drink called Long Island Iced Tea. I don't know the ingredients, though I'm told a bit of everything goes into the making, including a flavoring that imparts the look and taste of tea. I do know it's an extraordinarily potent drink. We would gather in the hotel bar in the evenings and I'd toss down one or two L.I. teas. I seemed to handle them amazingly well and never got woozy or giggly. I'd get up and have no trouble walking to the elevator and going up to my room. Ah, but from that point on there was trouble. I could not get to sleep and suffered from insomnia every night. I'd get up in the morning and drink strong coffee all day long to keep awake. The caffeine and alcohol put my body into a kind of fuzzy neutral. When we left Iowa, I stabilized, and from then on I avoided mixed drinks. Straight liquor was easier to handle.

Though I limited *my* intake during March, April, and May, drinking went on around me. Don't get me wrong. We were not boozing it up. Liquor, however, played a role in our camaraderie. A member of the press staff recently told me of her experiences in the last months of the campaign. She felt drinking was tacitly encouraged. Nothing was ever said, still, she detected a subtle undercurrent—if you drank, you were part of the in group. I wasn't aware of this atmosphere at the time. Looking back, I think she might have been correct. Drinkers can bring pressure to bear on others to join with them. I must have been giving signals. I know we all eagerly anticipated that cocktail hour in the plane.

In those last three months, members of my staff would leave the bottle of Stolichnaya in my hotel suite, usually in an adjoining room. At night, I waited for everyone to leave or to be occupied elsewhere. Then I'd sneak into the room, grab that bottle, and take it into my bedroom. I'd pour myself a shot and return the bottle to its original spot. I left a trail of three-quarters-full vodka bottles. My behavior was a perfect example of an alcoholic losing control of her drinking. Impaired control is one of the primary symptoms of alcoholism. Basically, my schedule determined my dosage. I could not chuga-lug as I wanted because I had places to go and appointments to keep. The bottle was made available by my friends, my enablers. They had no idea I had a problem.

Late in the campaign, I began to think about what I was doing, how drawn I was to the vodka, how necessary it was for me to have a drink. I tried to dismiss the thoughts, but they would not completely vanish. For many years I had lived with the guilt of taking diet pills; now I had this small voice inside warning me about the drinking. Small, indeed; I reduced the sound to a feeble squeak.

During September and October, I was very down. The polls were not in our favor; everything seemed to be tinged with melancholy. While in St. Louis, I talked to a friend for hours. He saw my despondency and was concerned enough to telephone Bonnie. He told her he thought I was in very bad shape and headed for a real depression. In truth, I already was suffering from depression. Bonnie was wonderful all during those trying times. Officially, she was my executive assistant and took care of all the campaign details. Beyond that, she was a good and true friend and tried her best to look after me. Before she could take any action to help me, I managed to pull myself together. Activity kept me on the go. I could run away from my thoughts, from my feelings, and from my fears. And so I did, until November 8, 1988. On that day I ran right into the brick wall of defeat.

The day after the election, on November 9, my staff had a party for everyone who had worked for me during the campaign. The day after the party, on November 10, I became an episodic, binge drinker. An alcoholic can contain himself for only so long. When a crisis hits, the restraints snap.

I made furtive stabs at getting back to work. I'd go to

the State House and putter around unenthusiastically. Most of the time, I left the office early and returned home. After a while, I didn't bother to appear at my office. I confined myself to Perry Street. My procedures were typical of alcoholics. According to a recent CBS news program, 8 percent of problem drinkers never seek help. My behavior was also quite typical of what happens to alcoholics of my sex. All over the country there are women who closet themselves at home and drink without anyone knowing. We are the best deceivers in the world. We have to be. While all alcoholics are disparaged, women are particularly stigmatized. Yes, public awareness has been heightened and we've come a long way in the past few decades, still, there's a long way to go. The numbers of women in treatment programs does not reflect their numbers in society. A much larger group of alcoholic women is out there and they're not seeking help. I can empathize with the dilemma because I went through the same hell right in my own home.

On a typical day on Perry Street I would rise, wait till my husband left, and, by nine o'clock in the morning, cancel all my appointments. I would go to the liquor cabinet in the dining room, bring the bottle into the kitchen, measure out three or four ounces of straight spirits, and drink it down. Then I'd take a newspaper or magazine, go upstairs, shut the blinds, unplug the phone, and read till I passed out—a process that usually took no more than ten minutes. Two and a half hours later, I would wake up and repeat the process. I did it all day long. If I had an evening engagement, I'd stop drinking around 2:30 in the afternoon.

In the early- and mid-stages of hitting bottom, I would drink for two or three days straight and then pull myself together for the next few days. During those periods of sobriety I'd tackle projects like the book Bob Barnett was attempting to sell. I never drank when I was traveling; whether I was on the road with Michael or going to New York City on business, I didn't touch a drop. The heart of my drinking was in my own house.

To make matters more complicated, we were facing a personal crisis at home. On August 16, 1987, my son John married a wonderful young woman named Lisa Thurmond, and she and John worked together on the campaign. In the middle of September 1988, complications midway through her pregnancy forced her to leave the campaign. Lisa was ordered to bed for four months. She and John moved into Perry Street and lived with Michael and me. Because she was around the house all the time, Lisa became the first to be suspicious of me. She relayed her fears to John.

On December 15, Michael and I took a trip to Florida. The afternoon before we left, I had a big drinking episode. I sobered up before Michael got home, but not enough to get things ready. I wandered around the bedroom dejectedly, looking at the clothes in the closets and drawers and at the empty suitcases on the bed. I could not make a move. I was like the character Mary Tyrone in Eugene O'Neill's play *Long Day's Journey into Night*, wandering around addicted, stupefied, and miserable.

"There's no way I can pack," I said to my husband.

"You've got to," he answered, "Come on, I'll help."

I wouldn't let him. We were scheduled to leave at 8:00 the next morning and I didn't begin packing till 1:00 A.M. Somehow, I got everything together. I must have gone into automatic packing pilot, a condition left over from all the campaign trips.

I had an awful hangover the next day and my headache didn't improve much over the next five days.

We had vacationed often with Stratton (Tyke) and Vivian Sterghos—he is Michael's cousin and a successful doctor in Ft. Lauderdale. In the past we had always enjoyed visiting with them, but this time the Florida trip was grim. During our stay, I drank a little wine and, on one occasion, I snuck a bit of vodka. Michael and I took long walks. Neither of us could work up much enthusiasm. I was so very low and Michael was only beginning to come out of his postelection dejection. From Florida we flew to San Francisco where Michael was being honored.

I remember I went through the motions of Christmas shopping. It was like pulling teeth. We celebrated Thanksgiving and Christmas at Perry Street. Usually, we go to my sister's for the holidays because she and Al have such a large family. That year, I invited everyone to Perry Street as a kind of defense mechanism. The preparation and activity would keep me busy; I wouldn't be able to think. Also, I *wanted* to be active. I couldn't bear the empty days. My public platform had collapsed under me and I desperately needed a new rostrum. In late December, I invited my neighbors Todd and Rose Jick and Rose's mother, Dorothy Zolteck, for dinner. Dorothy was visiting from Canada. She's a Holocaust survivor and a marvelous woman. They're all wonderful people, and I enjoyed very much the Jicks' darling daughter Zoe. It didn't matter. I dragged myself through the meal, wished everyone a good night, and, after they left, went into the kitchen to clean up. As part of the cleanup, I systematically drank the remaining wine out of every single glass. In every way, my life had reached the dregs.

The next day, December 28, I stayed in bed. I got up only to get to the liquor. By year's end, I had given in to alcohol. I didn't stop in the afternoon anymore, I couldn't. I drank anything I could get my hands on. I never had to go out the front door to satisfy my thirst; everything I needed was on the premises. As governor and first lady of the state, we entertained periodically and kept a large supply of liquors and wines. The stuff had been in the house for ages and no one ever checked it. Our closet could have kept me going for at least three months. In little more than a couple of weeks, my life assumed its alarming pattern.

In the initial stages, I had taken precautions. I'd wait for Michael to leave in the morning, make sure John and Lisa were in their room, and then go for the bottle. Vodka was my drink of choice but I had no true allegiance. When the vodka ran out, I switched to gin. And when the gin disappeared, I turned to scotch, then to bourbon, always without skipping a beat. If anyone had told me six months before that I would be swallowing scotch and bourbon, I'd have laughed in his or her face. I had never tasted them until I ran out of vodka and gin, and, in fact, I didn't particularly like the taste. It didn't matter what I was drinking as long as I got the desired effect—oblivion. I drank straight, too, no water, no ice. When the vodka, gin, scotch, and bourbon were gone, I drank brandy. I was gone.

I knew the liquors gave off strong aromas. They say vodka has no odor. That's a myth. To cover up the stench, I took baths all the time, brushed my teeth, and ate foods I thought disguised the odor. In my sophomore year at Penn State, the housemother of my sorority was the president of the local Women's Christian Temperance Union. When we came in at night she'd be standing at the door. Most of us would have had a beer and we didn't want her to smell it on our breath. One of the sorority sisters claimed that peanut butter absorbed the liquor, so she carried a jar and we'd scoop a few table- spoons into our mouths before signing in. The sign-in room smelled like the Skippy factory and the house- mother never said a word. Remembering this, for a while I tried peanut butter on Perry Street. Then I began to use antiseptic "chasers" and flooded my mouth with mint-flavored breath enhancers. Scarlet O'Hara covered up her drinking by swigging cologne; Rhett But- ler caught on right away. It didn't take long for Michael Dukakis to get my number, either. Michael told me that, when he got into bed at night, although he was over- whelmed by the tangy fragrance of toothpaste and mouthwash, he also detected the scotch and bourbon underneath.

I wasn't fooling anyone, anymore. By Christmas, the entire family realized what I was doing. Michael came home and found me in the bed, out cold. He had difficulty waking me. I awoke and blamed my condition on a mi- graine. It was a vicious circle. I was in denial, and my family kept hoping I'd stop. They clung to the belief that my drinking was a temporary, not a permanent, condi- tion. We were all in complete denial. This is not an un- usual circumstance. Many people deal with alcoholics by avoiding the issue, hoping it will pass.

Then came the appalling incident when John found me unconscious in my room, lying in my own vomit. Michael rushed home, not certain if he'd discover me dead or alive. I was out cold. That's when he washed and cleaned me. Hours later, when I revived, I swore I'd never have another drink. I meant it, too! The next day, I kept my promise; I was so sick it was easy. The day after, I felt better. I forgot how bad it had been and I forgot my promise and began to drink again, assuring myself that *this* time it would be different. It wasn't. The progression was typical; my disease had beaten me again.

Michael and the children began a "liquor watch." Whoever was in the house was supposed to keep a vigilant eye on me. They thought they could discourage me simply by catching me in the act. It doesn't work that way. I was confronted, and couldn't stop. In January 1989, I started having blackouts and couldn't remember how much I had drunk. It didn't prevent me from continuing my raids on the liquor cabinet.

One morning I slunk past the kitchen where John was sitting on guard duty, went into the dining room, and opened the liquor cabinet. The door squeaked loudly. I was furious that I hadn't oiled it. John appeared at the door. He stood there with his hands on his hips.

"What are you looking at?" I demanded.

"Why are doing this, Mother?" asked my son.

"Because I can't help it!" I answered honestly. I grabbed a bottle from the cabinet, brushed past him defiantly, and went into the kitchen.

Statistics show alcoholism progresses much faster with women. Men produce a stomach enzyme that allows them to metabolize alcohol more quickly. Within weeks, I absolutely had to have a drink every two or three hours. Though many believed it was the campaign that started me drinking, the campaign actually had had a restraining influence. During that period I had been high on activity. The campaign was wonderful in almost every way. There were ups and downs as there are in any kind of roller-coaster experience, but the presidential race was a very positive undertaking. Then it was over. I began drinking when I was faced with a gaping emptiness I could not endure.

Alcoholism is one of the loneliest diseases in the

world. You build up all kinds of defenses and feed off them. You find yourself going deeper and deeper into denial about the disease and the effect it's having on you and on your family and friends. You cut yourself off so your defenses can function. Denial and isolation become your companions, your drinking buddies. They're bad company.

In one sense, I was a "fortunate" drinker. The disease progressed so rapidly I hit bottom relatively quickly. Perhaps my addiction to pills had something to do with the accelerated pace. I have met many recovering alcoholics who had long histories of alcoholic drinking with all the pain and suffering and physical effects that go with it. Some have gone on for twenty-five years and more. I confess, I still find it difficult to understand how people can go through years and years of alcoholic drinking. I could not have gone on that way for any length of time. I would have died.

I had shared my awful secret with Bonnie Shershow and Sandy Bakalar right before Christmas. I told them I was an alcoholic. They have since told me they didn't believe me at the time. I had talked about chemical abuse enough during the campaign to understand what was happening. As humiliation, self-pity, and self-hatred overcame me, I drank more. I became very withdrawn and began to isolate myself for days on end. Under normal conditions, I spoke to my father and my sister every day. Now I stopped calling. I wouldn't talk to my friends. I wouldn't answer the phone. I unplugged it.

In early January, Michael spoke at a press conference at a facility for people arrested for drunk driving. I managed to attend. I had been through several days of serious drinking and was churning with conflict. I couldn't get over the irony of the fact that here was the governor's wife at a press conference on alcoholism, when she was nothing more than a drunk herself.

I saw Dave Mulligan, then head of alcoholic services for the state, standing in the room. Though I didn't know Dave well, my brother-in-law spoke highly of him. Almost without thinking, I went over to Dave and said, "I need to talk to you." My voice choked and tears came to my eyes.

"Where do you want to talk?" he answered.

I asked him to come back to my house. After the conference we went to Perry Street and sat in the living room. I told him what I was doing, and, for the first time, I cried. I'm sure he must have been shocked at hearing the sordid story of the governor's wife. He tried to be helpful and put me in touch with a woman who runs a recovery program. She came to counsel me several times and was terrific, but it wasn't enough. I couldn't handle my situation on a one-to-one basis in my living room. The visits petered out. Nevertheless, by admitting I had a problem, by seeking help, I had taken the first step. I wanted to get well.

Originally, my daughter-in-law, Lisa, was scheduled for a cesarean section on January 5. On January 4, she went to her doctor for a final checkup. The examination revealed happy news. Her placenta previa had reversed itself; the baby could be delivered naturally. The doctor told her she could get out of bed. The turn of events happened in a matter of hours and made a big impression on me. I was all set to be a grandmother, come January 5. Now I had to wait. You really can't plan ahead because you don't know what twists and turns can occur. Now Lisa was scheduled to deliver on February 1.

A few days before this date, I decided to enter a recovery program. On January 29, my husband, sister, and brother-in-law sat with me in my bedroom at Perry Street. The topic of discussion was my sorry state. This was not a classic intervention when loved ones, and often a professional, confront the alcoholic. Later, I met people in recovery who had gone through bona fide interventions. Some were furious and fumed for days. Eventually, they got over their anger and concentrated on getting better. Knowing loved ones care enough to intervene means something. In my case, I didn't need full-scale intervention; I already wanted to get help, I was ready to go. I needed my family to force the issue, not to bring it up. And they did give me the necessary boost.

What had held me back more than anything, I think, was my abject shame at confessing to my alcoholism after a long period of touting my recovery. I felt like a complete failure. Despite my fears of public humiliation, I couldn't avoid taking action. Anyway, my family would not let me off the hook. Indeed, we were all in this together.

I remember Al saying, "Alcoholism is a family disease."

Michael reacted violently: "I don't care what kind of disease it is, my wife needs help."

Michael has since learned Al was right. When my loved ones met with me, I planned to reenter Hazelden. Then I thought it over. I decided I preferred to go some place closer to home. Al had worked at Edgehill Newport while getting his M.S.W. from Simmons College in Boston. He felt it was the place for me.

Then we ran up against an obstacle in deciding my entry date. My family wanted me to go immediately.

"No way," I adamantly told them, "I'm waiting for my grandchild to be born."

They tried to convince me otherwise, but I wouldn't budge. It was Sunday; the baby would be induced on Wednesday. After that, I'd go to Edgehill Newport. My family argued vehemently because they were afraid I'd back down. I was determined to hang on. I told them I would not drink anymore. No more stealthy trips to the liquor closet. Finally, I was allowed to do it my way. Late that afternoon, I began to shake. My body was trembling uncontrollably. Michael was frantic and asked Al what to do. Al said I needed a little liquor to get through it. He gave me two ounces of brandy. Poor Michael nearly collapsed watching me gulp the brandy down. It killed him to see me drinking even though he knew it was necessary.

We called the doctor. He came and prescribed Librium. Jinny took time off from school and stayed with me every minute until Michael got home. She stayed with me for five days. My dear, faithful sister played the role of watchdog brilliantly; she never let me out of her sight. I took naps with her on the bed beside me.

January 30, 1988, was my first sober day. On February 1, Alexandra Jane Dukakis was born. Four days later, her grandmother, Katharine Dickson Dukakis, entered Edgehill Newport. I was a totally ashamed and thoroughly terrified woman. Michael, Jinny, and Al drove down with me and stayed until the admitting process was over.

Michael kissed me good-bye, then asked, "Is there anything you want?"

"Yes," I answered in a voice so meek I didn't recognize it as my own, "I think I don't want you to go."

THIRTEEN

In 1982, at Hazelden, I had concentrated on the problem at hand—addiction to diet pills. In 1989, at Edgehill Newport, I had to address my alcoholism. I could not hold myself aloof thinking I had only one problem; as my actions had shown, dependencies can be changed or exchanged. I went from diet pills to alcohol. I was no trailblazer; the switch from other drugs to alcohol is an old story for the chemically dependent. So is the switch from alcohol to other drugs. Physically, I had no idea how bad off I was until I got to Edgehill Newport. The examining physician's report revealed a bombshell. My liver was beginning to show signs of damage. I couldn't believe it. I had been drinking alcoholically for barely three months; I didn't think that was long enough for anything to happen. I was further shocked to learn that, had I continued any longer, the damage would have become irreversible. I would have developed cirrhosis of the liver. (Fortunately, the doctor did say my liver would get almost 100 percent better during my stay.)

Again, an old story for alcoholics. Progressive destruction and regeneration of cells and increased connective tissue formation induced by excessive drinking results in liver failure and death. When the doctor said the words, I was dumbfounded. I wanted to cry out in defense, "You're crazy. Jewish women don't get cirrhosis of the liver!" The doctor was far from crazy. I learned, among other things, the myth about Jews not being drinkers is no longer valid. Jews really have assimilated and so have their drinking habits. That's only one shattered illusion; much of our thinking about alcoholism has changed. For one thing, we are more aware of the genetic influence. Programs have been established to help the children of alcoholics who, statistics show, have a far greater potential for alcoholism. I also discovered there is no prototype of an alcoholic. The skid row bum sitting in the gutter drinking out of a brown paper bag is no more an alcoholic than the banker with a flask nestled in the glove compartment of his Mercedes. It is an equal opportunity disease.

When I entered Edgehill Newport, the induction procedure was similar to Hazelden's. All my bags and clothes were checked for alcohol and/or drugs. They took away my breath spray (alcohol), my razor (suicide), and, to check the wiring, all electrical gear like my hair dryer and radio. I had brought my thyroid and hormone pills, and, once again, my medication was taken and then re-given to me. I was put on "Close Observation," the name for the detox unit. C.O. is the umbrella unit for all new arrivals. I didn't have to be detoxified, I'd been through it at home as had several others in the group.

I entered on a Sunday night and spent some time in the living room and the rest in my own room. While I was downstairs, I heard someone say, "Kitty?" I turned and looked. A man was standing there. He looked familiar. "How do I know you?" I asked. It turned out I knew him quite well—I just didn't recognize him. He was not in my unit but I would see him in exercise class, on walks, and in the cafeteria. If I couldn't measure my own stay on a personal level, I was able to watch the change in this friend. That first morning, he was almost unrecognizable. Slowly, he began to improve, physically and mentally, and by the time we left, he looked great.

Monday night I was in my unit sitting with my confreres in the common room. There were about fourteen of us in C.O. We began as strangers, but then, little by little, we began to bond. The link was augmented and forged even stronger when we were assigned to our units. There are six units of up to twenty-five people at Edgehill. We were a disparate group in terms of background, religion, race, and education. One man was incapable of saying a sentence without using four-letter expletives. I remember thinking, "How am I going to have anything in common with these people?" I soon realized I had something very powerful in common with them—we were all alcoholics, drug addicts, or both.

I was very, very nervous that Monday. Earlier in the day, Michael had called a press conference and made the announcement about me. I heard it had gone well; still, I was a bit shaky. I was sitting and talking to the others when a man reeled into the room. The new entry was absolutely looped. He put out his cigarette on the rug and proceeded to talk garbled nonsense in my direction. All of a sudden I was surrounded by the others. He tried to get to me but couldn't break through them. I realized they had formed a circle to protect me. I was touched.

Five days later I was standing in line at the cafeteria when the fellow who made the scene took a place behind me. I didn't think he'd remember anything.

He tapped me on the shoulder and said softly, "Kitty, I'm sorry."

I turned and said, "What are sorry about?"

"I scared you when I came in. I apologize."

I couldn't get over the change in the man. He had looked and acted so awful, and now he seemed so much better—one of many cocaine addicts and alcoholics who stopped using and started getting better. Wasted by cocaine when he entered, by the end of the month, he filled out and looked normal.

It's funny how you mark the transformations in others just as they note yours. Several of my C.O. compatriots advised me I was a wreck when I arrived. Let's put it this way, nobody goes into recovery looking and feeling his or her best. Usually, it's the other end of the scale. Some people are drunk when they enter. I was sober; still, I wouldn't have won any Mrs. America contests. My appearance was a reflection of the way I felt. I had spent nearly two years putting my best foot forward and part of the deal meant looking my best from head to toe. In the months since then, I had lost interest in grooming. I'd gotten so used to having my hair done and my makeup put on, I didn't think I could do it on my own. I honestly thought I'd never look decent again.

I was very fragile. What little confidence I had was nearly shattered by one of the men on my unit. A week or so after my arrival, this man came across a picture of me in an old issue of *Life* magazine. He didn't know the magazine was eight months old because he couldn't read.

"Look," he shouted, "here's you." He was all excited because he thought he was showing me something I hadn't seen. He leafed through the pictures and said, "Boy, you looked really good here. Your hair looked terrific."

Well, I went nuts. I just blew up. I had only just started to feel as though I could do things myself and to look okay, and he opened up the old wound and filled it with salt. I was upset and talked to my counselor. In the end, I spoke to the man himself.

"You know you really hurt my feelings," I said in a therapy session.

"How, what did I do?" he asked.

I proceeded to explain how he'd attacked a very vulnerable side of me. He was very apologetic. He had no idea how strongly I was affected. It was a good lesson for me. I didn't have to crumble before every innocuous remark.

One of the most remarkable aspects of any recovery program is hearing other people's stories and, of course, identifying. The variety of tales reaches Scheherazadian proportions. I thought I had problems. I thought I was deceitful about my drinking. I learned to what extent people go to hide the truth. One woman always carried a pocketbook big enough to hide a fifth bottle. She'd walk along and the bottle would go *glugga-glugga-glugga*. She was afraid the noise would attract attention, so to drown the sound, she bought about fifty keys and put them on a ring. As she walked, the sound of the jangling keys overwhelmed the sloshing liquid. One man revealed his elaborate scheme of deception. He kept a bottle of antifreeze in his garage—except it wasn't antifreeze. He dumped the original contents and filled the container with vodka. To keep things looking kosher, he added blue coloring. Another man went an automotive step further. He kept vodka in his car by pouring it in the windshield spray container. "I spent a lot of time with my head under the hood," he laughed.

I couldn't believe what I was hearing. My furtive forays to the liquor cabinet were simplistic compared to the master plans unfolded by my peers. In truth, you don't have to have elaborate tales of deception to be an alcoholic. Some of the simplest lies are the most effective—and the most deadly. Whatever the tales, it's a relief after weeks and months of imposed solitude to be able to tell the truth, the whole truth, and nothing but the truth. It's necessary.

You have to bring a willingness to the program, a willingness to share and to work. And it is work. In essence, you've got to voluntarily give yourself over, humble yourself. I had trouble with certain aspects, some of which had more to do with my religious beliefs than my willingness. The program asks participants to get on their knees. As a Jew, I found this action difficult. I spoke to the head counselor of my unit and told him my feelings. "Look," I said, "I go to Catholic churches all the time, but I don't kneel because I'm not a Catholic. I'm a Jew, and spiritually I can't see getting down on my knees before God."

The counselor reasoned with me. "You have to focus on being an *alcoholic*," he advised, "and that means you need the help of a higher power whether you want to call it God or not. Think about getting on your knees as a period of time to reflect rather than worship." What he said made sense, but I still wasn't exactly comfortable with the notion or the process. However, I placed my need for sobriety ahead of my reluctance to kneel.

Sophisticated and educated members of the program have a tendency to put down whatever they deem naive. We try to intellectualize rather than feel. It doesn't work. You have to feel things in the gut, not the brain. It's easy to take potshots because everything is kept as uncomplicated as possible and the simplicity is subject to much scoffing. The program abounds in slogans and acronyms; at first, I couldn't take them. "HALT" was a word I relearned. It stands for *H*ungry, *A*ngry, *L*onely, and *T*ired. Any one of those conditions can provide an impetus to drink. I thought it was dumb, but I went along with it. "KISS" is another popular acronym. It means *K*eep *I*t *S*imple, *S*tupid. Eventually, I could respond to the words. I stopped wasting valuable time deriding the slogans and used them. They're easy to remember and they pack a wallop. I grew to respect KISS. I'm even trying to apply its principles to this book! I took the chip off my shoulder at Edgehill Newport, and wholeheartedly embraced the program. I learned so much, it's tempting to just run down a list! I know my own attitude helped.

Every morning we were awakened at 6:40 by the person assigned to the job of rapping on our doors—the town crier. The last person to hold that position complained his knuckles hurt from all the tapping, so he got a pan from the kitchen and used it to bang on the doors. You could hear the noise all the way down the hall. I used to rise at 6:15 and throw my door open before the pan hit it. I'd shower, get into my leotards, tights, and sweats, and head over to the gym. There was an early-morning exercise class for cocaine addicts—atrophy is one of the side effects of snorting cocaine and the recovering addict needs lots of physical activity. I joined the class because I wanted the exercise.

At Edgehill Newport, I noticed a difference between alcoholics and cocaine addicts. There were more "triggers" for the latter. Many things would remind them of the stuff they were trying to forget. One day a group of us were sitting in the kitchen. A woman, a former cocaine addict, was fooling around. She poured some salt on the table and made a line. There were two other addicts sitting there, and, at the sight of the narrow, white path, they turned pale, got up, and left. We were shown a film on drugs. I watched the addicts and they were going crazy. I could look at bottles of alcohol and it made no difference to me. I had the feeling the drug addicts had a harder time with visual reminders.

There was a difference, but there were many similarities. An addict is an addict is an addict. Whether it's alcohol or a pill, you share many character defects. You hide things. You're dishonest with yourself and with others. You vacillate between pomposity and grandiosity on one end of the scale and plunge to low self-esteem and self-loathing on the other. The object of the addiction may be interchangeable, the results are the same—poisonous.

The early-morning exercise class, a wonderful way to wake up, lasted for forty minutes. There were different degrees of difficulty to the classes; I felt good afterwards no matter how easy or hard it had been. I needed a strong physical workout and Edgehill Newport brought me back. When the class ended, I'd return to my unit and head directly for a hearty breakfast. At 8:30, we each performed a therapeutic task. My job was room inspection. My official title was "Bed Ripper." My orders read, "You are responsible for making room and bed checks. Please make sure that each patient is making his bed daily and rooms are kept orderly. Rip beds of patients who have not made their beds by 8:45 A.M. On Sundays, the patients have until 12 noon to make their beds and clean up their rooms." Bed ripper, or stripper, as we used to call it, I knew my job.

At nine o'clock we'd have peer evaluation, with one of us in the group chosen as the subject of discussion. The night before, we had been given a slip of paper with twenty-five character defects listed, and were instructed to check off those that applied. We would assemble and the person being evaluated would sit in the center of the room. The rest of us would form a circle around him/her. The senior member of the group would open the meeting by reading the rules about what was expected. We'd each introduce ourselves. I could say with full conviction, "I'm Kitty, I'm an alcoholic and a drug addict." Following the introductions, we'd go around the circle and tell what we'd checked off. I won't go into the evaluations my peers received, but I will say that when my turn came, I scored highest on the trait, "Always wants to be right." The meeting lasted till ten and then we'd close with the serenity prayer. "God grant me the serenity to accept the things I cannot change, the courage to change the things I can, and the wisdom to know the difference."

From ten to eleven, a meeting of Alcoholics Anonymous was held in the auditorium and all the patients were required to attend. After that we'd have a variety of appointments, with our counselor or recreation therapist or psychiatrist. That would last till 11:30 or 11:45 and then we'd go to lunch.

After lunch there was a free period. Often, I'd take a walk. I was known as the speed demon because I moved so fast the others had to run to keep up with me. I found out later, several people in C.O. sat around waiting for the walking group just to catch sight of this funny woman in her red wool hat go whizzing by.

At 1:30 we would have small group meetings. The large group was divided into smaller therapy groups. The counselor-in-chief would read the rules, give the date and time, and then we'd introduce ourselves. The counselor would tell us, this is your meeting to deal with what you want to talk about. Hands would go up and people would raise different issues. About the second week, my counselor gave me what is called a "greeting." Every time I introduced myself in group therapy I had to read this greeting, which said in essence, "Do I know my worth and am I willing to let people see the real Kitty?" The counselor wisely assessed how much politics had influenced my interaction with others. I had learned to tell people what I wanted them to hear and I didn't go any further. I didn't tell them what I was really experiencing—that I felt lousy or that I was crying inside or that I didn't believe I was a worthwhile human being. I wanted people to like me, so I said what they wanted to hear. I was always up. Two and a half weeks passed before I could admit in the therapy sessions that I felt uncomfortable, or sad, or vulnerable.

The 1:30 session ended around 3:15. I'd rush to my room, get into my leotard and tights, and join an aerobics class. At four, I'd return to my unit. Sometimes I'd take another walk, or I might have an appointment with my counselor or some homework to do. We were given assignments all the time. Often we'd interview our peers. Gradually, I began to add an occasional nap. When I took my first nap at Edgehill Newport, I couldn't believe I'd actually fallen asleep naturally. I was so used to drinking myself to sleep during the day. A lot of people in recovery want to sleep all the time. I was lucky. I could get by on five or six hours a night. However, I found I needed a nap in the afternoon. This has carried over. For the first time in my life, I'm able to take rests without feeling I should be doing something else.

Dinner was served at 4:45. Guess who often was first in line? We'd finish around 5:30 and I'd go back to my room, sometimes alone and other times with a friend. I'd stand at the window and watch the sunset. I loved to see the sky streak with color and then fade into blue-black. It was beautiful and comforting. By the second week, I was noticing my surroundings with renewed interest. I could see the buds on the trees. I realized how alcohol had interfered with my appreciation of the everyday world. I had fallen away from all the good things and been mired in those loathsome months of drinking. A short time ago, from sunrise to sunset, I hated the days. Now I was sorry to see them end.

At 7:00, we'd have a film and a lecture in the auditorium, or perhaps a meeting. Then at 8:00 we'd return to the unit and be free till 9:00. At that hour, someone told his or her story. You were called upon a week after being on the unit. (I remember those sessions well. Many of the stories moved me to tears, and I had shed very few tears since the election.) That session lasted anywhere from a half hour to an hour. Afterwards, you might have an assignment and call together four to ten people to talk about a particular problem. We talked a lot. We ate, too. I had tons of celery and carrot sticks. Sometimes we played games like Trivial Pursuit or Pictionary: We laughed a lot. To laugh without alcohol was great. Peer evaluations, homework, special assignments, or reading would keep you occupied until 11:30 or 12:00; then you wrote down your significant events of the day. I'll share a few entries:

2/7/89: Having opportunity to move out of CO and particularly walking outside and exercising in the gym! Those were my significant events for the day. Grateful to be here and that the publicity from the press was positive. Pleased at being welcomed warmly and lovingly. I am too tired to write beyond this and think that bed rest and a good night's sleep is as important as writing more.

2/10/89: Listening to others has been somewhat helpful. I feel stronger physically because of activity and regular eating. Tonight I'm beginning to understand that it's ok to take time off to laugh and have good-better feelings about me . . . I also am beginning to think more clearly about not having to be productive every minute. Taking time not to reflect feels acceptable.

On February 15 I discussed the election for the first time: "It felt like the beginning of some real work and lifting the huge feelings of grief I'd been carrying around." My counselor wrote on the bottom of the sheet, "Bravo Kitty, keep sharing. You've waited a long time to begin the journey."

I've saved my entries because they are the mirror of my stay. I can measure my own growth. To have the word "significant" applied to my days was uplifting in itself.

On Saturdays, we were allowed to have family visitors. Michael came down with Kara, Jinny and Al, and Dad. I talked a lot with my father. Dad had been rocked by my alcoholism. For some reason, he wanted me to tell him exactly what I drank. I went down the list from vodka to brandy. Each time I brought up a different alcohol, he'd say, "No, no," and shake his head.

When I finished, Dad burst out, "That does it! I'm getting rid of all the alcohol in the house."

"Dad," I said, "there's no need to do that; you don't have a problem."

"It's a terrible thing. I'm not going to keep any alcohol," he reiterated.

I said, "Dad, that's ridiculous. Suppose people drop in and you want to have a drink with them?"

"No," said my father, "I don't need it, I don't want it."

My father was attempting to shut the barn door after the horse ran out. Actually, the horse hadn't even been in his barn! Nevertheless, he wanted to take on some of the onus. His reactions continued to be interesting.

After I came home, Dad, Jinny, and I went to a meeting and then had dinner at a restaurant.

Driving back from the meal, Dad announced jovially, "It's such a treat not to have a drink!"

I laughed so hard. Still, my laughter was bittersweet. The fact remains, my family and friends enabled me to drink by not recognizing my disease. From the time I left Hazelden, they kept assuring me I was not an alcoholic. I accepted their view because it was what I wanted to hear. I wanted "not" to be an alcoholic.

While at Edgehill Newport, I learned to put myself and my sobriety ahead of everything else—a complete reversal of my previous thinking. I always had directed most of my energies toward others. That's what you do when you are in public life. Sure, there's an element of ego gratification as well as altruism; you get lots of attention and those perks, too. Basically, though, you are interested in the welfare of others; anyway, you should be. In the recovery program, I had to make a psychological U-turn and direct my energies toward myself.

I had to deal with my resentments. Alcoholics build up and feed upon resentments. We collect them, hoard them, and regularly trot them before our egos as an excuse to drink. You start with one bitterness and begin piling on the others. Then, when this resentment monster of your own making stares you in the face, you drink to obliterate it.

At one of the early meetings, our group was asked, "How many of you have resentments?"

Everyone in the group raised a hand, except for an older man in the back of the room. One of the counselors looked at him, quizzically. "You mean to tell us you have no resentments?" he queried.

"That's right," answered the gentleman, "I have no resentments. They all died."

The truth is, while people die, resentments don't necessarily get buried with them. I had an army of resentments, and the commander-in-chief was my mother. Now it was time to shake off the burden. In the small group-therapy class, I was able, at last, to deal with my feelings about her. Mother was such a strong force in my life. Though I no longer spent an enormous amount of time blaming her for my problems, I did harbor a swollen measure of rancor. My counselor told me to write a letter about my mother to Kitty the young child and to express all my feelings, both as a child and as an addict.

I resisted for several days. Then I complied. I poured everything into the letter. Typically, when it was finished, I wasn't satisfied. I didn't think it was good enough. Whatever I thought, I read it during our session. Writing the letter was helpful; reading it to the group was cathartic, an emotional and painful experience. Once I finished, it was like a great weight had been removed from my back. The very act of publicly venting my feelings about Mother eased them.

I wasn't the only one to experience a dramatic purging. Others read letters penned to an important person, and each went through the same purification process.

Edgehill Newport helped us realize how self-defeating it is to keep looking back.

It can, however, be equally paralyzing to focus on the future. If you start adding up the days, months, and years, it can loom awfully large and awfully somber. That's why staying in the moment is so important.

A friend of mine called from California to offer his support. "You mean you can never have a drink again?" he said, mournfully.

I answered, "I can deal with that today, not tomorrow, or the day after tomorrow. But, nothing is terrible if it's one day at a time."

"Oh," answered my friend.

Oh, indeed. For people with my disease, a day at a time is a sound and comforting philosophy.

I finished the program at Edgehill Newport and returned home to my husband and my children. I attended my first fellowship meeting the day I came home; the woman who took me became my sponsor and I speak with her daily. My family helped in every way, as I knew they would. Michael, Dad, Jinny, and Al periodically went with me to meetings of my support group.

My children also joined me at various sessions. We discussed and shared our problems in ways we never had before. They are, after all, the adult children of an alcoholic parent, and they must bring that fact to bear on their own lives.

Michael joined me in a couples program and we met regularly. I came out and spoke in public on drug addictions, and related problems. I was eager to help others similarly afflicted. I was told by some I should wait. I told them I couldn't. I didn't want to wait. I knew I couldn't go at full steam, yet I felt I could at least get things moving.

One of my pleasant memories of this time occurred after I addressed a group of over one thousand high school students in Framingham, Massachusetts, on the subject of substance abuse. Offering myself as an example, I told them I started using when I was their age and continued for over a quarter century.

"I'm fifty-two, and I've begun to wake up," I advised my audience, "even someone as old as I can change." I finished my speech and was on the way out when a young man came running up behind me.

"Mrs. Dukakis! Mrs. Dukakis!" he cried.

I turned and said, "Yes?" I thought perhaps I had touched a responsive chord in a boy who needed help.

The young man stopped and smiled. He was out of breath. "I just wanted to say," he panted, "you look pretty good for fifty-two." He turned and ran off.

I have to say, I felt pretty good for fifty-two. For the first time in seven years, I looked forward to a fall and winter free of depression. Imagine, my first Thanksgiving, my first Christmas, my first Hanukkah without harboring those morose demons in my own dark mind. Just imagine.

IV

HERITAGES

FOURTEEN

A few months after leaving Edgehill Newport, I kept an old promise I made to myself. I wanted to clear up the mystery of my mother's birth, once and for all. I felt, somehow, if I could unlock the secret of her background, it might open new doors for me. I had talked about investigating Mother's origins with other members of the family, and at one point Mother herself had suggested I do some research. My father couldn't understand why I was so eager to carry out this search, and my sister never felt as compelled as I did to track down our ancestry. On one level, Jinny was curious, but not enough to actually go after the facts. Not I! I had to know.

After the presidential campaign, at a social gathering in New York City, I was introduced to Charles Galbraith, a genealogist. When I discovered Charles's specialty was Irish genealogy, I hired him to track down

Mother's antecedents. After months of painstaking effort, the question of her real parentage was resolved. Her natural father was George Washington Byrne. The Byrne family had immigrated to the United States from County Clare and George and his siblings were born in New York City. After his youthful liaison with my grandmother, Margaret Buxbaum, George Byrne married and settled down.

Charles Galbraith discovered that there were distant relatives in Ireland and closer ones nearer to home. George Byrne's three legitimate children, my mother's half-sisters and -brother, our aunts and uncle, lived no farther away than New York City.

One sunny summer morning, my sister, Jinny, and I went to Manhattan and were introduced to our aunts and uncle—Grace Kuchlin, Frances Molinaro, and Edward Byrne. Together we looked at family albums and saw pictures of their father—our grandfather.

Along with Jinny and a few friends, I went to Ireland to meet our distant cousins, Michael and Maura Byrne, and their children. We were taken on a tour of our "ancestral home" and visited the grave of our great-great-grandfather. All the Byrnes, the American and Irish branches, are wonderful people, kind, smart, and loving, and so willing to embrace Jinny and me. I'm sorry my mother didn't have the joy of knowing them. The mystery of Mother's natural parents was solved and a new era had opened for our family.

I had so hoped this revelation might help me to get myself firmly on course. Now I knew where I came from. However, the successful end to this search was not enough—an old and dread adversary was waiting for me.

When I returned home from Ireland in June 1989, I

felt really good. I thought the unearthing of my mother's, *my* past, was the missing piece of my life. Now that it was in place, I had a sense of accomplishment and fulfillment. "Know thyself," said the ancient Greeks, and I believed I did. I no longer recoiled from the recent past, either personal or political. I could look back on the presidential campaign and take justifiable pride in what was accomplished. Michael hadn't won the election, and that was sad, but how fortunate I was to have been so intimately involved with the workings of democracy. To this very day, in spite of all that has happened, I wouldn't give up the experience for anything. I'm not being Pollyanna, either; some incidents still bother me. Distance may soften the focus of memory, but it doesn't obscure completely.

No need to go into those events again, however. No. What happened to me was not a result of the campaign; my ills were there long before. The race for the presidency was a crisis situation and, as always, I dealt with the immediate tasks by squelching, to the best of my ability, my own pressing needs. I learned part of this lesson at Edgehill Newport, and when I left there I was to have nine months of sobriety. The big trouble started when I felt the first intimations of the inexorable grip of depression. I thought those moods were over, and the sense that they might be coming back was unbearable. I did not know if I could handle them.

Years earlier, after Hazelden, I began suffering periodic depressions. My diet pill habit had been erased, but it was only one aspect of my dependency. The depressions I began to experience were related to my being an alcoholic. There's no question about the correlation; that's the way we alcoholics deal with things. Deprived of alcohol, my body went into despair.

My depressions came in the fall, persisted through the winter, and went away as spring progressed. Oh, but while they were there it was agony.

Many have tried to describe depression. John Milton rightly characterized "loathed Melancholy" as being "of Cerberus and blackest Midnight born,/In Stygian cave forlorn,/'Mongst horrid shapes, and shrieks, and sights unholy."

People undergo varying degrees of depression. Some can function for a time, as I was able to do. Then the process of living turns grim. You close the shutters and retreat into yourself. Energy is low and there is a noticeable lack of affect. The future looks bleak and nothing is going right, nothing feels right. Sometimes there are specific causes, like a loss or an illness. My depressions, however, were nonspecific; I could never pinpoint what was causing them.

Nonspecific depressions are the toughest to treat. When my depressions started in the early eighties, I began seeing a psychiatrist, and have gone to him periodically, ever since. Because of the severity of my illness, I was put on an antidepressant called Norpramin, which I took with varying degrees of success. Under Norpramin, the depression was alleviated; there were, however, side effects, including constipation, urine retention, dry mouth, and slurred speech. I was taking Nopramin during the presidential race until the side effects really got in the way. I was on a fairly high dosage when I went to West Virginia and campaigned with Sharon Rockefeller. I was having difficulty getting my words out, and equal trouble urinating. I got some of the slurs out of my speech but could do little about my bladder problem. Indeed, I think the urine retention might have been part of the troubles with my spine, which eventually led to my neck surgery. The side effects were too gruesome for me to deal with. Under medical supervision, I gradually stopped taking the pills. By the end of the campaign I was off Norpramin . . . and turning to alcohol.

After the election, the gloom returned. I went to the psychiatrist and told him I was feeling very low. I did not tell him how much I was drinking. He prescribed another antidepressant, Prozac. I took the medication but was unable to stop the drinking. Thus, I was doing both. I knew it was dangerous to combine the medicine with the alcohol, and that I had to give up one of them. I chose to sacrifice the Prozac. What ensued were those shameful episodes on Perry Street and my eventual admission to Edgehill Newport, where I was put back on Prozac.

Prozac didn't give me the euphoric feelings I experienced with amphetamines. Instead, it provided a kind of balance. I just felt normal.

I continued taking the Prozac after I left Edgehill Newport. An antidepressant is a drug, and though I was under doctor's care, I never said anything publicly. I didn't feel the need to, I suppose, because I didn't want my depressions up for public scrutiny the way my drinking had been. I felt my personal problems had had enough exposure.

By May of 1989, I was doing so well, I decided there was no need to stay on medication. I spoke to my physician and he agreed to phase out the Prozac. Over the next three weeks or so, I gradually decreased my intake until I stopped completely. Though I was free of actually taking a drug, the effect of Prozac has a long afterlife, and I remained reasonably content throughout the summer months.

I faithfully attended meetings of the fellowship and much of my time was taken up with lecturing and traveling. The Irish experience was refreshing as well as revelatory. It was followed by a refugee mission to England and a brief sojourn to Greece. Everything was looking up.

Then, in mid-September, I began having negative thoughts about myself. I've come to learn that these feelings were the precursors of my illness.

Depression, for me, doesn't come all of a sudden. It's not a quick wipeout; rather, it's an imperceptible process. I felt it was under way and consulted with the therapist Michael and I had been seeing together. I told him I was low on self-esteem and energy, and, as usual, didn't know why. We discussed a possible alternative to medication.

Back in May, on a speaking trip to Denver, I was introduced to the director of the Colorado Outward Bound program. He invited me to come on a trip anytime. I had mentioned this to Michael and the therapist. Now seemed an opportune moment for me to use Outward Bound to pull myself out of the approaching depression.

I signed on for a seven-day women's invitational rafting trip on the Colorado River through the Cataract Canyon in Utah. Outward Bound was full of activities that tested self-reliance, and proved to be one of the most impressive experiences I have ever undergone. Like the presidential campaign, it was one of those situations where you really don't foresee what's going to happen until you're physically involved. God knows I was ready for a challenge, especially a physical one as opposed to all the emotional trials I'd been through.

Kara had been on a National Outdoors Leadership

Program in Wyoming for four weeks and we had lots of family discussions about my impending wilderness adventure. She went into great detail about what she had done, and questioned whether, at my age, I would be able to handle a similar situation. Naturally, that made me more determined to go.

I remember filling out the forms, wondering how many women would be as old as I. It turned out half of our group was over fifty. Medical forms had to be completed to show what kind of shape we were in. I was in good shape from walking, low-impact aerobics, and exercising, but I was concerned about my neck and back. My doctor told me not to worry, just not to overdo.

On September 21, I flew to Grand Junction, Colorado, took a walk in the afternoon, got to bed early, and the next morning was up at six and washed my hair very thoroughly, since this would be my last opportunity to shampoo for a week. Two friends from Boston had come with me, and we met the rest of our party as we boarded the bus—nineteen of us in all, plus six staff members. My friends and I were the only East Coasters; the rest were from Colorado, California, and Wyoming. The group represented a cross-section of middle-class American life and included whites, blacks, Hispanics, businesswomen, teachers, social workers, and so on. It was like a platoon out of one of those war movies I used to see when I was a kid, only we were all women. I was happy to be with females. In coed groups I think men often take the major share of the physical action simply because it's expected of them. When women are on their own, they have to do what the men do.

We arrived at our destination and sat around in a circle on the shore of the river. The unfamiliar scenery was especially breathtaking to the three New Englanders. The terra-cotta mountains, ridges, and mesas that are so much a part of the western landscape were a revelation to us.

The first day was easy. The sights along the river were unbelievably beautiful. The sun came in and out and all sorts of colors played around the huge canyons. That first night there was lots of talking. The next morning we were up at around six and had a cold breakfast. No coffee. That hurt.

The second day was more difficult, I think because I was feeling the effects of the first day. Still, the open sky was glorious, and if I had any tinge of doubt, I had only to look up and be renewed.

That day we did a little climbing—a simple walk up to the crest of a low mountain. Later we learned to belay, or climb with ropes. We sat at the top of the mountain and talked mostly about our fears, what concerned us about the trip. I said I was terrified of the "solo"—the eighteen-hour period each of us was to spend alone. I wasn't kidding, I really was concerned.

The second evening we made camp and gathered wood to cook the meals. I was eager to undo my gear, take a bath, and have dinner. We were told that the next day we would be using backpacks that weighed about twenty-five pounds. I explained to a staff member that I'd had neck surgery; she told me not to worry, that they would fix my pack to sit on my hips. And that's what happened: I went hip-packing.

The climb was difficult, but the belaying—which was done as a partnered activity, with one person climbing while the other held the rope—was even more difficult. Nonetheless, I gave it a try. My first attempt was unsuccessful, and I ended up being stuck partway up for about fifteen minutes. I went back down and said I'd try later.

There were only two other women left when the instructor asked if I wanted to try again. The group yelled encouragement as I struggled this second time. I kept falling and was soon covered with bruises and scratches —but I kept at it. After much perspiring and many tears and lots of tugging, I finally reached the top. I was exhausted.

In the end, all nineteen women, half of whom were over fifty, had made it. It was a tremendous feeling of accomplishment.

That night we were to begin our solo period. We had to leave our watches and all reading material behind, bringing with us only our journals in which to keep notes. The solo began with all of us walking away from the camp. One by one, a good distance apart, we dropped off at different sites. I was the second to be left off. The instructor pointed out a ledge and told me to sleep on it. The group left and I gingerly made my way to the rock.

Each of us had been given a piece of fruit as our only food. I had an apple . . . and I was starving. Intrepid frontierswoman that I am, I sat down and immediately ate the whole thing, knowing full well I wasn't going to have anything else to eat until the next afternoon. Oh well. Someone had given me a couple of mints, I'd make do with those. I rolled out the sleeping bag and placed my canteen and flashlight nearby. I wrote in my journal and watched the sunset as the sky became a riot of oranges and pinks and then was gone. Stars came out and glittered. I fell asleep.

I got up several times during the evening. I could hear small-animal noises around me, but I wasn't afraid. I'm sure I would not have been so calm if I had heard *big*-animal noises.

I lay there under the stars and contemplated recent events. I thought about where I had come in my sobriety and what the last year had meant. I thought about Michael and each of my children and my granddaughter and about the gifts I had been given and how much I had to be grateful for, and how fortunate I was to be having this experience. There are healthy and unhealthy ways of being alone. At that moment I was free of "wrinkled care," and able to enjoy my solitude. This experience was not pushing others away as I did when I was drinking. This was a sound isolation, a communion with nature and with the strongest elements of my own character.

The rest of the trip strengthened my positive feelings about myself. I recall so vividly the group's spirit, and how it helped each of us do things even when we weren't sure we could.

I returned home refreshed and invigorated, with a very positive outlook. Just the way I had felt after the trip to Ireland. I wanted that feeling to last. It didn't. It couldn't. It couldn't because the other feelings, the deep-set ones that refused to fade and disappear, came to the surface. And this time, I was more dejected, more lost. What could I do? Where could I find a lasting peace? Where?

FIFTEEN

When I set out on my speaking rounds in October 1989, I was still feeling the salutary effects of my Outward Bound venture. The farther I got into the lecture tour, however, the more my optimism faded. I could not sustain the good spirit.

I had scheduled a backbreaking number of engagements, ten in less than a month. I thought it would be like the campaign and that I would gather the necessary strength as I went on. The presidential campaign, however, is special; the cause is so overwhelming, you seem to draw from a bottomless well of adrenaline. Now I was in everyday circumstances and the accelerated tempo was out of place. What was I running for?

The idea of pacing myself never occurred to me; I wanted to cram in as many events as possible. With hindsight, I can see how mad it was to assume such an agenda.

In my lectures, I talked about substance abuse without touching on my own alcoholism or treatment. Some of the lectures were okay; still, as the weeks went by, I had less and less sense of accomplishment or pride. On the contrary, I was forcing myself to get through and deriving little satisfaction. My measuring stick of worth was warped. The lectures were received with warm and generous applause, yet even the clapping sounded hollow. Afterwards, people would come up to say how much my talks meant to them; I didn't believe them. While in fact I was doing well, in truth I felt like a fake.

I came back to Brookline and started slipping again. Oddly, I wasn't thinking so much about drinking. My thoughts were more centered on *not* wanting to drink. I still went to fellowship meetings but I was detaching. I went through the motions, but without any of the necessary emotions. I wasn't yet at the point of hurting, but I was withdrawing.

As a favor to my friend Joe Grandmaison, I spoke to his political science class at Boston University. I didn't want to go in the worst way, but I couldn't disappoint Joe. I sat in front of the class and answered questions, mostly about the role of the press in the campaign. I felt like a zombie.

My last speaking engagement for that period was on the first of November. The next round would come in February, March, and April. My pattern always had been to think about what I was going to do next, to go from one kind of excitement to another. Now I didn't care about the future lectures. They were far off. I began to draw away from the very things I needed to hold me up. I hid out on Perry Street.

The situation in the State House was sapping Michael's energy. Even so, he never ignored my predicament. He tried so hard to help. There are people in the program who say my husband enabled me too much because he didn't detach enough. His love for me coupled with his natural compassion caused him to accede to my demands.

Despite Michael's attempts to reach me, I couldn't give anything back. I needed love, yes, but a special variety called "tough love." I had no answer to "What's wrong, Kitty?" Anyway, it really wasn't Michael's issue, it was mine. I desperately wanted to be strong for him because I knew how much he was being hammered. Trapped by my own helplessness, I became worse and worse. I think this was the major problem for me, this inability to say, "I'm hurting, I can't handle it myself." I was in despair. I should have been in therapy, but I had stopped seeing my psychiatrist. Michael and I had continued to see a therapist together, only less frequently.

There was talk of my going back on the antidepressant, but I had a sense from a number of people in the program that it wasn't a good thing to go on medication. I've since learned, if you don't treat depression the way it needs to be treated (in my case with both therapy and medication), then everything shuts down. And that's what happened to me. I simply couldn't get beyond the doom surrounding me.

Monday, November 6, I was scheduled to work on the last details of my book. Pleading illness, I had canceled appointments with my writer the previous week. I had skipped a number of social engagements as well. Everyone was told I had the flu and I hid behind that excuse.

Although I hadn't had any liquor, I was experiencing the same pessimistic forebodings associated with drinking. These feelings encompassed everything, including my book. I liked the book, I wanted to finish it, yet I couldn't deal with it. I felt I had nothing to say. And so, I canceled Monday's appointment. Michael was very worried when he came home that evening. People, including my writer, had called him to express their concern. He tried to get me to talk about what was bothering me, and, again, I could say nothing.

After dinner, Michael was in the kitchen and I went upstairs to the bedroom. I lay there praying for sleep. It didn't come. I wanted something to put me to sleep. I needed something. I got out of bed and went into the bathroom. I opened the cabinet under the sink. I didn't expect to find anything because the house had been stripped of dangerous substances. It was just another futile gesture. Then I saw a bottle; the word "alcohol" leaped out. The word "rubbing" was right above it and I saw that, too. Alcohol, that was the answer. I knew rubbing alcohol was different from the drinking kind, but I only thought it was "different," not harmful. I just thought if I took some, just a little, I could sleep. I had no plan to kill myself; I only wanted to sleep for a while. I wanted relief from the pain of being awake.

I took the bottle from the shelf, unscrewed the top, put my lips on the mouth of the bottle, tilted my head back, and took a small gulp. I could see my actions mirrored in the looking glass over the sink. It was like watching a movie on television. Who was this woman and what was she doing?

The alcohol tasted horrible, horrible!—like fire going down my throat. I put the bottle down. Dear God, just a day ago I had received my nine-month sobriety chit at a meeting. Nine months and now this!

I didn't want to think about it anymore. I lifted the bottle and took another swallow. Fire on top of fire.

I put the cover back on and returned the bottle to the

cabinet. I was lucky; I had drunk only a small amount of the rubbing alcohol. I staggered back into the bedroom and groped my way into bed. That's all I remember; the oblivion I prized enough to break my sobriety for, enveloped me. Michael noticed my breathing seemed strange. He couldn't rouse me. The scene was hideously familiar.

He called our family physician, who came right over. The doctor unsuccessfully tried to shake me awake. They knew something was terribly wrong. They had no idea what I had done. The doctor called for help. Around nine that evening, an ambulance came and I was taken, unconscious, to the emergency room at Brigham and Women's Hospital.

The next thing I recall is someone saying, "Mrs. Dukakis . . . Mrs. Dukakis . . . Kitty! Did you take anything? What did you take?"

I didn't want to answer. "I don't know, I don't know," I mumbled and drifted off again.

The doctors figured I had taken something. From their observations, they concluded I hadn't ingested enough of whatever it was to make the situation a life-or-death matter, so instead of pumping my stomach, they gave me a charcoal solution. The charcoal goes right through your system and gives you the runs for days.

The doctors then urged Michael to return home, saying it would be a while before I woke and that he should get some rest. During the night, I was tested and traces of the rubbing alcohol were revealed. When Michael came back to the hospital early the next morning, I had revived and was being questioned by the doctors. They confronted me again and again, asking if I took rubbing alcohol.

I kept saying, "I don't remember. I don't remember." I remembered. I was so humiliated I could not talk about it, let alone admit it.

In the meantime, the media had gotten wind of my hospitalization and a circus atmosphere prevailed. Outside the hospital Michael was besieged by the television cameras and reporters.

On the second day, I was moved from intensive care to a private room. A security person was outside my door. Flowers began to arrive. I lay there in the bed desperately trying to think of something to do or say to get me off the hook. I really hadn't realized rubbing alcohol was lethal. (I wasn't the only one. Afterwards, Jinny and some of my friends told me they had no idea, either.) Nonetheless, the potential consequences of my action hit me more and more. I was so mortified, I could not confess.

The staff doctors and psychiatrists, and my therapist, kept at me. "What did you take, Kitty? Come on, tell us. It will be better for you. You took rubbing alcohol, didn't you? Come on, Kitty, admit it."

By Wednesday, I could hold back no longer. Michael, my sister, and the doctors were there and I began to talk. I didn't care what they thought of me, I just wanted to get it out. "Yes, I did it, I drank rubbing alcohol. I'm so ashamed. I took it because I wanted to go to sleep. I couldn't stand the pain."

The doctors wanted me to realize the seriousness of my action. "Did you know you could have killed yourself? Did you want to kill yourself?" asked one of them.

"No, absolutely no!" I replied truthfully. "I only wanted to sleep. I only wanted to wake up feeling better."

Brigham and Women's Hospital doesn't have a psychiatric unit as such and I stayed on a regular floor for a week. By then, the room was filled with flowers. I was surrounded by hundreds of beautiful blossoms and barely noticed them. Later, I was grateful, but then . . . all the flowers in the world couldn't have made a difference. I was too down on myself to observe anything. I couldn't think about anything, not even drinking. I just wanted to be left alone.

When you're a public person, however, and you do something like I did, the chances of being left alone are slim. At first Michael and I had decided not to say anything. Then, remembering that, for the most part, there are no secrets in this business, and rather than having the press ferret out the story, we decided to tell the truth. Michael released the facts and printed pandemonium took place. Thank heavens, I didn't see the headlines until much later.

I was confined to my room at the Brigham and someone was with me at all times. I found it annoying to have a constant presence but it was necessary. The hospital would have been liable if I did anything to myself.

My visitors were limited to members of the family. I remember telling Michael I didn't want my children to see me under such circumstances. Anyway, Kara was studying in Spain and Andrea lived out of state. Toward the end of my stay, John and Lisa came by for a quick hello.

On November 13, we celebrated my dad's eighty-first birthday in the room. Jinny brought a cake and Chinese food. Everyone was putting on a good front, but I could see through the cover-up. Dad was heartsick and in real pain. All of them were, and no one was more distressed than I.

I was the cause of the sorrow. I couldn't cry, though.

I didn't seem to have any tears in me. I can recall crying just a bit when I was alone with Michael, somewhere around the third or fourth night. I saw he had tears in his eyes and mine filled up, too, more for him than myself. I couldn't really let go though the shame, the disgrace of what I had done to my family, those I loved the most, overcame me. Rather than cry, I began to do a number on myself. No-good Kitty had done it again. Not surprisingly, my self-deprecation didn't help matters.

Everyone knew I needed more help. The doctors, Michael, and I talked about further treatment. I was willing to go for it, but not far away. I wanted to remain close to home and stood firm on that point. The others, anxious for me to get therapy as soon as possible, acquiesced. We decided on the nearby Deaconess Hospital where there was an affective disorder unit. The next hurdle was getting me there.

The media practically camped outside the Brigham and Women's; no one could get by the phalanx of photographers and cameramen, least of all the object of the bivouac. Sneak tactics were mandatory. Six o'clock one morning, my sponsor drove into the basement of the Brigham and Women's. She came up the back way to my floor and into my room where I sat packed and waiting. Together, we snuck down the back elevators into the basement. We got in the car and drove around the corner to the Deaconess. My stay there turned out to be a holding period. I wasn't really comfortable. I felt out of place. While I was a patient, the average age on the affective disorder unit was eighty. I spent most of my time in my room.

I wasn't taking any medication because it was important for the doctors to do a thorough workup. Eventually, I began seeing a psychopharmacologist as well as my therapist. I was given a dual diagnosis. I was suffering from depression and alcoholism. Prozac was prescribed and this time I did not fight it; I now had a better understanding of medication. If my depression wasn't alleviated, I would turn to alcohol or drugs, so I had to be medicated. It was as simple as that.

I did a lot of talking to a lot of doctors at the Deaconess. Michael, my sister, my father, and my sponsor came to see me every day. Eventually I left the hospital and became a kind of outpatient, going back and forth for treatment. We went to celebrate Thanksgiving at my sister and Al's place on the Cape. I still felt pretty crummy. I sort of plugged along, trying to make things work.

After Thanksgiving, I did two public events, one commemorating the Holocaust memorial in Boston, and the other honoring me for my work with refugees and the homeless. I felt pretty good about both appearances.

Meanwhile, I continued to see my therapist twice a week and the psychopharmacologist once a week. I went to meetings too, but not enough of them. Things still weren't right. I could not shake the feeling of impending doom.

I was impatient for the medicine to kick in. Typical of my impatience, I wanted relief fast. Incredible as it sounds, I began to fall into the old destructive routine. I was going to the doctors, all right, but I was also hanging around the house. At the few meetings I attended, my commitment was tepid.

Gloomy feelings flitted in and out of my head. I was haunted by them. They frightened me more than ever because they were still there and I was under a doctor's care.

On the sixth of December, I found a bottle of Tylenol

with codeine in a bureau drawer. The summer before my hospitalization, someone in the family had had dental surgery. The pills were prescribed, then tossed away under a pile of clothing. The bloodhound instinct of the addict is remarkable; it's as though I sniffed out those pills.

I thought if I took a few, I could get some sleep. Sleep was my only solace.

I swallowed a handful and went to bed. When I awoke, I got up, went for the bottle, and took a few more.

What the hell was the matter with me? I was diagnosed, I was on medicine, why didn't I call the doctor instead of repeating a practice that had proved to be fruitless and dangerous?

Of course I should have called the doctor, or Michael, or anyone. However, "should have," the seasoning of addiction, is sprinkled liberally over perverse behavior. I should have, but I didn't.

Again, I was overcome with a sense of shame, a sense of worthlessness and isolation. I should have been in a psychiatric program, one of the options presented by the Deaconess, but I hadn't wanted to commit myself. I had wanted to come home, to be with my family, and to work things out with them. As a result, I again put my health in jeopardy.

Michael telephoned me all the time, now. On this day, after futile attempts to reach me—the phone was unplugged—he called Jinny. She came over immediately and found me in the bedroom. I had been vomiting repeatedly and was quite sick.

Jinny was beside herself. "What's the matter, Kitty?"

I shook her off and said something about food poisoning.

Jinny sat with me in the bedroom.

Then I said I had to go to the bathroom. I went in, grabbed some more pills from the bottle and quickly downed them. I began gagging and throwing up again.

"What's the matter, Kitty?" Jinny cried.

I told my sister I was taking pills.

She was so shocked, so sad. Jinny got the bottle and put it aside to show the doctor. She called Michael and he rushed home.

I was dehydrated and very weak when he came into the bedroom. Michael was furious. "You can't do this to yourself! You have to go back to the hospital!" he shouted.

That night, I returned to the Deaconess.

My therapist contacted the executive medical director of the Four Winds Psychiatric Hospital in Katonah, New York, and made plans for me to go there. I urgently needed psychiatric help and I accepted the fact.

We had another family conference at the Deaconess to figure out how I was going to get to Four Winds. We had to keep this from the press. I could not endure another media free-for-all, none of us could. Everyone was determined to keep this latest disaster out of the papers.

I was scheduled to enter the facility on Friday, December 8; because Michael had a full schedule, Jinny and my sponsor elected to drive me to Katonah. I left the Deaconess and went home to get ready. I had my hair cut. It was too short and I got very upset—as if anyone would care about my hairstyle! Jinny helped me get my things together. What a strange scene. Two sisters packing a suitcase for the one who was about to enter a mental hospital.

The many thoughts churning in my brain boiled down to, "What will people think?" I answered my own query:

I'm a very sick person. I need help and there's no other way to get it. The most pressing question, however, I couldn't answer—would I ever be well again?

The drive down to Katonah was scenic and beautiful —and I couldn't have cared less. The Four Winds is a physically attractive place, but then, so were Hazelden and Edgehill Newport. My many mansions were all beautiful places.

A psychiatrist welcomed us and talked to me, Jinny, and my sponsor. The subject of keeping the press at bay was broached. The psychiatrist suggested I take an assumed name. He proposed "Abigail" and then someone else added "Adams." And so, Kitty Dukakis, aka Abigail Adams, entered a psychiatric hospital. It was about time.

The people on my unit were advised that "Abigail Adams" would be joining them. They were told her real identity, too. The pseudonym was used to protect me from outsiders. The only people likely to telephone me were Michael and the children, my dad, my sister and brother-in-law, and my sponsor; they'd be asking for Abigail Adams. It sounds terribly cloak-and-dagger, but the ruse worked and the press didn't get to me. I read later I had reportedly gone back to Hazelden, Edgehill Newport, or some unnamed facility in Connecticut. I'm very thankful I was able to keep my whereabouts unknown.

I began intensive therapy in the hospital program and saw the psychiatrist six days a week. One of the things I'd been skeptical about was the kind of help I could get from psychotherapy; it was part of my warped thinking. I hadn't given very much to therapy before because I was afraid to go back and really look at myself. I wasn't sure I'd be able to handle it and be honest with myself.

At Four Winds, I was still dubious. I felt guilty, too, surrounded as I was by others whose histories seemed far more severe than mine. I did not come from a dysfunctional family. I had a loving husband, wonderful kids, financial security, and a position of prominence. I had everything, and I had nothing.

There were more stringent rules and regulations at Four Winds than I had experienced in either of the rehab centers I had been in previously. The stress was on security. Before I went to my room, my belongings were checked very carefully, just as they had been at Hazelden and Edgehill Newport. At Four Winds, however, certain objects were taken away from you. A special place called "sharps" was set aside for glass items, scissors, tweezers, or anything else that might be dangerous. Your "sharp" possessions were put in there and you had to ask for them, even if you just wanted to tweeze your eyebrows. The staff was very gracious about giving you any item; still, it was closely observed.

I noticed too, there were no wire hangers of any kind in my closet. I sort of blinked at that, but I never asked why. Electrical equipment is taken away and inspected for safety reasons. I had to do without my hair dryer and radio for a couple of days.

Upon arrival at Four Winds, you're assigned a mental health worker who acts as an escort and stays with you a good part of the time. You're checked every fifteen minutes. Later, the check-in occurs every thirty minutes. And, no matter where you are, you have to make your presence known. Phones are located all over the extensive grounds and, even if you just take a walk, you still must call in.

For the first twenty-four hours at Four Winds, most people stay in their assigned unit, or living quarters.

Meals are brought to you until it's time to venture into the dining room. I came on a Friday and brought some books with me. I don't even remember what I read. I only remember it was very quiet on the weekend; there weren't many people around.

Those who were there were kind and friendly, and we played gin rummy. They knew about the Abigail Adams story, and while they were protective and helpful, I sensed they were a bit frightened of my being there—just as I was frightened about being there. They later told me they had expected me to think I was better than they were, and they were sure I wouldn't participate—the same sort of stuff I encountered at Edgehill Newport.

In addition to reading and gin rummy, that first weekend I slept a lot; in fact, sleeping may have been my primary activity.

At Four Winds, patients are issued passes and can go off grounds. This was different from Edgehill Newport and Hazelden, where you stayed for a prescribed period of time. When you returned to Four Winds, your urine was tested immediately.

We were monitored even in our rooms. All through the night, every thirty minutes, someone knocked on the door, opened it, and beamed a flashlight into the room. At home, I had cut myself off from everyone by removing the phone from the hook and holing up in my bed. Here, there was no opportunity to isolate myself.

Every day there was a staff and community meeting on the unit. There were fifteen people in my section. Meetings on the weekend began at eleven so we could sleep late, but I was up a lot earlier to receive my medication. Sometimes, I'd take my pills and go back to sleep. You could have breakfast in the kitchen unit or the dining room. I ate all my breakfasts, such as they were, in the unit. Then, I'd shower, get dressed, make my bed, and prepare for the day.

Many activities came under the heading of occupational therapy. O.T. provided a variety of art opportunities such as oil painting, drawing, ceramics, watercolors, and the like. The first day I worked with clay, which wasn't my medium. I tried other avenues and then discovered watercoloring. I don't want to sound corny, but I really did find much solace in watercoloring. It became very important to me and I want to study further. I'm not saying I'm going to become a great artist—that's not important. What is important is my wanting to work at it from the ground up. Some twenty-five years ago, I took an oil painting class at Brookline High School and had liked it well enough, but not enough to keep it up. Using the watercolors was different. I was much more comfortable in this medium. I painted flowers at first, with lots of bright colors. Then I started experimenting with distance and perspective. My efforts were primitive, only the beginnings, but I was encouraged by the instructors and my peers. What I learned was, I didn't know enough to really do what I wanted. I needed the instruction and solid training that leads to, if not a mastery, then at least a good control of the medium.

After the O.T., there were meetings on the unit. These sessions covered personal issues or unit business; it was an opportunity for people to discuss issues that were bothering them. Although there were alcoholics on the unit, alcohol was not part of the discussion. We spent a lot of time talking about conduct. I have to say, there was far more destructive behavior represented at Four Winds than at either Edgehill Newport or Hazelden. I admitted I was sick with depression. At these meetings, "status" changes were noted. Unlike the rehab centers, people started on a certain level and then would move up. S.O. was the entry level. That's when you had an escort accompanying you to all your activities. G.O. was the next step—no escort. I moved to G.O. quickly, on the first Monday, in fact. At the meetings, the presiding officer would ask if there were any status changes and then there would be a dialogue. You didn't just move up, either—you could go the other way. When infractions occurred, your status could be dropped.

Along with the unit meetings, special meetings for particular problems and disorders were held. I balked at attending the one on chemical dependency. Such a session was fine for people who had never been in a program, but this group was composed of beginners and veterans. I had been going for nine months and knew the basics. After all of us complained long and loud; the session was dropped.

I learned something from that experience, too. When you enter a facility like Four Winds, you have to yield somewhat to your surroundings. I have a tendency to want to control things. At Four Winds, I learned that I could surrender and still be my own person. I had private therapy sessions every day and joined group therapy three times a week. I remained uncomfortable discussing my personal problems with others. Though I was able to relax and ended up being able to speak more freely, I still find it difficult. When you've been in politics for twenty-seven years, you develop a protective armor. I trusted people; on the other hand, I was used to protecting my feelings. There was no dramatic breakthrough for me in group therapy; it was a gradual process. I talked about some of the difficulties of being a public person and wanting to be treated the same. I never mentioned the presidential campaign; it just wasn't an issue anymore. I talked about my depression and its causes. Those causes were becoming clearer to me in private therapy.

I had never focused on how much "running" I had been doing in my life. I was in a hurry all the time. Anyone who knows me will attest to this. I spent time talking about why I was in such a rush, why I needed to have something going on every minute, and why I had to put on a happy face to cover up powerful disappointments and sadnesses. Healthy people learn how to deal with such things. They can be sad or angry, appropriately. I got into trouble because I had to hide so many feelings and try always to keep a smile on my face. Look, sometimes you don't have a choice, you have to put on a public face. However, if you dissemble all the time, it's destructive.

I've always been a good listener; now I was learning how important it was to talk to others and have them listen to me. This has been helpful in my relationship with my husband. We've always been very close, but Michael has had a tendency to answer for me. He is used to calling the shots, and sometimes he takes control. And while our marriage is one in which there is an equal distribution of responsibility and decision making, often we tend to talk *over* each other. Probably it will happen again, but now at least I'm conscious of the dynamics. Moreover, we're both aware of the need to listen to each other—really listen.

I also learned not to have such high expectations for myself, for Michael, or for our children. I reinforced what I'd learned in the program, namely that I can talk to people and tell them when they've done something to upset me. What I can't demand, or even expect, is that they will change. I can change myself if I choose to, but that's all.

This realization has been a great help for me, because for years I'd hold everything in and then lose my temper. If only during my growing-up I had possessed some of the tools for living that I'm equipping myself with now —I think it would have made such a difference.

The psychiatrist told me that when I came to Four Winds I was like a piece of camouflage without any understanding of who was behind the mask. The need to hold on to that cover was, perhaps, the real story of Kitty Dukakis. He felt my basic problem was in my feeling of inadequacy, and we went into my history to figure out why I felt this way about myself.

No question my mother had something to do with it. I learned early on it didn't pay to fight my mother too much because I could never hope to win. Giving in to her wishes was a compromise toward peace, toward survival. She certainly wasn't evil or destructive by intent, she was simply, for her reasons, an extremely controlling person, one who exerted influence over my life until the day she died. Some of that influence remains.

My own strengths and talent were tempered by my sense of not measuring up to expectations. I was a student leader in high school and in college. This success came fairly easily, almost naturally—I seemed to get recognition without paying my dues. And while it was gratifying to be popular, I lived in fear that if people knew the real me, they wouldn't like me. My public image and my easy success allowed me to cover up the inadequacies I felt.

In the course of treatment, the special qualities of my family relationships became clearer. Even as my husband tried to be helpful, his needs highlighted the negative self-image I had, and underscored my sense of inadequacy. He would praise me to the skies at a time when I felt like two cents. The more he tried to be helpful and supportive, the greater the gap between the image he created and where I was mentally. This made me cover up more. Eventually this game of cover-up and deception became a life-style.

So much became clearer to me while at Four Winds. Significantly, I realized that going from excitement to excitement was a continuing opportunity to escape; a very dangerous and destructive opportunity. "Knowing" doesn't mean I'll never make the same mistakes again, but at least I now have greater insight into the mechanics.

Unfortunately, having an understanding of the mechanics doesn't mean that you can make things work. Things seemed much better, but they really weren't. Not yet.

Michael came to visit the second weekend and stayed at an inn close by. We went out for dinner. After the meal I went back to Four Winds and he went to his lodgings. We had breakfast together the next morning. I started talking about Christmas and how I wanted to be home for Kara when she returned from Spain. My therapist had reservations about my leaving so soon, but I was adamant. I felt it was my duty to be with my family during the holidays. I was granted a leave. The therapist was right. I wasn't ready. My four and a half days in Brookline turned into a nightmare.

On the twenty-third of December, Michael and the girls came to Four Winds. After an excellent family therapy session we left for home. On the drive, I began feeling anxious. I started thinking about Perry Street, what had happened there, and what a mess I'd made of other people's lives. The closer we got, the worse it got. We reached home in the late afternoon. I was exhausted. It was dark and that terrible feeling welled up in me— the morbid, lonely, almost strangling kind of feeling I so dreaded. Worse, I held my feelings in. I never told my family. I hadn't learned my lesson.

I walked in the front door and was overcome by the familiar ache. I went upstairs and lay down. We had dinner and talked about Kara's trip. I participated in the conversation, but only marginally. John and Lisa dropped by with the baby and I tried to appear cheerful and interested. The awful thing was, even my precious grandchild couldn't change my mood. I went to bed early and the next day, the twenty-fourth of December, I stayed in bed.

I could see my family was apprehensive, particularly Andrea and Kara. Michael assumed I was tired. Christmas Eve, I didn't do anything. I was in bed with visions of nothing in my head.

The next day I got up about six-thirty in the morning to wrap presents, gifts I had bought for everyone while I was in Ireland. We had fourteen people coming for dinner, and Michael, the girls, and I prepared the meal. My dad, my mother-in-law, Jinny and Al, a few of their kids, and Al's dear mother, Ohma, joined us. I got through the meal, but with real difficulty. We cleaned up and I retired to my bed.

The next day was my fifty-third birthday. That morning, the children came up to our bedroom with a coffee cake studded with candles. We always celebrate birthdays that way. I opened presents and then excused myself. I went right back to sleep. Sleep.

I awoke on December 27, 1989, and all I wanted to do

was go back to bed again. I wanted to forget I needed a fix.

I started looking around the house for anything containing alcohol. I was on a search that could destroy me. There was of course no liquor in the house. I did find some substitutes, though. It's humiliating for me to put into print what I took. I'm only doing it because it shows the depths to which I had fallen.

In my desperation, I reached for virtually anything in sight. I drank mouthwash, after-shave, and, God help me, nail-polish remover. I didn't take much of anything, fortunately, not even enough for them to show up in my urine test at Four Winds. Then I got back into bed and fell into a troubled sleep.

Later, I heard Andrea moving around the house. She was supposed to drive me back to Four Winds in a rented car, and then continue on to New York City. I started to get up and stopped; I just couldn't do it.

Andrea and Kara took one look at me and called Michael. He canceled all his appointments and telephoned the psychiatrist at Four Winds. The doctor told Michael to get me there even if they had to use an ambulance. "You've got to be tough," he said. "If Kitty won't do anything, you've got to do it for her."

Michael came home. He was in tears. I lay in bed and wouldn't move.

Michael got me dressed and put me in the backseat of our car. Andrea drove back to New York in the rented automobile, and Michael and Kara drove me to Katonah.

I looked like hell. I felt like hell. We arrived at Four Winds and the doctor came out to see me. He was upset that Michael hadn't called him when my condition was obvious. Again, Michael had been hoping against hope that things would be okay. Hope really does spring eternal.

Michael and Kara left for Boston and I was put under strict supervision for the next twenty-four hours. I had put myself and my family through another siege of horror.

I spent close to three months, off and on, at Four Winds. At the time, I sincerely believed I was looking at the truths about my condition. Now I know I was simply fooling myself—again. I had been a con artist for so long, I was buying my own inventions. Nothing, neither therapy nor medication, seemed to be working. I was still in a fog, and still functioning at a very low level. My depression never completely lifted.

I returned home and my suffocating melancholy continued. I slept fitfully during the nights and walked like a zombie through the days. I attended fellowship meetings and went through empty motions of recovery. I spoke to my sponsor. I even got on my knees and prayed. I tried; I really tried. Nothing helped. Scarcely a month had gone by when the inevitable occurred. One morning, about five days before the running of the Boston Marathon, I woke up, looked ahead to another stretch of pain, and said, "Screw it!"

I could not, *I would not*, endure it anymore. I had to escape the pain, and the "help" I needed could not be provided by family or friends. I put together a disguise, tying a kerchief over my head and drawing a huge mole on the side of my face with an eyebrow pencil. A large pair of dark glasses provided the finishing touch; then I went out to buy "relief." I drove to a package store on the Brookline-Brighton border and bought a bottle of vodka. If anyone recognized me in my disguise, they didn't let on. Nonetheless, I shook, the whole time.

Once home, I hid the vodka in the laundry basket in Kara's closet. While I didn't drink that night, I felt better knowing the bottle was available. The next night, however, I took a few drinks. I was alone; Michael had gone out. My only thought at the time was, I don't care. Over the next few days I continued to drink from the bottle and from virtually anything else that contained alcohol. Each time, however, I was careful not to drink "too much."

Monday, Patriots' Day, Michael and I were at the Marathon finish line with family and friends. I returned home exhausted, even though it was still early afternoon. Michael was busy with some work. I got busy, too. I went to Kara's closet, took a few swigs from the bottle and crawled onto my bed. I passed out. Around five o'clock, the phone rang. Michael answered. It was Alice Mayhew, editorial director at Simon and Schuster. Michael came into the bedroom, woke me, and told me to pick up the phone.

"No," I said, "I can't."

"You've got to talk to her," Michael answered, adding, "what is the matter with you?"

"I've been drinking," I said. Michael's face dropped; his whole body sagged.

"All right, all right, I'll talk," I groaned. I dragged myself off the bed and went to the phone. I don't remember the conversation. I do recall asking Michael if I sounded okay. Immediately after, I called my sponsor and she said I had to get to a meeting the next day. Michael was obviously depressed and upset, but there really was nothing he could do. I told him everything I had done. How I had checked every bottle in the house for alcohol. How I had gone through the vanilla extract and other obvious sources. The last thing I swallowed was hair spray—I just pulled off the spray top and gulped the ingredients. Yes, I was well on the way to hell—again.

Michael called my sister, told her what had happened, and asked her to come to our house . . . and to bring a bottle. Better to drink real booze than to down all those potentially harmful substances.

Jinny came over with the liquor. The sadness in her eyes was as deep and terrible as my own. After she left, I began to drink. I went to sleep and when I awoke the next morning, I immediately began again. The old pattern—drink after drink after drink. Only this time I did not unplug the phone. Later that day, Michael phoned from the office. I have no recollection of the call; it was my first total blackout. Michael came home and found me passed out on the bed, lying in my own vomit. It was an all too familiar sight for my beleaguered husband.

Since my first relapse on November 6, my sponsor had been telling me that there was one place where I should go; one place that really would help me. She believed Hazelden, Edgehill Newport, and Four Winds, although useful, were merely stops along the way to the help I really needed. Thank God, on April 9, I took my sponsor's advice. I called Mary Lee Zawadski, the Executive Director of Self Discovery, Inc. That evening I flew down to Atlanta and was driven just over the border to Roanoke, Alabama. I entered the facility, which is housed in the Randolph County Hospital.

I describe Self Discovery, Inc., lovingly as a cross between a convent and a boot camp. It is a program of such unrelenting intensity, it makes all the other places in which I'd been seem like country clubs by comparison. It was precisely what I needed. I spent twenty-eight days there and during all that time I was told repeatedly that I was a mess, and that if I didn't take control of my life I was going to die. I heard it so often, I finally began to believe it. Once I believed it, I could act upon it.

It was painful, it was horrible, but at last I knew the truth.

During all my trials and tribulations, somehow I always retained what I called a glimmer. I'd never totally lost hope—not when I was using, not when I was drinking, and not even when I was ingesting substances that might have killed me. Those dreadful acts obscured the glimmer, but when I was sober, the spark remained.

Slowly, this glimmer, this buried promise, began to surface. I started working with my therapist with renewed determination and a deeper and firmer perception of what I had to do in order to be healthy.

At the beginning of this book I said that if my husband had been elected president it would have been dangerous for me.

Now I know I was right.

But I also know the run for the presidency did not create my problems; it merely compounded them.

Long before the campaign there were harmful patterns in my behavior, patterns that were established before I met Michael Dukakis. I had spent a lifetime dodging the truth and running from my own feelings. Clearly, what happened to me would have happened whether or not Michael ran for office. Although the campaign was, in many respects, an emotional battleground, I was able to answer many challenges and am able to look back at the experience with a strong measure of pride in what I accomplished. I don't blame the campaign. It didn't cause the inevitable—it postponed it.

Politics is a tough arena for someone carrying the burdens of substance abuse and depression. I spent too much time trying to hide. Now I know I cannot stifle the legitimate problems that assail me. I must address them. I must adopt a wider, wiser perspective and apply it to myself among others, rather than on others alone.

The demands for perfection that my mother extended were impossible for me to meet. I know now I cannot apply her exacting standards to my life. I know now I must take responsibility for my own actions, good or bad. Now I know the search for my mother's roots was, to a great extent, an attempt to establish some sort of identity for myself. What I didn't realize was, I had an identity, and along with it, I had an illness. I am aware of that illness and am attempting to deal with it head-on.

In order to stay well, I cannot drink. That's number one. I am an alcoholic and must maintain my sobriety. To do this I have to go to meetings and continue with counseling. I want to do this, I'm willing to do this.

Now I know it's not just a question of alcoholism. I am a manic-depressive.

When I addressed the American Psychiatric Association about the stigma of mental illness, I didn't realize how close to the bone I was cutting. Now I know I suffer from depression. I cannot use therapy as a stopgap measure, applying it like a Band-Aid every time I begin to feel low. I cannot allow my emotional life to seesaw; it must be balanced. Awareness and willingness are my watchwords. Right now I am on lithium and it seems to be helping.

The healing process is going to take time and it's hard, hard work. I have no doubt the results are worth the effort. Even so, I cannot say for certain that I will not make errors. If I do make them, please remember, it will never be because I *want* to.

I know that in the past I have done things that have hurt others. I have a particular sense of sadness at the pain I've caused my family. I know what they went through because of me. I must take that knowledge and go on.

The idea of changing myself is very much with me. It's very humbling to recognize you don't have all the answers. I'm learning to let things happen and not try to control everything. It's tough, and I'm still having ups and downs.

While I cannot indulge in the luxury of calling myself cured or recovered, I have found a measure of ease through understanding. And, when the time comes, I want to take my knowledge and my experience and put them to use. I want to be with my loved ones and continue to work in all the areas that interest me—perhaps adding a few more. I want to put things together in a positive way and stick with them.

Good things are happening.

In the spring of 1988, I was asked by the Soviet-U.S. Joint Conference on Alcoholism and Drug Addiction to welcome the first delegation of recovering alcoholics from Russia and escort them around New York City. As part of the joint program, I hope to visit the USSR in the future.

In January 1990, President Bush reappointed me to the United States Holocaust Memorial Council. I was so pleased and proud and grateful.

My husband will be leaving office in January of 1991. We are looking forward to being with each other away from the pressures of public life. We each have been offered lecture and teaching positions and are seriously considering them. I still believe the best thing that ever happened to me was meeting Michael Dukakis.

. . .

Obviously, the story isn't over. I am still struggling to resume my place—with one important difference.

Now I know, before I can do anything for anyone else, I have to take care of myself.

On May 30, 1990, my father sent me a letter. In it he wrote, "I think I'm not going to worry about you in the future and let you take hold of your own life." And that's exactly what I'm doing.

Now you know my story—as much as I know myself.

AN AFTERWORD FROM
JANE SCOVELL

One crisp November after-
noon, a classmate and I were walking through the
quadrangle at Brookline High School. A band of under-
classmen were laughing and talking in the far corner of
the quad. As we passed by, I could see the boys in the
group dancing attendance on a winsome brunette standing in the center. Her brown eyes sparkled as each of
the youths stepped toward her and offered a comment.
Whatever they said, she responded with a dazzling smile
and a whooping laugh. Though there were other attractive coeds in the pack, this one stood out.

"Did you see that girl over there, that's Kitty Dickson," my friend informed me. "She's a sophomore and
she's seeing a Harvard guy. She went to a dance at
Dunster House last night."

"Big deal," I said. Actually, it was a "big deal." I was
a senior and had yet to date a Harvard man. This girl
was in my sister Pinky's class. The idea that a contemporary of my kid sister had leaped ahead of me in the
dating game was almost too much to bear. "She must be
fast," I commented to my classmate. That evening, I
casually asked Pinky if she knew Kitty Dickson.

"Yeh, sure, she's a friend of Wilma Greenfield's."

"What's she like?" I inquired further.

"She's really nice. Kind of shy. She does stuff with the Girls' League. Everybody likes her. Her father's with the Boston Symphony."

"The Boston Symphony!" I gasped.

"Yeh," answered my sister, "he's a violinist." At that moment, I hated Kitty Dickson. Except for being a sophomore, she was everything I wanted to be. She was pretty, she was popular, her father played with the Boston Symphony, and she dated Harvard men. Fortunately for my ego, I didn't have much contact with her during our overlapping high school careers. From everything I heard, though, had I known her, I probably would have liked her. No one had a bad word to say about Kitty Dickson.

Two decades later, I attended a fund-raising party at a friend's house. Mike Dukakis, also a graduate of Brookline High, was running for governor and meetings were being held to introduce him to the voting community. I walked in and saw a group of men and women clustered in the far corner of the living room. They were gathered around a vivacious woman with large brown eyes, a radiant smile, and a hearty laugh. I recognized my old, unwitting nemesis, Kitty Dickson—the girl with everything. Well, she still had everything: She was pretty, she was popular, her father played with the Boston Symphony, and she had married a Harvard (Law School) man. I joined the group around her and, like the others, was won over; my long-ago adolescent envy was completely wiped out. Kitty Dukakis was lively, cordial, very informed, and enthusiastically supported her husband's candidacy. I couldn't help liking her.

Michael Dukakis was elected governor. Four years

later, he lost the party primary in his bid for a second term. I thought he had been a good governor and was saddened at his defeat. I was glad, therefore, when he made his stunning comeback four years later. And I was positively bowled over when he became the Democratic candidate for the presidency of the United States. Although he lost the election, his wife won the heart of the American public. And for good reasons. We sensed her innate decency and delighted in her outspokenness. Strong-willed and tough-minded, she was also womanly and appealing. We watched as Kitty Dukakis lavished energy on her family, her friends, her home state, and the entire country. Her triumphs made headlines all over the world. Then, without warning, everything swerved the other way; triumphs turned to travails. Piece by piece, Kitty Dukakis's private hell was revealed, and bit by bit, she's fought to come back. She humbled herself before us, confessed her shame, and sought help. No one, not even those closest to her, understood the agony she suffered all those years. When she began this book, we believed, as she believed, her worst struggles were over. The story was complete. We were wrong. The worst was yet to be. Kitty Dukakis met the awful truth and is still fighting. She has updated her narrative with characteristic candor and force. Her tale goes way beyond the frenzied arena of politics or the glamorous realm of celebrity, and its protagonist emerges as a true heroine.

In the nearly forty years since I saw Kitty Dickson Dukakis standing in the Brookline High School quadrangle, a delightful youngster has became a brave and remarkable woman. I have been privileged to witness this process and assist in writing her inspiring story.

ACKNOWLEDGMENTS

KITTY DUKAKIS
To all my friends and staff who provided guidance during the writing of this book;
to Paul Costello, my press guide and close friend;
to Bob Barnett, the quintessential lawyer/agent whose advice and caring were always there;
to Alice Mayhew, Michael Korda, and Chuck Adams for their patience and guidance during the writing and editing of this book;
and to Jane Scovell for her wonderful combination of professionalism and love.

JANE SCOVELL
Thanks also to Joy Harris, Laura Marshall, Ann Gordon, Freddi Crystal, Hal Meyer, Nick Bazas, Susanna Margolis, and Andrew Crystal. Special thanks to Louis Scovell, Lucy Appleton, and Bill Appleton. The perceptive comments of Sidney Sheldon Welton and Amy Appleton were much appreciated. I also would like to thank Alice Mayhew, Michael Korda, and Chuck Adams for their insightful guidance. Very special thanks to Victoria Skurnick.

PHOTO CREDITS

1, 2, 3, 7, 8, 9, 10, 12, 14, 20, 23, 26, 31, 33. Author's Collection
 4. Lenscraft Photos, Inc.
 5. Photography by Bill Coleman, State College, PA.
 6. John Brook
11. *Boston Herald* photo by Leo M. Tierney
13, 15, 16, 17, 18, 19. *Boston Herald* Photos
21. Copyright © Alice Kandell
22. Courtesy of John J. Keller
24. © Ira Wyman
25. Photo by Mark Kelley/Juneau Empire
27, 30. Copyright © 1988 Richard Sobol
28. Copyright © Mikki Ansin
29. Photograph by Robert A. Cumins
32. Jane Scovell
34. Brian Stocker
35. Larry Laszlo/CoMedia